First published in the United State of America by
Rockport Publishers, a member of
Quayside Publishing Group
100 Cummings Center, Suite 406-L
Beverly, MA 01915
Telephone: (978) 282-9590
Fax: (978) 283-2742
www.rockpub.com

ISBN-13: 978-1-59253-545-3
ISBN-10: 1-59253-545-3

10 9 8 7 6 5 4 3 2 1

Design: HVANDERSON DESIGN, Louisville, KY.
Produced by Crescent Hill Books, Louisville, KY
www.crescenthillbooks.com

Printed in China

REALLY GOOD PACKAGING
explained

BEVERLY MASSACHUSETTS

Top Design Professionals Critique 300 Designs & Explain What Makes Them Work

ROCKPORT PUBLISHERS

Bronwen Edwards
Marianne Klimchuk
Rob Wallace
Sharon Werner

BE

bronwen
edwards

Design or Decoration?

Great design has an extra element: an idea behind it. Injecting a truly original, relevant idea into a design transcends subjectivity.

What makes great packaging design? This is a tough brief. What pearls of fresh wisdom can I impart here on a topic that has been the subject of endless debate? No doubt you have read and absorbed a vast number of opinions on the matter throughout your careers, and no doubt you have views and opinions of your own.

This book however, contains examples to aspire to and lessons to learn from.

The issue here—as with all creative industries—is that what makes great design is subjective. There are no definites, no secure ground; all work is subject to the personal opinions of a vast, differing audience. There is much debate to be had, but no firm proof, which means that people can believe pretty much what they want to believe. Because of this, some great designs never see the light of day, victims of a client for whom a safe decision is preferable to a brave one.

Some people confuse design with decoration. Sadly, there is a lot of decoration around in packaging. Decoration tends to be the most conservative of the design outputs, mainly because of client demands. Great design has an extra element: an idea behind it. Injecting a truly original, relevant idea into a design transcends subjectivity. It incites a striking engagement that is instant, indisputable, and appeals to clients' instincts rather than their tick-lists.

Good design not only captivates an audience's attention, it makes them linger. Great design means that the audience will connect with the brand, want to engage with and then remember that package later on. This is often achieved by having a great idea at the start—and at the heart—of whatever you do.

Ideas can come from any direction: They can be softly witty, intellectually playful, or something that breaks all boundaries yet is still sharply relevant. The best ideas are easily spotted—when they're someone else's—by that horrible feeling in your stomach when you think, I wish I'd done that. I had a fantastic tutor during my degree who drummed into me the importance of ideas over simply style-led designs—a design must speak for itself. Outside the studio, nobody is going to be there to explain to the consumer the intricacies and deeper meaning of subtle color reference. The best work needs no explanation, so if you're ever in doubt, ask someone who hasn't seen it before if they "get it." If you need to talk them through it or convince them of its worth, go back to the drawing board: Your wider audience will be the same. Styles and trends will come and go, but a good idea, beautifully executed, will last forever.

Q & A
with Bronwen Edwards

My favorite package designs inside this book are...
Gu (page 76) and Honey Pot (page 73). Both have really innovative structures and graphics.

You know a package design is really good when...
It's iconic, redefines a category, or you buy it just to have it, not to consume it.

The best thing a client ever said to me was...
"You're the expert; I trust you."

And the worst ...
"Sorry, my wife doesn't like it."

For creative inspiration, I...
usually turn to other creative disciplines, such as illustration or advertising—they can spark off interesting thoughts—or stroll through central London, which is always full of vibrancy and creativity. Failing that, I sit in the bath and hope!

The smartest thing I ever heard anyone say about package design is...
"You have to see it to do it."

The best career advice I ever received was...
"Styles come and go; ideas live forever."

Most designers probably don't know that...
There's more to life than packaging!

10 Mistakes Designers Make When Designing Product Packaging

BY BRONWEN EDWARDS

1. **Not following the brief.**
First, and let's start at the beginning here: not following the brief properly. I'm guilty of this myself. It's easy to get selective amnesia over certain details that you find uninspiring and to hope that somehow the client will share this memory loss. Sadly, they rarely do. This usually results in a painfully convoluted process where you have to go back and re-address the design. It devalues the work you did, even if it's the best idea you've ever had and you're busy dusting off the trophy shelf. Most important, you lose the client's trust, which is bad for business and also makes it much more difficult to push for ideas in the future—the client will not believe you have the brand's best interests at heart.

2. **Approach.**
Some designers give up the minute they start a project "Ugh, this is going to be rubbish; they insist on this, and that, and it's got to have…." It's up to us as designers to challenge every brief, to push every aspect of a design. If you start with the attitude that the design is destined to be uncreative, then it's doomed from the outset. Some of the most award-winning work has come from heavily restricted briefs, which force us to be more imaginative in how we get around them: The gauntlet is thrown down.

3. **Reaching for the mouse.**
Right: You've read the brief; your brain is sharpened, raring to go…then you get straight onto a computer. WHOA! These days, with the industry revving up at a scary rate, time demands becoming an increasing pressure, and the ease with which we can now translate our thoughts digitally, the worst thing you can do is head straight for the computer. Sketches are the medium of ideas, and no matter how dandy you think you are with a mouse, you can never thoroughly explore the ideas you are capable of on a screen. It's impossible to do so without addressing the style, which should be the next stage, not the first. Sketches should be rough, scribbled, quick, expressive, and—as long as you can read the idea—then, and only then, should you flex those Photoshop muscles.

4. **Not challenging preconceptions.**
There are two sides to this: a) the category; and b) the physicality.

Category: There is normally a category language. For example: It's fruit juice, so, unsurprisingly, everything has big, predictable photos of fruit on it—how dull. Challenge everything without losing credibility in the genre.

Physicality: Just because you know it should be in a certain format, try to question every aspect—structure, finishes, substrates—use every opportunity to break existing preconceptions. Although this is not always appropriate, try, whenever possible, to push for the unexpected.

5. **Style over content.**
Don't be seduced by whimsical styles. Never-ending trends sail through the ever-evolving sea of design, all of which can be used as a vehicle for an idea. But if you rely solely on these to carry your design, you'll look back in two years' time and cringe. It won't be original; there will be others just like it; and it will date horribly. It's incredibly lazy to rely on trends: They don't last. But a great idea transcends its execution.

6. **Not just a pretty front face.**
When thinking about packaging, whether structurally or graphically, it's easy to forget that it's more than just a shelf shot; it's a 3D object. Sometimes when the brief is restrictive on the selling face, you can be more creative with the other aspects. For example, there's been a great surge of witty barcodes, evocative copy, and legal iconography. These are lovely after-thoughts that are often overlooked and can make the concept come to life in an unexpected way. Ideally, the front face is only the immediate side of the packaging; the concept should involve its entirety.

7. **Seeing the pack out of context.**
    It's easy to forget that our designs are heading for the big, wide world out there. They live in a consumer environment crowded to within a hair's breadth with other people's designs. It's in store, in a shop, not sitting pretty on a white backdrop. It's also taken home, held in the hand. It serves a purpose and has a journey from purchase to disposal. Successful designs consider the entire process and use it to their benefit. Be aware of what's out there—visualize it in its future environment, consider its function—and you'll end up with something that has difference.

8. **Designing for awards.**
    Designing for designer's sake, purely for awards, is really tough. We all love a bit of industry recognition, but focusing on this rather than the brief in hand never seems to get great results. Try not to put that pressure on yourself. Turn that drive toward the job in hand, try to create the most innovative solution for that category or problem, and the awards should take care of themselves.

9. **Knowing which battles to lose in order to win the war.**
    It's a subjective industry, and clients are rarely visually literate. Sometimes it can feel like a constant battle to get the right results through. Remember, the secret is knowing which fights to pick. Getting precious about kerning on the subsidiary copy or angering a client who is stubbornly attached to pink is never going to get the bigger concept across, and sometimes you have to lose a few soldiers in order to win the war. Being able to compromise shows open-mindedness and builds trust with clients. It's difficult, but try to step back from the job, focus on what really constitutes the big idea, then figure out what can be sacrificed in order to get a great result, even if that kerning makes you wince.

10. **Taking yourself too seriously.**
    This might upset some people, but what we do really isn't rocket science. We're designing for a business and a consumer, not for ourselves. We're privileged to be paid to happily do what we love, which—let's face it—in the long term will be redesigned, and in the short term ends up straight in the bin. If you can't have a bit of fun, take criticism objectively, and keep getting excited about briefs, then you're destined either for burnout or for unbearable conceit. (By the way, I will be signing autographs...if you're lucky.)

World traveler Bronwen Edwards is half Welsh but was born in Belgium and spent her childhood in Istanbul. After art school, she went directly to Coley Porter Bell, a design firm in London, and is currently an award-winning designer at Brandhouse. She has a penchant for vintage clothing and wants to own a sloth one day—they're good for the humor, she says. Her 2008 photography exhibition, New Dawn— a collection of portraits of Ethiopia—was attended by the Ethiopian ambassador. She lectures for design courses and blogs for the top-rated packaging design blog TheDieline.com. Bronwen is 6'2" in heels, and, she claims, over 7' on a ladder.

with Marianne Klimchuk

My favorite package designs inside this book are...
Bootleg/Turner Duckworth (page 133). I'm not sure
if this design classifies as a double entendre or if
there can be such a thing as a triple entendre, but
nonetheless it is exceptionally rare to find a packaging
design that is clever on so many levels. I visualize a
pretty fun brainstorming session...Italian = country
shaped in a boot, fashion design, wine, fabulous
designer shoes, avant-garde style, leather, zip-up
boots...you get the picture. The outcome is magnifico!

Domaine De Canton/Mucca Design (page 115). An
instant icon! The architecture and luminescence
of this bottle is stunning! Every detail is handled
perfectly, from the line weights, the typefaces,
leading, kerning, and dingbats to the slight label-
shape detail. Decorative, simple, elegant, modern yet
classic, and definitely transporting...should I go on?

You know a package design is really good when...
There is no simple answer and no established
measure to tell you if your packaging design is
good. Being a designer today means having well-
honed critical-thinking skills. In a world of tastes,
perceptions, values, and expectations that are
changing faster than ever, you realize that even with

all the necessary skills, producing something that
is really good is extremely difficult. There are basic
criteria for "good," but even if you had a checklist, it
would not guarantee a successful end result.

Good package design goes beyond strategic problem
solving and beyond being straightforward, inoffensive,
innovative, recognizable, comprehensible, trustworthy,
truthful, or sustainable. Good packaging design
is distinguished by emotional reaction or perhaps
emotion in action, since this ultimately drives results
and perhaps even inspires. However, once a design
induces that connection, the relationship between
good packaging design and the audience won't last
unless the design also functions, protects, preserves,
transports, and informs.

Designers often choose attractiveness or physical
appearance over a conceptualized strategy to problem
solving. Really good design takes time to build and
can rarely be identified without a serious commitment
to a well-conceived design process. Good design has
resonance, commands attention, and may not actually
be perfect—but good design is lasting.

The best thing a client ever said to me was...
"We have had a very successful end to our fiscal year. Thank you."

And the worst ...
"It's a really good idea but just not for us."

For creative inspiration, I...
teach design in New York City. I experience the endless sense of wonder, the breadth of imagination and fountains of ideas that come from fresh minds, the freedom of experimentation unconfined by clients or real-world restrictions, and the energy that comes in rooms full of creative minds working together to achieve their best. Every week I encounter amazing concepts, incredible talents, inspiring uses of materials, technology, typography, and resources. When it's not happening in the halls of academia, there are few places in the world with the diversity, energy, and stimulation of New York City.

Outside of that, raising two teenagers keeps me ever-so stimulated, and escaping to the Berkshires allows me to quiet my mind and be inspired by nature.

The smartest thing I ever heard anyone say about package design is...
"A designer knows he has achieved perfection not when there is nothing left to add, but when there is nothing left to take away." –Antoine de Saint-Exupery

The best career advice I ever received was...
The best career advice came not verbally, but from living with and watching two exceptional individuals and highly successful professionals—my parents. They said: "Find what you love to do and then do what you love."

The next inspiring advice was derived from reading Steve Jobs' commencement speech at Stanford.

Most designers probably don't know that...
Creative thinking is a muscle. The more you use it, the more you build it. It needs to be exercised regularly.

Age brings experience, but not necessarily wisdom. There is much to be learned from people who challenge convention or see the world from a different perspective.

10 Mistakes Designers Make When Designing Product Packaging

BY MARIANNE KLIMCHUK

1. **Failing to discuss money up-front.**
Would you work with a plumber, carpenter, dentist, doctor, or lawyer if you didn't know how they bill? Money, sales, and contracts are not what designers are trained to discuss and therefore, it's a matter too often avoided until countless hours have been invested in a project and the desire for fair compensation creeps in. When designers can clearly identify their strategic process and how their creative value serves a client's identifiable needs, then the value creation is clear. It is only then that they can define the variables that determine fee structure.

2. **Jumping onto the computer before brainstorming, researching, sketching, collaborating or experiencing.**
Thinking that the Internet makes up for real-life research and experience is a mistake. Actually, it's called laziness. Certainly there are thousands of inspiring works right at our fingertips, but nothing can take the place of interpersonal, experiential, and sensory experiences. In fact, the mindset that makes us jump onto the computer—being overwhelmed, feeling a lack of creative thinking, not having a clear sense of direction or organization—is precisely what often leads to a great sense of frustration (or even design plagiarism.) With the breadth and diversity of information at our fingertips, we are bombarded by sensory overload and time is lost in this Internet vacuum. This is also when design plagiarism can occur. A great brainstorming session, researching analogous or dissimilar subjects, or collaborative mind-mapping can increase productivity. Designers make better decisions when they have a clear, well-informed, well-organized, yet varied problem-solving process.

3. **Failing to design with the end in mind.**
Not only is this all too common, but add to that failing to work with a printer or production professional at the onset of a project. From size, material, and production processes to retail environment, lighting, shelf positioning, and consumer demographics, too often designers move forward in the design process uninformed. Designers should not be afraid to have a backward design process, to ask questions and advice from manufacturers and production professionals, and to use all potential recourses and collaborative opportunities to advance a design process. There is no road map for the designer who fails to understand or articulate the essential outcomes of a project.

4. **Thinking that design aptitude can compensate for communication skills.**
Designers need to be not only walking visual thesauruses but also world citizens. On a macro level, they need to be informed about the workings of the global business world, the financial transactions, management, and business environment of their clients, and the impact the global economy has on design. On a micro level, they must be able to articulately communicate a clear design strategy behind an aesthetically pleasing solution. Communication skills, including writing, speaking, and critical thinking, have been significantly altered with the integration of new communication technologies. Although new ways to express ourselves have emerged, the ability to articulate effectively in an oral or written format will always be an essential and highly regarded value in our society. Young designers, in particular, should be given opportunities to witness great orators presenting or reading exceptional examples of business writing, and they should be provided with plenty of opportunities to practice these skills themselves.

5. **Losing touch with innovation and creativity and falling prey to the same design routine or a stale design process.**
Too often, designers and design firms lose perspective on themselves and their work. They produce similar work for a wide variety of clients. Certainly, directors and peers are critiquing designers internally, and clients externally, but among external designers and design firms, there are few opportunities to share and receive feedback. The speed of innovation breakthroughs in the technology sector far surpasses any minute advances in our own profession. Designers need to change perspectives, turn processes around or even upside down, look at the designed environment from a new, younger (or older) perspective, and take risks. Common sense and pragmatism have been drilled into us over the years, and the sense of imagination, playfulness, inventiveness, and rule-breaking that were hallmarks of childhood are lost to systems and rigid processes.

6. **Thinking that taking responsibility for the environment and humanity is their clients' issue.**
Certainly for many designers, this issue has changed their process, business focus, and mission; however, creating lasting and positive change is critical for the future and direction of our design profession. We need to look at clients and designers as partners and share common goals in this effort. Information relevant to health, environmental and production considerations, alternative materials, technologies, and processes should be shared freely. One more thing: Designers should not let more violator labels—FSC (Forest Stewardship Council) or otherwise—infringe on the face of good design. Once these labels get into packaging design, it will be hard to get them off. Designs that are environmental friendly should live it, not wear it.

7. **Devaluing their craft by participating in spec work.**
Other than doing pro bono work, which in packaging design is a rare opportunity, doing spec work (free design work) cheapens our profession. Any designer willing to work without a guarantee of appropriate compensation should consider a career change. I have heard plenty of potential clients argue that viewing a project submission by a number of firms allows them to compare evenly. Can you imagine asking five painters to each paint one wall of a room to see who has the best approach? If a capabilities presentation, portfolio, and interview are not evidence enough, then the client is fishing for freebies.

8. **Taking themselves and their work all too seriously.**
Comic relief—or at least a bit of wit—in our everyday environments is desperately needed. I truly believe that humor and wit (used with good judgment) not only sell but also add levity to tension-filled existences. What I am referring to is the visual marriage of ideas that communicate in a clever, visually interesting, artful way. Although there are psychological, social, and aesthetic differences in the interpretation of wit, using humor and wit in ways that are open to common interpretation by audiences of globally disparate perspectives can make for highly effective visual communication tools. Although there would be nothing worse than every design attempting to be funny, I believe that consumers are beginning to slow down and appreciate the nuances and expressions of creative thinking that witty designs communicate.

9. **Designing based on an old set of rules and philosophies.**
Design is about creating new experiences, not simply conforming to the competition or to pre-set parameters. Don't get so caught up in a project, a style, or a philosophy and forget to cultivate a new perspective, a new relationship, or a new approach to thinking about the world in which the design and consumers live. Reframing a problem and the approach can often make it more interesting and solvable. Designers should be encouraged to break away and break rules. With the utilization of clear communication skills, based on innovation, designers can collaborate with clients on solutions that are part of a more meaningful consumer experience.

10. **Thinking that anyone with any design background can do it well.**
Packaging design is a focused discipline that takes education, experience, and a lot of hard work. It takes an extensive breadth of qualities beyond the ability to graphically lay out a pdp or create a three-dimensional structure. With all the requirements and functions that are integral to packaging designs, it is not simply about the *what* but about the *how*. Yes, as Primo Angeli asserted, it's about making people respond, but there is nothing simple about that.

Marianne Rosner Klimchuk has been the chairperson of the Packaging Design Department at the Fashion Institute of Technology for the past fourteen years and an instructor of design for over nineteen years. She has been a visiting lecturer at the University of Pennsylvania Wharton School's Jay Baker Retailing Initiative, is a contributing writer to industry magazines, and co-authored Packaging Design: Successful Product Branding from Concept to Shelf. She is a design consultant with a focus on design strategy, integration, and best practices. When not at work, she is carefully navigating her kids through their teenage years, herself through life, and her husband through all these phases.

with Rob Wallace

My favorite package design inside this book is...
Chivas Regal 25-Year-Old Original (page 94). It is
often much more challenging to evolve an existing
identity than to create a new one. I admire how
well this design pays tribute to its heritage while
recasting it in a contemporary, relevant, and ultra-
premium context.

You know a package design is really good when...
It drives an initial purchase, it serves as the key
visual mnemonic of the brand, and it unifies all other
brand communications. At the end of the day, it all
comes down to engaging the consumer at the point
of sale. Now, if a package can do this and elevate
consumers' sensibilities at the same time, then the
design is truly great.

The best thing a client ever said to me was...
They wanted me to help make them more
courageous in their design choices. Large
corporations are often too conservative. They
are looking to make significant change in their
consumer perceptions, and yet they only allow us to
tweak their existing identity. Now more than ever,

consumers not only embrace change, they expect it!
Keeping your brand relevant often means periodic
re-invention. And only design-led, synthesized brand
communications and courageous clients can do that.

And the worst ...
"I showed this to my wife, who is an interior designer,
and she thinks that it lacks a certain something."
While everyone is entitled to their opinion, non-
specific, subjective design direction derails an
otherwise efficient process. How do you prevent this?
Every design project should be initiated with a visual
positioning. If you predetermine the visual strategies
that best evoke the consumer experience *and* get
consensus on these strategies with the client, the ad
agency, the promotion firm, and all your consulting
counterparts before you start designing, you'll never
have to deal with your client's interior designer's
opinion again!

For creative inspiration, I...
brand analogies. How can we make this brand the
Dyson of its category? What would Apple do to this
brand? Who owns the Venus positioning in this

category? Would a *New Yorker* personality work for us? How would a Lean Cuisine aesthetic work for our brand? Well-defined brands are the visual symbols of their own distinct positioning and the visual tools that evoke them. They can easily be used as analogies to inspire completely nonrelated categories.

The smartest thing I ever heard anyone say about package design is...
"It needs to be quantified." We need an empirical measure to determine how many dollars of incremental profit come back to the brand owner for every dollar invested in design. I'd imagine that many of the brands in this book are not supported by advertising, and package design is their only form of consumer connection. Even among heavily advertised brands, package design is the most permanent part of their brand message, and the one seen by the most consumers. Really good packaging design continues to drive brand affinity throughout multiple advertising campaigns, countless promotions, numerous changes in brand management, and all the other elements of a brand's evolution.

The best career advice I ever received was...
from my dad, co-founder of Wallace Church (and my mentor), who said, "Follow your passion." This industry ain't for wimps. You have to fall in love with it in order to succeed. And the industry is blessed to be populated with passionate and talented people, as evidenced in this book.

Most designers probably don't know that...
Brand identity/package design generates the highest return on investment of any marketing communications effort, bar none. Most designers might feel that this is true but not know how to prove it. Most marketers probably don't know this. Our goal as an industry is to prove to ourselves, our clients, and the general business community that (to quote Thomas J. Watson) "good design is good business." Only then will design and the design process have best practices. Only then will design consistently receive the proper time and resources required to do it right. Only then will design consultancies be able to justify proper compensation for their contribution to brand success. Only then will design be respected for what it is—the single most effective and cost-efficient branding tool!

10 Mistakes Designers Make When Creating Packaging Design

BY ROB WALLACE

1. **Stop listening.**
Designers are so viscerally intuitive that they often get an immediate vision in their heads about the perfect solution before the client has fully explained the project. Great designers suspend their creative minds for a bit and use their analytical skills during briefs and design critiques. They listen while clients describe their issues, and they put them into a hierarchy. They ask questions, lots of them. They present alternative directions. With a good designer leading the discussion, clients often solve their own problems. And then, the designer can be much more efficient in giving them exactly what they want.

2. **Giving them what they want.**
OK, so after you lead the client to articulate exactly what they want, you just do that, right? Wrong. Great designers go beyond the expected and create effective solutions that also elevate consumers' design sensibilities. The objective of every brand-identity assignment is to sell the product and build a long-lasting emotional connection with the consumer. However, every assignment should also seek to raise design literacy, literally teaching consumers to respond to better design.

3. **Misunderstanding design research.**
Regardless of how much you and the client both like your concepts, package design's first true test of success is qualitative and quantitative consumer research. If the designer is not involved in determining the methodology and the questions being asked, the results can be not only confusing but also misleading. Research teams all too often want one primary valuation: purchase intent. Would you buy this? They don't care as much about the reasons why. Research respondents, on the other hand, are biased by their relationship to the existing brand—or competitive brands—and what they remember from the store. Optimizing package-design research is a much larger issue—perhaps worthy of its own book—but designers must also look for and correct the trapping questions. They must attend and help interpret research findings, and they must fight for the actionable insights that will improve their work.

4. **Designing for themselves.**
It's pretty rare that a brand's target audience is an exclusive group of highly evolved, elite visualists. Designers are not your brand's target market, so what appeals to you may be quite irrelevant to your audience. Think like them. Get into their heads and determine the visual cues that motivate their behavior. When we look at designers' portfolios, we want to see a high level of diversity, proving that they can design well beyond their own personal aesthetic.

5. **Not managing expectations/Selling through/Managing up.**
Needless to say, design is exceptionally subjective. What you and your design manager love, their marketing team and executive management might pee all over. Designers need to be storytellers. You need to have an articulate rationale for every decision you make, and you need to be able to tie that story back to the brand. If you can justify your opinions, you'll have a much higher degree of success in selling a concept through an organization.

6. **Limiting your influences.**
Great designers get inspiration from everywhere, not only through the 'net and the competition entries but in the way that the wrapper of your buttered bagel is folded. Get your head out of the annuals and get into a supermarket, a drugstore, a big-box retailer and open your eyes. Inspiration is everywhere, and everything—literally, everything!—can be redesigned to be better. Reinvent the ordinary. Reject the jaded. Celebrate the unexpected.

7. **Falling in love with your work/Knowing when to stop.**
Don't get me wrong. Passion fuels great design. So fall in love with the process, but understand that design is a business. You need to be compensated for the value of what you do. Ambitious designers are often too close to their work. They present several variations of ten to twelve concepts and thereby completely confuse their clients. Each design should achieve each individual objective in a different and relevant way. This leads to fewer but more focused and powerful concepts. When in doubt, leave it out.

If the client asks if you tried X, Y, and Z, you can then pull out those additional roughs and explain what worked, what did not, and why you abandoned them to concentrate on the most effective solutions.

8. **Not telling a story**.
An effective design presentation is a performance: It has a beginning, a middle, and an end. You are not only there to simply verbalize what your clients can already see; you are there to delight and inspire them. Tell them about your influences and what worked and why. Tell them the different emotions that will be evoked by each element of your work. Present several truly discrete and articulate solutions, but also have a strong and credible point of view. Lead them to your recommended design strategies and engage their passions.

9. **Not collaborating between disciplines.**
Package design is the cornerstone of an integrated brand communication architecture. While consumers might learn of the brand on the 'net or television or other commercial media, it is their engagement at the point of sale that's the most relevant. They decide to buy the product because of the package. They take it home. They interact with it whenever they are using the product. The consumer engages the brand. And yet, package designers and advertising creatives and Web developers and social-network craftspeople rarely meet to share ideas and synthesize their efforts. *Get out of your discipline and learn how brand communication design works.* Invite these counterparts into the package-design process. Collectively discover the visual strategies that will synthesize every consumer touchpoint.

10. **Overreliance on your tools**
Computer-aided design is a blessing and a curse. Yes, we are able to immediately gradate backgrounds and dimensionalize type, but we are losing design craftsmanship in the process. As a result, there are fewer and fewer designers who still have incredible hand skills.

Dust off your airbrush. Hand-letter your next logo. Experiment more with cut paper and vellum. With credit to the amazing advancements in design technology, if you can't communicate your solution with a felt-tip pen on the back of an envelope, you're relying too much on your computer.

As managing partner of New York City–based brand identity, strategy, and package design consultancy Wallace Church Inc., Rob Wallace works with some of the world's smartest and most successful consumer brand marketers, including Coca-Cola, Nestle, Kraft, Heinz, Miller Brewing, Dell, Colgate-Palmolive, and Brown-Forman.

Rob began his career at Grey Advertising and worked for several marketing consultancies before joining Stan Church in 1985, bringing his strategic insights to the firm's award-winning creative process.

Rob is on the board of advisors of the Design Management Institute, and a member of the distinguished faculty of the In-Store Marketing Institute. He speaks at dozens of marketing industry events and lectures at Columbia Business School, Georgetown University, and other post-graduate programs.

Brand identity is Rob's passion. The guru of design's return on investment, Rob focuses on proving that brand identity/package design is a marketer's single most effective tool.

When not traveling or entertaining with his wife and three daughters, Rob plays a wicked blues harmonica and a truly terrible game of golf.

sw

sharon
werner

Really good package design is elusive

A package that just does its job of holding the product and providing a surface for listing product attributes is not taking full advantage of the opportunity to tell the brand story.

What makes a package "really good"? I must have asked myself that nearly 200 times while reviewing the work for this book. Since the goal of this book is to get at the guts of that very question, I wanted to find a consistent answer. If package design were an exact science, dictated by formulas of color and type layout, this book would contain thousands of examples. But the fact is that really good package design is elusive.

The critiquing process was excruciating, exciting, and enlightening. With some examples, it was immediately clear what made it good, or even great, and that was made evident by the consensus of all the authors. With others, it was much more difficult to discern the exact element that made it go beyond just good to really good. Sadly, there were some that it was difficult to find anything good about. And of course there were many that were just okay, which is actually worse than bad, in my mind. It's like a wallflower at a junior high dance; it might have a great personality and be really fun, but if it's not exhibiting all those wonderful qualities, it will rarely be noticed.

So what *does* make a package really good? I used my own set of criteria which included :

- Did it make me wish I had designed it? There were several that I envied and secretly (and now not-so-secretly!) hated the designer for doing before I even could think of it. In addition, it was great because it was perfectly appropriate for that client or product.
- Was the design solution smart? Did it solve a problem that competitive products hadn't? Was there an aha! moment? Those are rare moments in design, but finding them is what keeps me trying every day.
- Did the package tell the brand story? We've all heard this before... blah, blah, branding, blah, blah. I wanted to connect with the package and the brand. I wanted to care to find out more and then be rewarded for taking the time.
- Did the design feel authentic and real to that story? On some of the submissions the design was nice but it didn't feel like it had a soul, it didn't feel real to the product or the brand. It felt like a copy-cat brand. Honestly with some packages it was a gut feeling, but it was very clear that others mimicked a competitor.
- Did the package feel like it belonged in the product category, and yet was unique to the category? Did the product have the visual cues of its category—for instance, did the milk package look like milk and not like motor oil?
- Was the package exciting and interesting to look at? Would it compel me to pick it up or even notice it? This is probably the most subjective of my criteria and this is precisely why there are four distinctly different authors for this book. At some point "good package design" comes down to personal taste.

No, this book isn't the ultimate doctrine on making a package really good. It doesn't give the scientific formula. It doesn't have all the answers. But it is a tool that dissects and puts into words what four authors from various backgrounds think about packaging. So agree, disagree, hate us or love us, but hopefully, you will come away with a broader perspective and your own criteria for what makes a really good package.

with Sharon Werner

My favorite package designs inside this book are...
Help Remedies (page 199). I wish I had designed
this package.

You know a package design is really good when...
It makes you (and, more importantly, consumers)
pick it up off the shelf. Getting consumers to
even notice the package (does it stand out from
its competition?) is a great first step. Then, is it
intriguing enough to get them to pick it up? Is there
an emotional connection or payoff? And, lastly, does
it make them want to purchase it? As a designer, if
your package design has accomplished those critical
things, you've done your job. The rest is up to what's
inside to make it a successful product.

The best thing a client ever said to me was...
It's not exactly words, but more of an emotional
response. It's sort of our secret goal to make
clients cry—with happiness! Many of our clients are
start-up businesses, and they are passionate and
heavily invested, both financially and emotionally,
in their product. So when they see it coming to life
with branding and packaging, they are often moved
to tears. It's the best feeling. We know we have
done our job.

And the worst ...
"I want it to win awards!" What that says to me is that
the client wants something they have seen before,
such as in a design annual or magazine. Generally,
that means it's at least two years old and, well,
frankly, it's already been done. That's a signal that
the client doesn't really want to be a leader but
somewhere just behind the leader.

For creative inspiration, I use...
I've always been a magazine junkie. I love magazines,
and now I include blogs: fashion/art/design/whatever
blogs. I can get completely lost for hours and come
away inspired, but in a very muddled, unclear sort of
way. Sometimes it's really more inspiration for what
I don't want to do, since it can be so overwhelming. I
also spend hours in the grocery store doing research
for new projects.

The smartest thing I ever heard anyone say about package design is...
"A great package design is the fastest way to kill a bad product." A great package raises the consumer's expectations of the product inside. They may make the purchase once, but if the product doesn't perform to those expectations, they won't make that purchase again.

The best career advice I ever received was...
"Sneak up on a design solution: It doesn't have to come all at once. Work your way around it; try some different approaches; turn it upside-down and sideways in your mind." Whenever I am stumped for an idea, I think of this advice and it immediately takes the stress off.

Most designers probably don't know that...
They have the power not only to design a lovely package but to direct the entire perception of the brand. Even the smallest package carries great weight in informing consumers about the product, who the company behind the product is, and what they believe. This is incredible power: Don't squander it!

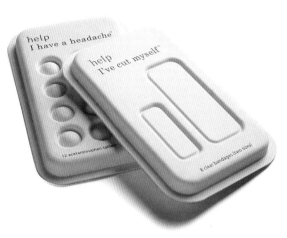

10 Mistakes Designers Make When Designing Product Packaging

BY SHARON WERNER

1. **Not knowing the product category.**
   What are the important visual cues within the category that communicate the product type? These product category cues are most obvious in a liquor store environment; the brown-goods category (whiskey and scotch) looks very different than the white-goods category (vodka and gin.) That difference is due to visual cues; they may be subtle or more overt, such as a brown versus a clear bottle. Every category has them; it's what makes foods look appetizing and hardware look masculine. As a designer you can certainly decide to break away from these cues, but you need to do it with the knowledge of how you are then going to guide the consumer in understanding your product.

2. **Not understanding what motivates a purchase.**
   In an ideal setting it can simply be a cool-looking package, but often it takes more to motivate a consumer to make a purchase. Before designing a package, it's important to be a student first. Become a student of the grocery store, the department store, the gas station, the entire world. Understand how and where the product will be sold. Observe people make purchasing decisions; see what they have in their carts and baskets. Look at how a package performs on the top shelf, middle shelf, and the bottom shelf of a fully stocked grocery aisle. This isn't something that can be gleaned and completely understood from a branding book; you have to immerse yourself in the experience.

3. **Ignoring product merchandising.**
   Determine the locations where the product could potentially sell and keep the details of that in mind. For instance, when deciding on a bottle for an energy drink, be aware of the maximum height of the shelves. Although an extremely tall, slender bottle might look great, if it's too tall for the store's shelf height—which is based on other energy drinks—that's a problem.

4. **Not knowing the product.**
   What makes it special? Why is it better than a competing product? What is the history of both the product and the company? How is the product used? How does it make you feel? Where does it come from? What are consumers' expectations of the product? What do consumers need to know about the product? Why should consumers care about the product? Etcetera, etcetera, etcetera!

5. **Not using the information you have.**
   Many designers gather all this information and charge clients for this phase of work, but then they don't know what to do with it or, worse, they choose to ignore it. Remember to use the information to build a brand story that becomes the guide for the entire brand and all variations of the packaging. So many products look nice but are soulless; they have no story. Create a story for the brand and bounce every decision to be made about that brand against the story. Does it fit? Is it appropriate? Ideally, that story is built on something that is real and inherent in the product.

6. **Being afraid to break the rules.**
   After you've followed rules 1-5—ignore 1-5. Many designers are afraid to venture away from the research and branding talk, but the best packaging often comes from intuitive thinking and instinct. That is a place that falls in between all the research and is often the place that moves a category forward, but it's also a very risky place to be.

7. **Falling into the trend trap.**
   Generally, it's best to avoid trendy design solutions that will feel dated in a year or two. Of course, this doesn't necessarily apply to limited–time offer packaging or trend-based products. Brand equity is built in part by the consumer's exposure to the package; if the package becomes dated-looking and has to change every year to stay fresh, this interferes with product recognition.

8. **Not thinking about the entire package.**
   Leave no side ignored. Think about the whole package, all the sides, top, and bottom. Don't simply apply 2D graphics to a 3D package, think about the entire form. Use the real estate to communicate a message, to add personality, or to give the package some needed breathing room. It's nice to add a touch of surprise to the package—something hidden under a flap, or something that reveals itself only when you see a shelf of product. A hidden message inside a package may not sell the product, but it will create a memorable experience for the consumer.

9. **Over-packaging.**
   Never over-package, no matter how cool it looks. This really doesn't need additional explanation. Avoid packaging forms (such as clamshell and blister packs) that are complicated to open, require tools, and can cause injury. Although it is not always possible to avoid them, these types of packages can create an unpleasant experience for consumers and do nothing to build consumer brand loyalty.

10. **Don't over design.**
    Keep it simple.

Sharon Werner founded the Minneapolis-based design firm: Werner Design Werks, Inc in 1991. The company specializes in combining strong visual language with sound design solutions to create work that not only impacts commerce but also culture. This creative and business strategy has attracted and gained praise from clients including: Target Corporation, Mohawk Paper, Chronicle Books, Mrs. Meyer's-Clean Day, Blu Dot Design and Manufacturing, Nick at Nite, VH-1 Networks, Levi's, Minnesota Public Radio, Ogilvy, Comedy Central, and Urban Outfitters.

food

TESCO

INGREDIENTS

SEA SALT FLAKES 200g℮

Roasted Sea Bass: Take a whole sea bass, slash twice on each side and insert fresh rosemary. Rub fish with olive oil and sprinkle with Sea Salt. Roast in the oven.

TESCO

INGREDIENTS

DRIED PORCINI MUSHROOMS 40g

Pasta Porcini: Soak Dried Porcini Mushrooms in hot water and drain. Sauté garlic in olive oil, add salt and pepper, tomatoes and the mushrooms. Simmer. Serve with cooked pasta.

One-quarter of a pack rehydrated contains

Calories	Sugar	Fat	Saturates	Salt
66	**4.2g**	**0.8g**	**0.1g**	**trace**
3%	8%	4%	<1%	<1%

of your guideline daily amount

"The black and white imagery helps to make this range look upmarket, and they all work brilliantly as a range that has to comprise a huge number of products."

— Bronwen Edwards, page 54

TESCO

INGREDIENTS

WHITE BALSAMIC CONDIMENT 250ml ℮

Tangy Vinaigrette: Blend extra virgin olive oil with White Balsamic Condiment, crushed garlic, mustard and ground black pepper. Add a splash to a simple green salad.

Each tablespoon contains		
Calories	12	1%
Sugar	3.1g	3%
Fat	trace	<1%
Saturates	trace	<1%
Salt	trace	<1%
of your guideline daily amount		

TESCO

INGREDIENTS

KAFFIR LIME LEAVES 2g

Thai Fish Cakes: Place fish, boiled potatoes, spring onions, garlic, chilli and Kaffir Lime Leaves in a food mixer. Mix well. Form small patties from the mixture, dip in beaten egg and flour and fry in a wok. Serve with a squeeze of lime.

…IENTS

…LLA
…S
…DS

…l Custard:
…anilla Pod,
… the seeds
… gently in a
… double
…move the
…d whisked
…, cornflour
…r. Mix until
creamy.

TESCO

INGREDIENTS

TOASTED PINE NUTS 100g ℮

Boardroom Chicken: Fry Pine Nuts in a dry pan, add chicken pieces and flash fry. Place in an ovenproof dish with olive oil and sundried tomatoes. Bake in the oven.

One-quarter of a pack contains

Calories	Sugar	Fat	Saturates	Salt
179	0.9g	17.3g	1.2g	trace
9%	1%	25%	6%	<1%

PRODUCT	Canned Vegetables, Pasta & Pulses
DESIGN FIRM	Turner Duckworth
LOCATION	London, England and San Francisco, CA
CLIENT	Waitrose Ltd.

 All hail yet another glorious model of simplicity. A design architecture that is this stripped-back can be polarizing. What some see as elegant and contemporary, others can see as generic. When there are only a few elements to play with, every one of them has to be optimized. Here, the considered colors and the straightforward typeface allow the product presentation to carry the message. In this case, the food-as-hero strategy also has an inviting tone. Never having considered buying canned celery hearts over fresh, this identity would convert me. Congrats to Waitrose for being this courageous.

 The graphic quality of these cans get every detail absolutely right; simple center-stacked typography with very simple product names (no fancy descriptive adjectives), and the graphic layout of the photos (beans aren't glistening in a bowl but rather laid out so we can appreciate the shape and color of each fresh bean). The unusual colors of the labels go against almost every text book description of what colors "sell food," but these are handsome and enhance the food images.

PRODUCT	Lake Champlain Chocolates - 5 Star
DESIGN FIRM	Optima Soulsight
LOCATION	HIghland Park, IL
CLIENT	Lake Champlain Chocolates

PRODUCT	18 Rabbits Granola
DESIGN FIRM	Eric & Christine Strohl
LOCATION	San Francisco, CA
CLIENT	18 Rabbits Granola

 Needless to say, a design architecture has to be flexible. It has to adapt to every brand offering and every different consumption experience. Here we have the brand experience in an everyday, bite-sized expression. While its logo is well designed, I'm not sure that the 5 Star sub-brand is relevant to this everyday experience. And even if it's required to differentiate these products from the organic line, I'm not sure its size or relation to the brand banner is appropriate. When elements are too similar in visual impression, there is no organization. If everything is big, then nothing is. A design needs to control the perception, guide the eyes to the most important elements in their proper hierarchy. I'm just not sure that the 5 Star sub-brand adds that much to the brand promise.

 This brand name just begs the question, "What's the brand story here?" It's not revealed on the front of the package. I hope the back panel reveals the mystery. Regardless, this well-constructed design architecture, radiant dual-color palette, and controlled product presentation promises a straightforward, premium-quality and honest-to-goodness wholesomeness. I love the choice of the black boxes to signal the unique selling features—impactful but not intrusive. The overall appeal is attention-grabbing but not at the expense of being garish or overstated.

 I visited the 18 Rabbits website, because I was so curious, first off, about the name. Evidently, it's about a rabbit that was briefly left to its own devices outdoors by the company owner (a child at the time), tempted by the aroma of her mom's freshly made granola. Well, soon there was a family of 18 rabbits (oops.) Overall, I really like this package, but there's something just a bit too slick about it. Maybe it's the metallic quality of the material and colors. The brand story, which is not communicated on the front, is actually really sweet and personal, and this feels more "big brand." With that said, I like the type treatment, the clear labeling system for product attributes, and the detail of the repetitive lines at the edges, simulating the crimped edge. This package was enhanced by the website, because I understood the brand story better. Not sure if consumers will take the time to do that.

PRODUCT	**Oloves**
DESIGN FIRM	Cowan London
LOCATION	London, England
CLIENT	Oloves

 Strong idea, strong name, strong iconic branding, and strong execution. Yep, I'm a fan. The silver background does a magnificent job of throwing forward the gloriously hyper-real olives and ties together beautifully with the sailor tattoo–style mnemonic. Strong color differentiation, yet the strong simplicity of this design makes them all sing together as a range. Good enough to eat!

 What's not to love? A wonderfully clever twist on the Forever Heart Tattoo. This design is a great example of an "aha" moment when you see a design that nails it! The ribbon-wrapped, full-bodied illustrations are entertaining, and their highlights, color-coding, and heart-pounding background burst are absolutely palpable! These animated products really look like they love each other. I can practically visualize them nestling inside this flexible pouch. Perhaps Pixar could make a movie about them.

 How could you not fall in love with this packaging? One of food branding's cardinal rules is "make the product the hero." Here the stylized product illustration takes center stage with a color-banding system that immediately signals flavor differentiation. The all-cap logo has lots of impact but perhaps could have been a bit more crafted. These graphics more than compensate for the somewhat industrial pouch structure.

PRODUCT	**Heinz Baby Food Range**	PRODUCT	**Lake Champlain Chocolates - Premium**
DESIGN FIRM	Cowan London	DESIGN FIRM	Optima Soulsight
LOCATION	London, England	LOCATION	Highland Park, IL
CLIENT	Heinz	CLIENT	Lake Champlain Chocolates

 Really simple, really strong, and very endearing. All the ingredients for a successful children's product, and I'm sure those eyes follow you 'round the room! Keeping them really unfussed, colorful, and leaving the characters as the heroes with just a simple descriptor and product shot (which I'm sure was one of those client compromises) makes them iconic and playful, and using the keystone makes them entirely ownable.

 A round of applause for another fresh set of designs that is sure to create a buzz. What a clever adaptation of the keystones into simple animated forms! With eyes on these characters that look over the viewer's shoulder, these cans leap off the shelf. A can as a great interactive experience is brilliant! I can see kids wanting to take them home, eat the contents, and then ask to sleep with them at night.

 I applaud Heinz for having the confidence in their established brands to have fun with the well-known icons. The keystone animal faces are hilarious and might make the drudgery of grocery shopping actually enjoyable. The slightly metallic label paper makes the clean, bright colors almost glow, giving the eyes of the animals even more sparkle. The typography strikes the right, kid-friendly balance—sending the cues that this is a baby product—without being so extreme and over the top that it's difficult to read. It just looks—friendly.

 There is a rich experience conveyed by the diversity of elements that is very appealing. The initial impression is of an aesthetically harmonious combination of colors. The sleeve colors against the rich chocolate structure have a palpable quality. The elegant brand mark nicely balances the unusual yet attractive variety panel and romance copy. The cocoa bean illustrations add an artisan feel. The layers of visual information give the sense that there is much to be enjoyed inside the box.

 What I liked most about the organic bar design—specifically the misfitting, hand-lettered type—I find just a bit too refined in this execution. I certainly understand the objective to evoke a more giftable occasion, and this design succeeds in that way. However, it's all just a bit too slick. I'm curious about the choice to have the brand name inside a banner where it more freely floated on the bar. I like the ripped paper/ rough silk-screened appeal of the flavor banner and greatly admire the choice of color on each pack. The subtle and inconsistent texture of the base box contrasts well against the overwrap sleeve. It all feels just a bit too formal and controlled and, as a result, less indulgent.

PRODUCT	Heinz Beanz 'n' Balls
DESIGN FIRM	Cowan London
LOCATION	London, England
CLIENT	Heinz

 These are slightly controversial; they've gone down brilliantly over here in the UK but may be lost abroad if you don't realize these are based on cheap newspaper headlines and aimed at students and the like. They're highly amusing, the design itself sticks with the Heinz branding unit, but the idea here—and its success—is in the copywriting. I applaud Cowan for managing to get 36pt-type *"RED HOT BALLS"* on an established family brand with full blessing! It certainly livens up cooking time; the cans are covered with witty little stories, innuendo, and some serious tongue-in-cheek. Bravo.

 A wonderful bold, defiant, and edgy solution! Really—a smart design concept that has what it says it has—this must have been such fun to work on! The design stays true to the concept from beginning to end, from the Heinz masthead through the banner headline, blurbs, date, edition, tag line, provocative photography, and sensational copy—so perfect!—and its disrespect of traditional category cues is great fun!

PRODUCT	**Fortnum & Mason Jams**
DESIGN FIRM	Pearlfisher
LOCATION	London, England
CLIENT	Fortnum & Mason

PRODUCT	**Asda Extra Special**
DESIGN FIRM	Core
LOCATION	London, England
CLIENT	Asda

 MK In a category filled with monotonous, rectangular labels, sometimes a unique die cut can be the defining feature that breaks through the clutter. The architecture of this label brings the eye down through the information, with a focus on the last element (unusually positioned below the mandatory copy), to a number that indicates the product's number within a collection. Elegant typography, precise details, harmonious colors, and precious illustrations capture the brand's luxurious positioning.

RW At face value, there's nothing revolutionary or unique about this identity, apart from its interesting label die cut. But, to me, that one element is almost enough. It's every design firm's dream to work on a specialty jam. Don't we all have one in our portfolios? And so I imagine that this initial design exploration tried to push the limits of what has already been done—and overdone—in this visually fussy category. While many consumers may not immediately discern the colored, white, and black backgrounds as the value tiers (good, better, and best), and fewer still might make the connection of the shape to a Georgian garden marker, it's still a pleasure to see how one single, well-crafted element like this label shape can have such an influential impact.

 BE The virtue in this design is the subtle idea in the logo, which, on closer inspection, is a lovely discovery. The photography style does make those sausages look extremely tasty, I have to say, and the white-on-white backdrops allow the colors of the food to punch out, making it feel fresh and delicious. The little imperfections make it feel real and unforced.

 MK To quote a colleague of mine (in reference to packaging design): Keep your audience entertained! This design solution—not unlike a cooking channel—does exactly that by using the food as the simple and authentic story. Oranges are not particularly attractive once squeezed, and a meal is not always that beautiful on plate. The beauty is in their unstylized beauty. They say, "Look at me: This is how I really am when I am ready to be consumed." With that, the colors and presentation effectively create genuine appetite appeal. The pure white background, simple sans serif type—set open and printed in a light color—and the amount of open space convey a clean, perhaps even sterile, environment in which the food is prepared. I particularly like the "Extra Special"—as though any marketer does not think their product is extra special—but this one states it! In this case, in its handwritten script, it is a formal pledge.

PRODUCT	**Plum Kids Organic Frozen Food**
DESIGN FIRM	Brand Engine
LOCATION	Sausalito, CA
CLIENT	Tribeca Kitchen

 There is a nice evolution from the Plum baby food to this kids' line. The series of loops created by the dotted line captures the nonstop motion of a young kid and yet effectively navigates the viewer to the final message: organic food for the active child. There is a lot of information to be conveyed and although the numerous violators disturb the cleanliness of the design, the circular format of the secondary copy communicates a playful disposition.

PRODUCT	**Moment Du Chocolat**
DESIGN FIRM	Brandhouse
LOCATION	London, England
CLIENT	Moment Du Chocolat

PRODUCT	**Sahale Snacks**
DESIGN FIRM	Niedermeier Design
LOCATION	Seattle, WA
CLIENT	Sahale Snacks

 MK Can I bite into the packaging design? A colleague of mine says that packaging design should say, "Here I am," not overwhelm, and keep the audience entertained. This design does all that!

 RW I had my first sip of real hot chocolate in a café in Leuven, Belgium, and it ruined Hershey's Cocoa for me forever. This identity takes me right back to that unforgettable experience. The tapered cup structure marries well with the indulgent colors and metalized texture. Here's an engaging way to highlight the product and separate it from all the powdered mixes. My only build on this might be to emboss the chocolate with an ownable icon so that this icon could only belong to this yummy brand.

 SW This is clearly premium. All the premium cues are present—brushed metallic finish, minimal text with simple font selection, and an architectural form. It feels warm and rich, as hot chocolate should be. I appreciate the linework creating warm objects, but I'm not sure that what I assume is a hot-water bottle is as effective as the cup—when I think of a hot-water bottle, I think of being ill. Is that the correct message?

MK The American marketplace is saturated with poorly designed snack packaging. The dark atmosphere with ambient lighting is the first compelling aspect to this design. Then the beautiful, highlighted products, set in unique dishes on interestingly clothed and propped tables, appear both savory and mysterious. The brand identity is well designed and holds together nicely to add just the right ethnic feel without seeming too unfamiliar to sample. The overall communication is of a seductive snack experience.

 RW What I like most about this architecture is its ability to contain all the information in one organized device—an open invitation for the food to take center stage. There is a bit too much going on in the background of these over-stylized food shots that distracts from the central focus—too much sense of place and not enough food. I'm curious about the changing color bands: Why are the flavor banner and the ingredient listing in contrasting colors? I'm specifically bothered by the subtle inconsistencies in the photo angle and perspective—some more top-down, others more side-on. Missing on these details detracts from the overall appeal. Still, the organization of elements and the visual drama carry the day.

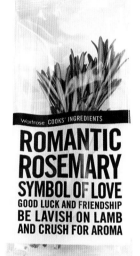

Waitrose COOKS' INGREDIENTS

THE BEAUTIFUL
BAY LEAF
SAVOURY OR SWEET
COMFORTING IN CUSTARDS, SUBTLE IN STEWS
INFUSE YOUR OILS AND PEP UP YOUR PIES
THE ESSENTIAL BOUQUET GARNI
OR 'BACCALAUREATE'
GARLANDS OF BAY TO HONOUR THE SCHOLAR

Waitrose COOKS' INGREDIENTS

COOL COOL
MINT
NOT JUST FOR JELLY!
INFUSE YOUR TEA, DRESS UP YOUR DRINKS
PAIR UP WITH PEAS OR SUMMER SORBET

Waitrose COOKS' INGREDIENTS

ROMANTIC
ROSEMARY
SYMBOL OF LOVE
GOOD LUCK AND FRIENDSHIP
BE LAVISH ON LAMB
AND CRUSH FOR AROMA

Waitrose COOKS' INGREDIENTS

MAJESTIC
BASIL
'KING OF THE HERBS'
ONCE REGARDED SACRED TO THE GODS
FRAGRANT BASIL STILL REIGNS SUPREME

Waitrose COOKS' INGREDIENTS

TANTALISING
TARRAGON
'FINE HERBS'
FAVOURED IN FRANCE
FAMOUS FOR TARTARE
MUSTARD AND VINEGAR

Waitrose COOKS' INGREDIENTS

BORAGE
HERB OF
THE WEEK
SOMETHING SEASONAL OR SIMPLY SPECIAL

PRODUCT	**Waitrose Herbs**
DESIGN FIRM	Lewis Moberly
LOCATION	London, England
CLIENT	Waitrose Ltd.

 Brazen, engaging, and compelling is what makes for a great headline and for an excellent design solution. This packaging design literally gets involved with the consumer. It's hard to explain; shopping for herbs is a quiet experience, but this design turns it into an event. Between what the text says and the clear-cut black (with the occasional red headline) text on a white background, the product looks simply irresistible.

 A complement to the Waitrose mustards and dry Cooks line, here the all-type execution is missing some of the system's approachable whimsy. A dash of sherry vinegar is real kitchen chatter in my home, and it makes the brand feel more authentic. I'm not quite as engaged by the more "editorial" language here. It feels a bit cold. I'm interested in the choice of red: Is that to signal a promotional item? Would a story about how and when to use borage be perhaps more appropriate? When I think herbs, the core determinant is freshness. While I applaud Waitrose's desire to brand items to their greatest commodity, I'm not sure that this effort is as compelling as the unpackaged—and therefore perceptually fresher— herbs sitting next to it.

 This is a far cry from the prepackaged herbs I find at my grocer—clamshell packs that lack significant branding of any type. The graphic nature of this bold, typographic approach—albeit a bit cold—is an intriguing contrast to the organic green leaves inside. It's interesting to compare this to the Tesco recipe additives—both typographic yet very different from each other.

Clearspring

APPLE & PINEAPPLE
ORGANIC FRUIT PURÉE DESSERT

Clearspring

APPLE & APRICOT
ORGANIC FRUIT PURÉE DESSERT

Clearspring

PEAR & BANANA
ORGANIC FRUIT PURÉE DESSERT

Clearspring

APPLE & BLUEBERRY
ORGANIC FRUIT PURÉE DESSERT

Clearspring

APPLE & STRAWBERRY
ORGANIC FRUIT PURÉE DESSERT

Clearspring

PEAR
ORGANIC FRUIT PURÉE DESSERT

PRODUCT	**Clearspring Organic Fruit Purees**
DESIGN FIRM	Mayday
LOCATION	London, England
CLIENT	Clearspring

 This is refreshing in more ways than one. First, it's an ingredients shot that actually looks stylish—usually something that designers groan at as a mandatory on a brief, but this uses it as the hero of the idea, and of the design. It's been shot consistently and brightly, adding to the fluidity of the idea—and the fresh juiciness of the fruit—across all the variants. Second, it's great to see a pudding that has so much deliciously colorful, clean, crisp fruit on it, with a white pack to magnify the fresh colors, and really simple, pared-down (no pun intended) typography that does only what it needs to, effectively. It's elegant and has huge taste appeal, with a modern, crisp feel that exudes real clarity and style.

 These well-crafted and carefully staged designs are stunning. White is beautifully used to showcase the tantalizing fruits and the simple band of copy. The masterful photography of the fruits is complemented by how they artfully become whole again. The color contrasts have a desire-inducing effect.

 What a delicious and delightful solution. I'm happy to see that it works equally well as a single fruit (e.g., pear) as it does in marrying such different fruit shapes as apples and blueberries or pears and bananas. Smart flavor type in complementing colors adds to the juicy impression. Imagining that the generic Clearspring logo could not change, I admire how it is grayed down so as not to visually interrupt the beautiful central focus of this impressive identity. Bravo!

SW This is an elegantly simple solution, from the square box to the simple, beautiful color photography and the thin sans serif typography. I especially like the choice of the ampersand, which almost becomes a logo of sorts.

PRODUCT	**Cadbury Chocolates**
DESIGN FIRM	Storm Corporate Design
LOCATION	Auckland, New Zealand
CLIENT	Cadbury India

 There's nothing admirable in the design here: It's the existing Cadbury logo, on the existing Cadbury color. The structure, however, does challenge conventions (although how it doesn't tip all the chocolates out when it's upended, I'm not sure!) I like the simplicity of simply cutting off an edge, instantly making it striking on shelf.

 Color and shape are a brand's core mnemonics. A red, contoured bottle can only be one thing. And nowhere (outside of that cola brand) are these elements better leveraged than in this concept. Chocolate assortments are the cliché gift. They define *special occasion only*, leaving lots of half-eaten boxes of candy to be tossed out. Here, however, the simple impression seems more *everyday* and for *me.* I bet the design firm wanted the chance to contemporize this logo but were turned down in favor of its equity. As with all visual communication, from fine art to graphic design, it's a true talent to know when to stop, and this design stops just in time.

PRODUCT	**Gardenburger Gourmet**
DESIGN FIRM	PhilippeBecker
LOCATION	San Francisco, CA
CLIENT	Gardenburger

 In the bustle of the marketplace, the combination of the regional-stamp designs and the appetite-appeal imagery establishes the product experience. Perhaps the stamps—with their artwork, use of typography, and detailed format—are a bit expected in terms of the communication of a cultural flavor, but the execution is handled impeccably. With so many poor examples of food photography and styling, this one is an excellent example of how to make a fairly unattractive product look especially appealing. It is the sum of the architecture of each of these designs, with all of their visual elements handled well, that makes this line work.

 I appreciate it when designers can take a specialty-brand aesthetic and make it work in a big-brand context. Beautiful food-as-hero photography eliminates the edges of the plate so as to direct your visual attention directly to the food. The postage-stamp/luggage-badge flavor device and their well-considered colors both violate and energize. I specifically like that the design firm did not "cheat" by removing the "NEW" flags before submitting this for consideration. These elements are often a reality, and smart design architectures provide a staging area for promotional messaging. Extra points for honesty!

PRODUCT	**Butterfield Market bag**
DESIGN FIRM	Mucca Design
LOCATION	New York, NY
CLIENT	Butterfield Market

PRODUCT	**Butterfield Market (Butterfield Box)**
DESIGN FIRM	Mucca Design
LOCATION	New York, NY
CLIENT	Butterfield Market

 The intricacies of this design are admirable in their own right; no cutting corners on this detailed piece of design! This splits itself into two halves—the logo and its surround, and the archaic illustrations that adorn the ephemera. First, the logo: The slightly odd, unusual, highly detailed "B" pings out on a sea of intricate bank note–style decoration. This gives the brand cues of enormous gravitas, heritage, care, and craft. The etched product illustrations also hark back to a heritage brand. They aren't too fusty, using the aubergine color from the logo to tie it all together nicely. I like their unusual positioning; I'm not sure they jump out, but this quirkiness helps pull it back to a modern feel, helped by the simple, duotone-color palette and single illustration color. It looks premium, but it has a little fun without losing any of its credentials or tastiness.

 Great care and detail have gone into the Butterfield packaging system—it's both handsome and pretty, modern and historic. This is obviously a premier grocery, and it's immediately evident in each of the packaging elements. The lovely calligraphic "B" of the logo, with its intricate in-line stroke, is distinct enough to be immediately recognizable. The color palette uses a masculine aubergine and balances it with the soft mint color—handsome *and* pretty. This detailed package has a historic feel— appropriate but ironically refreshing, as many premium products tend toward simple and sparse.

 Quirky and memorable. Given the history of rubber stamps as a marking device to add identification and information to products, they work well to communicate this historic market's local-community personality. The elaborate geometric background pattern behind the unusual monogram "B" adds to the ingenuity of this line.

This identity certainly evokes an impressive brand. I love replacing shopping bags with the box, a twenty-first century reinterpretation of the original grocery market experience. The tightly illustrated background behind the monogram "B" echoes the visual cues of currency, giving the brand mark a literally noteworthy impression. Nostalgic without being dusty, this identity is most certainly on target for its yuppie audience. I can just see the Upper East Side i-bankers eating this up.

PRODUCT	**Sweet's Gourmet Taffy**
DESIGN FIRM	Struck
LOCATION	Salt Lake City, UT
CLIENT	Sweet's

 A lovely and completely relevant structural design here, with some clever paper engineering that creates a definite difference. I particularly like the way they can stand horizontally or upright, making them flexible at the retail end. The graphics themselves have a retro vein that works well with the structure. There is a certain naiveté about it which has charm, and while I think the strength is in the structure, the design itself does have a nostalgic feel that adds to the overall sweetness of the packs (pun intended).

 The paperboard structure alone makes for a compelling design solution and captures the experience of twisting open the enclosed product. The pastel color palette, uncluttered Primary Display Panel, and product typography reflect a lovely mid-century aesthetic. The design of two Primary Display Panels, permitting the product to be positioned either horizontally or vertically, is an added bonus as it allows for optimal marketing of the product. The soft wave graphic and the shaded swirl backgrounds are appealingly consumer-friendly, although if the hue were bumped up a bit, the brand identity would be more easily recognizable.

 It's not enough sometimes to simply invent a unique package structure. A designer's job often includes securing a manufacturing partner that can create the desired effect within the client's budget parameters. I applaud the square shape and unique twist closure. The color palette, type, and illustrated icons evoke a whimsical nostalgia that is very much part of the taffy-eating experience. The horizontal and vertical orientations also provide merchandising flexibility.

 I am fascinated by this innovative structural design; I would purchase this product for that alone. I am dying to twist those ends open! I am impressed with the designer's ability to get this manufactured locally and affordably.

PRODUCT	**ChiliChaser Salsa**
DESIGN FIRM	Sudduth Design Co.
LOCATION	Austin, TX
CLIENT	Lava Foods

PRODUCT	**Jamba Juice Citrus Squeeze Fruit Sours**
DESIGN FIRM	Sudduth Design Co.
LOCATION	Austin, TX
CLIENT	Jamba Juice

 A design with an independent spirit that plays off two printing technologies—the chili art has the appearance of an ACL (applied ceramic label), while the Chili Chaser label design resembles an old-fashioned embossed label placed on top. The design nuances—the smaller *THE* next to the larger *ORIGINAL*, and the smaller *C* in *Chili* and larger *C* in *Chaser*—are an atypical way to establish the hierarchy of information. The bottle feels as though it reflects a time, place, and culture of the past and yet also feels modern. The value added is that this makes a great collectible!

 Tactile. Nothing revolutionary about the graphics (in fact I'm curious about the different type styles between *Chili* and the larger *Chaser*), but something quite special about the texture, inviting consumer to feel it.

 At first glance, this package made a good impression—I liked it immediately. But when I tried to write about it, it became difficult, as many of the details are not working together. Although I appreciate the vintage-style label and typography, I don't understand this choice of aesthetic for a chili product, and it doesn't work stylistically with the wood-cut pepper illustration. What's the inspiration, the brand story? The larger *C* on the word *Chaser* fits the label shape, but it doesn't make sense in the information hierarchy. Sorry, but it looks like a clone of the El Paso Chile Company's older, original packaging—which I've always liked.

 The use of retro graphics works well here, evoking a golden age when boiled sweets naturally came in tins. The name rolls beautifully off the tongue, which also helps with the retro feel. The debossing is what brings it all together, though, making this a little less expected, a little classier, and a lot more tactile for the consumer.

 The colors are so flavorful they create a real sensory experience. I can practically taste and smell the citrus. Definitely works as an impulse item.

 I'm a sucker, pardon the pun, for texture. I'm immediately drawn to this tin and want to feel its rich embossing. Once you get the product in the consumer's hand, it's a short trip to the checkout counter. The vintage graphics are an interesting choice for the otherwise contemporary Jamba Juice brand, but it seems appropriate for these sours. Where the tin structure itself has great heritage, I've often had problems opening traditional tins, allowing the product to spill out. Perhaps there might be a new opening feature for tins, like the ones in round containers for mints and gums, that would retain this authenticity and still elevate the user experience.

 The intensity of these colors makes my mouth pucker—that's a perfect response for fruit puckers. I love the embossed elements; they refract light just enough that the orange actually looks juicy.

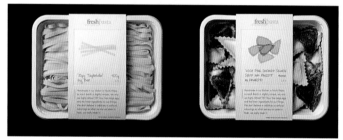

PRODUCT	**Fresh Pasta**
DESIGN FIRM	P&W
LOCATION	London, England
CLIENT	Fresh Pasta Company

PRODUCT	**Rylstone Olive Oil**
DESIGN FIRM	Landor Sydney
LOCATION	Sydney, Australia
CLIENT	Rylstone Olive Press

 Fresh, simple spring to mind. I'm not a fan of putting a picture of the product when you can clearly see the product—which looks rather nice—but it has an elegant illustration style which gives an impression of delicacy and specialness. The white adds to the overall feeling of purity.

 The only thing this beautiful pasta really needed was to be well-protected and creatively marketed and so this beautifully subtle packaging firmly establishes this stunning product. The bellyband as an artist-signed and titled print of an interpretation of the pasta truly elevates the product and packaging to an art form.

 While the fresh pasta category has for some time been thinking "out of the box," this tray structure borrows some of the fresh credentials from the meat and deli case. I like the brand band and the fine-art illustration style. I appreciate the simple differentiation between pasta cuts and styles. I imagine that this could have great presence in the deli case, but if it were to live in the pasta aisle, it would require special merchandising racks to allow consumers to first see these side-on, rather than stacked on top of one another.

 Shelf impact and recognizablilty are the strengths to this design, and its iconic label shape and strong graphic lend themselves to a powerful overall look. I struggle to read the typography, however, and beyond its impact there is little to this design. It's simple, yes; modern, yes; but it leaves me wanting a little more.

 The olive-shaped label, scaled and positioned masterfully on this elegant bottle, definitely commands attention and establishes the brand equity as innovative and modern. I question the white outline for an oil product and find that the type does not read particularly well against the contrasting colors, nor does it help define the personality. Nonetheless, the dramatic neck, gently sloping shoulders, and tapered sides of this green glass bottle add to the overall aesthetic of a producer with very high standards.

 This brand graphic will act as a beacon, drawing attention to this product from thirty feet away. It will become the primary brand mnemonic. I appreciate how the brand icon works with the elegant, almost wine-like bottle shape and black shrouded neck. I agree that the typeface is strong and simple and perhaps just a bit cold. Olive oil is an artisan product, made by craftspeople. Perhaps just a simple signature would have made this design that much more personal and approachable.

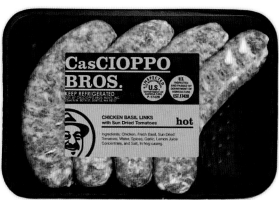

PRODUCT	**CasCioppo Sausages**
DESIGN FIRM	Turnstyle
LOCATION	Seattle, WA
CLIENT	CasCioppo Sausages

 MK Sam looks so friendly, I want to meet him and hear his stories of the days when the butcher made the sale and packaged the meat. The stamp format of his image serves to establish that personal relationship with the consumer. The brand architecture is well constructed and yet flexible enough to adapt to varied formats. The masculine color palette and bold Egyptian type not only conveys strength but projects a fashionably discerning style unique to the meat category.

 RW There is much to admire about this identity. I like the black foam container, now more common than in years past, as an immediate signal of something different from the generic meat counter products. I like the color blocking and the gloss graphics on matte black background. I like the combination of upper and lower case and all cap logo, suggesting the phonetics of an otherwise rather long and confusing brand name. I specifically like the caricature of Sam, lending his smiling face to his family name and adding to the brand's authenticity and integrity.

PRODUCT	**Heinz Salad Cream**
DESIGN FIRM	Cowan London
LOCATION	London, England
CLIENT	Heinz

 Ah, the cumbersome, unwieldy Heinz keystone—bravo to Cowan for managing to shake it up. They've given it relevance, an idea, and a welcome lift with this emotive take on a summer's day picnic. The green is perfect as the grassy backdrop—the core subrand color—and it feels fresh and tasty. The care and consideration that have gone into setting the scene—even down to having a deck chair for the ultra-light versus a heavy wooden chair for the core—all come together to create a considered and very English design.

 A prime example of how consumers interpret packaging designs based on their cultural backgrounds and why it is imperative for designers and clients to understand that not every product—or its corresponding design—translates globally. Although this design is beguiling in the American retail environment (in which I did see it on the shelf in the international section), it is primarily because the pastel colors so completely break the shelf set of typical category color cues. Nonetheless, this is a charming design concept that clearly speaks to a culturally infused brand. With a focus on the details (I especially like the wrinkles in the blanket/label), the effect is one that smartly positions the product as central to a lifestyle experience.

 Talk about refreshing an iconic brand! This identity absolutely owns a distinct "sense of place." The sun-drenched color palette and top-down photo perspective invite the consumer into this summer afternoon picnic, an invitation that I imagine would work all year long. What attracts me most about this identity is how well the Heinz logo and its signature "keystone" icon work—a strong brand badge that lives in concert with the rest of the identity's light, airy freshness. The neck label says it all: pourable sunshine, indeed.

PRODUCT	**Dorset Cereal**		PRODUCT	**Trident Sweet Kicks**
DESIGN FIRM	Big Fish Design Limited		DESIGN FIRM	Coley Porter Bell
LOCATION	London, England		LOCATION	London, England
CLIENT	Dorset Cereal		CLIENT	Cadbury

BE These were the first packs of cereals in the UK to really break the category expectations, with their natural, uncoated stock, die-cutting, and foiling on the logo. You can't actually see them from this image, but there are about six different variants, all with a natural, autumnal palette, that look really stunning together. The rustic simplicity fits perfectly with the product; the simple leaf die cut shows the muesli, so no forced photography is necessary. The silver foiling obviously adds premium, but the simple, considered type makes this feel fresh and different.

MK I agree. The die cut and the matte finish set a nice tone to this original approach. I also like the flush-left layout of the text and its positioning on the bottom half of the pack. Lovely use of scale and color to bring the viewer down through the design.

SW The leaf-shaped, die-cut windows work extremely well to reveal the product. The product manages to balance the line between communicating a natural, healthy, product in a modern aesthetic and not going too earthy. Normally, I'm not fond of the corner violators, but this bright, reddish-orange one balances the design nicely. Nice choice of type font—a thin, modern serif.

MK With the wide appeal of '60s design, these lips, the small pinup-girl silhouettes, and the flavorfully fluid background not only communicate a pop aesthetic but are seductive and mood-setting. I like that the Trident identity just so slightly breaks out of the boundaries of the lips as it subconsciously communicates a real mouthful experience. Notice how the lyrical background imagery, particularly the white highlights, nicely flows the attention around the PDP to focus on the brand. Definitely a fashionable design statement.

PRODUCT	**Lake Champlain Chocolates - Holiday**
DESIGN FIRM	Optima Soulsight
LOCATION	Highland Park, IL
CLIENT	Lake Champlain Chocolates

PRODUCT	**Everyday Truffle Bars**
DESIGN FIRM	Bungalow Creative
LOCATION	Kansas City, MO
CLIENT	Seattle Chocolate Company

 OK, now I'm back to the brand's essence. Turning down the volume on the color palette and warming up the illustrations immediately strikes a better balance with the brand. The unusual shapes and painted illustrations carry the festive message and better reflect the chocolate-eating experience. Here is a lovely example of the proper balance between brand authenticity and holiday sparkle. But where's the brand block? We are back to a floating logo in a different staging area, and this erodes brand consistency.

 I was immediately attracted to the color palette—it's bright, but just off enough to make it interesting—of course I always love chocolate brown for chocolate packaging. There is a nice retro style to the illustration, reminiscent of the days when visiting a good department store was an event and was treated as such. It feels special and worthy of gift giving. It doesn't bother me that, on this special-occasion package, the brand block isn't consistent or prominent—I think it's appropriately sized for a gift item.

 These work really well together, mimicking a stack of presents in a simple, graphic, decorative style. The logo itself doesn't do it for me, but the solid matte finish and the colorful patterns are certainly alluring.

 What a departure from the "everyday"! Nothing new here with the brand mark or flavor communication. In fact, much more could have been made of these elements. Still, the wallpaper textures and vibrant colors are a delight. Big brands might shoot this design system down for its lack of "shopability"—it's impossible to differentiate flavors—but after consumers engage this system for the first time, they may be drawn back to the colors and patterns of their favorite flavor.

 The design strength of these chocolate bars is really how they look as a group. I want to pick them up and own these lush colors as an object. But that's where the design starts to fall apart. The logo (which could use an update) seems smashed into position. The ovals don't relate well in size or shape to the overall package, and I'm not sure what the highlight (?) line on the left side of the oval represents. Individually, the patterns aren't that special, but as a group, they're beautiful.

PRODUCT	**Plum Organics Frozen Baby Food Product Family**
DESIGN FIRM	Brand Engine
LOCATION	Sausalito, CA
CLIENT	Plum Organics

BE This pulls on all the maternal strings—an adorable baby ambling towards a tasty, simple-looking product on an unfussy, modern utensil, combined with a charmingly playful logo that says "healthy" and "handmade"—bingo. The head shot of a spoon is a lovely touch, and overall it has a clean, cute, strikingly modern feel.

MK At first glance, I find the white somewhat contradictory for a baby food product (have you ever seen babies eat?) but then the purity grows on me. The brand identity's top-left positioning introduces this friendly line. The understated color-coding system keeps the focus on the full-color product. The beauty in this design is that an absolutely ordinary object, presented simply, becomes the most beautiful detail.

RW How can you not fall in love with this identity? Organized, efficient, effective, and absolutely adorable. There is little appetite appeal inherent in the product itself, but I love how it is presented, on a spoon just about to go into a baby's mouth. The black-and-white baby photo is a smart, iconic way to represent differing age ranges, and I love the side panels. Simply irresistible!

SW At first glance, this package didn't excite me, but the large baby face on the side sold me. They say babies sell products, and I guess they're right. It communicates "premium," with its spare white background and controlled food photography and silver spoon. I like that the crawling baby is different on each package. It would be a plus if the baby were older for less-strained varieties, as a cue to which food is appropriate at what age. There is something reminiscent of the Michael Graves for Target packaging.

PRODUCT	Tesco Ingredients
DESIGN FIRM	P&W
LOCATION	London, England
CLIENT	Tesco

 Putting recipes on the ingredients is a great idea, and the sans serif caps type looks modern and unfussed. I find the overall look a little sterile, a little cold, but the black-and-white imagery helps to make it look upmarket, and they all work brilliantly as a range that has to comprise a huge number of products.

 These are a knockout, and they glisten on shelf. A clever push-pull strategy that works with the design by providing instructions on using the enclosed ingredient—an added benefit, since consumers tend to purchase based on the recipe. The elements work: the light-color labels, readable two-color design, text sized for hierarchy and readability, the inset photos. The silver metal, foil, and clear plastic or glass are particularly alluring.

 Here is another sans serif type–driven "brand story" strategy. The sophisticated organization and black-and-white imagery make this one stand out. The matte silver and creamy paper stock echo a simple elegance, classic and timeless. American retailers are catching up to this UK/ Euro retail brand design aesthetic. Major CPG's will have to embrace high-end design to justify their price premium against store brands with a presence as lucid as this.

 I applaud the variety of expression in all of Tesco's privately branded products as well as the similarity in design sophistication that holds the brand together. That is a difficult balance that gives their brands room to grow and evolve. The unique containers, type-heavy labels, and monochromatic color scheme are rich and elegant, yet a bit industrial. I find the color of the toasted pine nuts hard to see and out of place in the color palette.

PRODUCT	Edna's Success Cafe Cookies
DESIGN FIRM	Sudduth Design Co.
LOCATION	Austin, TX
CLIENT	Edna's Success Cafe

PRODUCT	Simple Seed Organic Rice
DESIGN FIRM	Capsule
LOCATION	Minneapolis, MN
CLIENT	Gulf Pacific Rice

 Edna's artfully mimics the current revival and popularity of letterpress printing (a printing style that was the precursor to offset lithography) and echoes the affection for the design crafts. There are few instances in which the use of so many type faces works on a primary display panel, and this design solution is one of them. Although rooted in an old-fashioned spirit, this design is timeless and appealing. Love the small rolling pin as an apostrophe, the "Time to EAT!" clock, the overall color, and all the details that make the architecture of this brand work.

 Revolutionary? No! Pleasing? Yes! I am always attracted to this '40s-inspired, '90s-revived design aesthetic: large, drop-shadowed, slab-serif letters and compartmentalized product information. This makes me think any number of well-known paper companies may have ventured out to market a cookie brand. But it's still appealing, even if it's very familiar.

 The illustration on this is lovely, with its innocent and simplistic style which reminds me slightly of *The Little Prince*! The idea is all in the window—a great way to combine the product show-through—integrated into the concept. The clear and simple navigation system and simple, understated typography are a little floaty, but to me, what works on this pack is the illustration.

 A circle is a beautiful shape and, as a whimsical illustration from which seeds grow, it tells a beautiful story. An atypical brand design approach with sensitivity to the overall typography, right down to the "grown in the USA." Welcoming colors, a minimalist design, a graceful, modern solution that feels quietly optimistic. This simple seed has an imaginative, spunky, and distinct personality. I like the quiet little tag line as it politely speaks its message.

 This is a lovely packaging system. The hierarchy of information and color coding is easy to navigate. The use of the die-cut window, allowing the rice to peek through, is handled well. Even the regulatory copy looks good. However, I'm a bit confused by the illustration and what it's depicting; it appears that rice is a root or a bulb that grows under the earth. Is it a plant? A tree? Am I missing something? But I do like the color, mass, and whimsy the illustration provides.

PRODUCT	**Fortnum & Mason Tercentenary**
DESIGN FIRM	Pearlfisher
LOCATION	London, England
CLIENT	Fortnum and Mason

PRODUCT	**Seafood & Eat It Crabmeat**
DESIGN FIRM	Davies Leslie-Smith
LOCATION	Buckinghamshire, England
CLIENT	Seafood & Eat It

 This is elegant in its heavy use of black, its refined and hugely kerned typography, and the choice of imagery itself. I don't think you could find posher clock hands if you tried! I like the way it's not always the same clock, either, pulling it away from being elegant but bland. I'm not sure I would get "moving forward timelessly," but I certainly would get that daily biscuit reminder!

 This design literally stops time. Packaging design at its best conveys a sense of anticipation, and is there a more dramatic way to do that than with elements that express the times of day and their respective comings and goings? A sharp and minimalist design that makes beautiful use of delicate, ornamental, gold clock hands, the juxtaposition of the filigree on the black canister is strikingly handsome, and the elegant white script is perfectly balanced by the uppercase gold sans serif caps.

 How many identities desperately try to tie their brand to a specific "day part" or consumption occasion? This identity ties itself to a recurring trigger that reminds its consumers that it's time to indulge. Although the gold-and-black palette are certainly not proprietary, never before has teatime been more elegantly represented. I can almost hear the four rich, ringing chimes. How long is it before the 7 a.m. morning blend comes out?

 First, and most important: Great idea; it's seafood, so why not make the whole design out of sand? Cracking! They're passionate about seafood, so it's a lovely idea; the heart doesn't look forced or contrived. Second, what a bold use of color differentiation that clearly pings out on shelf, the black panel down the bottom giving a premium feel and making the whole thing strikingly simple to decode. The carefully crafted typography helps the premium, considered feel. Last, the strength in the crab icon, with its radiating sandy lines, makes the whole range so clearly hang together with impressive standout—in a classy, not brassy, way. I'm hooked!

 I'm not sure how intentional it was but, to me, the graphic resembles a close-up of a heart tattoo turned into a genial crab. With tattoos so the rage, this graphic is very vogue. The bold-to-regular type format of the brand identity and the well-scaled, well-positioned, contemporary white text on black is a format that I see often, but I like it—it's attractive, direct, and it communicates well. The pastel hues have a cosmetic feel—they remind me of an eye shadow compact—but I imagine that in retail, on a competitive shelf set, these make for great shelf appeal. Anyway, why shouldn't seafood be heart-poundingly sexy?

PRODUCT	Liberation Fairtrade Peanuts
DESIGN FIRM	P&W
LOCATION	London, England
CLIENT	Liberation Foods CIC

PRODUCT	Langage Farm
DESIGN FIRM	biz-R
LOCATION	Totnes, England
CLIENT	Langage Farm

(BE) I'm in agreement with Sharon's comment below that it's a real shame there isn't more variety between the flavors, a few different nutty poses, but this is lighthearted, fun, and a welcome release from the serious and worthy fair-trade genre. The heavy black instantly links it with the premium lines in this category, and the little hand-drawn additions add a quirky, friendly feel.

(MK) Protesting for liberation—these guys are really nuts! The graphics pop nicely against the black bags, and the use of the white chalk outlines fit nicely. The hand-drawn, marker-style type on the picket signs is the perfect choice, as is the exclamation point on the identity. The detail of the perforated line at the top of the package is an added bonus to this instantly recognizable and memorable design.

(SW) I like this concept for a fair-trade product—it's a serious business strategy, presented in a lighthearted and honest way. The addition of the hand-drawn line work to make the nut characters is funny and sweet. I only wished that there were more variety among the different flavors, creating a broader and more cohesive story on the retail shelf. The addition of partial nutritional facts on the front is interesting and visually works on this heavy black package. The accentuated "open here" line is a nice balance to the off-centered logotype. There is a lot of information on this package and it hangs together well.

(BE) Well looking up a cow's nostril is not what immediately springs to mind when thinking dairy products, but it's surprisingly amusing, with a shocking intimacy that really brings the ingredients to life! Let's face it, cows are just funny, and this design forces us to really get to know them on a one-to-one basis. Its success is the angle—the cow is literally looking down at you—and hence it is framed nicely by a backdrop of clear blue sky, adding freshness and a recognizable color that pulls it all together on shelf. With such an impactful image, keeping the branding and typography simple and clear allows the cow to do all the mooing—ahem—talking.

(MK) This is truly a blue-sky approach. I'm not sure how I feel about looking up the nose of a cow, but it certainly grabs my attention! The second take on this—that the cow is actually looking so closely into the lens that the viewer becomes the focus—is quite witty. Hey—what does he see? The Langage Farm identity adds to the positioning of a brand that clearly does not take itself too seriously. A colleague of mine said recently, "Sometimes it's good to disrespect the typical cues." This design definitely does that!

PRODUCT	Full Tank Baby Fuel Packaging
DESIGN FIRM	Turnstyle
LOCATION	Seattle, WA
CLIENT	Full Tank

BE Heh. I have to laugh at this rather cute design that uses one iconic illustration across the range to link them together. Nice little ideas like the gauge up the the side lift this into being a fun and engaging pack that, for a mum who just needs to feed and go, would be perfect, and probably a refreshing change from all the worthy-mumsy packs around.

MK Sometimes "really good" is when it makes you smile! These designs are a welcome new language and add much-needed levity to a generally ho-hum baby food category. There is a bit of disorder to the architectural hierarchy, but somehow it works. The activity of the Japanese tamagotchi-style character is perfectly on target in establishing a fun, interactive and thumbs-up personality that speaks to a new generation of technology-bred mothers. The various icons (other than the USDA symbol that disrupts this design) serve the communication needs effectively and the color break and gauge lines (empty to full) are delightfully consistent with this bubbly, on-the-go personality. Very original!

SW A welcome relief from the schmaltzy, over-the-top sweet tendency for baby products. This is cute and funny and adds a sophisticated spin to the baby food grocery aisle. The icon flavor system adds to the whimsy along with the flat, monochromatic color palette.

PRODUCT	**Camilo Olive Oil**
DESIGN FIRM	Watts Design
LOCATION	South Melbourne, Australia
CLIENT	Camilo

 The most attractive feature of this design is the landscape vignette. It is unusually violated by the brand identity, but that is exactly what is arresting about this design. The unusual hierarchy, however, calls for a more stylized product name and descriptor.

 This olive oil has a historic, Old-World feel, but with a modern touch. The lino-cut illustration style is interestingly interrupted by the mortised white block-out with a modern typographic treatment of the brand name. The curve of the block-out is mirrored in the die-cut edge of the label—I can almost feel the olive trees swaying in the wind. I have only a couple hesitations with this design: The script font seems expected for olive oil; and the stacking and spacing of the words feels awkward.

PRODUCT	**Gourmet Condiments**
DESIGN FIRM	Mucca Design
LOCATION	New York, NY
CLIENT	The Gracious Gourmet

PRODUCT	**Heinz Deli Mayo**
DESIGN FIRM	Cowan London
LOCATION	London, England
CLIENT	Heinz

BE A fruity beauty, indeed! The intensity of the colors is the real strength of this design, juxtaposing the historic illustrations—with their punches of almost neon-colored block overlay—with the simple, sans serif branding that has an almost editiorial feel. The white band through the middle holds them together, giving it freshness, and keeping the colors from being too overpowering. Tasty!

MK The horticultural illustrations set among striking light-spectrum color strips immediately establish the visual character of these clear-sighted designs. The clean break of the background with a white band and matching color codes serves well not only to clearly communicate but as a resting place for the consumer's attention. Beautiful typographic lock-up and colors. Lovely, striking, and very desirable!

SW The brightly colored overlays give the botanical drawings a new life and a quirky, lighthearted, modern quality, which partners well with the product type treatments. The hierarchy of brand placement versus product name, with the opposing flush paragraphs, works well, at least for these product names, but I wonder if it will always stack so aesthetically.

BE Again, the Heinz keystone, an immovable lead weight, is cleverly transformed here into a great little idea, employing the language of New York deli. I really like the almost cartoonlike illustration style, with its brassy black outlines and the strong, careful typography that all sits neatly in the keystone. It really enhances the strength of this design. Quite fancy a bagel now....

MK A design that expresses the entertaining deli experience of orders being yelled out and others communicated quietly. The painterly quality of the vegetable illustrations and the use of the keystone as their speech bubble are both so appealing. I love how they call out to you. Kudos to Heinz once again for allowing the designer some flexibility with their brand. Although it probably was not part of the plan, an aging consumer population and the need to easily locate this product in the refrigerator makes the billboard typographic approach a welcome solution. Alternating the bold brand name and variety with an understated, retro, personalized script balances the communication aspects skillfully. The fine details have been resolved well, from the color-coded outline around the keystone to the tamper-evident label band. The declarations at the bottom of the labels epitomize a deli perfectly but are communicated ever so tastefully.

PRODUCT	Camilo Olive Oil
DESIGN FIRM	Watts Design
LOCATION	South Melbourne, Australia
CLIENT	Camilo

 The most attractive feature of this design is the landscape vignette. It is unusually violated by the brand identity, but that is exactly what is arresting about this design. The unusual hierarchy, however, calls for a more stylized product name and descriptor.

 This olive oil has a historic, Old-World feel, but with a modern touch. The lino-cut illustration style is interestingly interrupted by the mortised white block-out with a modern typographic treatment of the brand name. The curve of the block-out is mirrored in the die-cut edge of the label—I can almost feel the olive trees swaying in the wind. I have only a couple hesitations with this design: The script font seems expected for olive oil; and the stacking and spacing of the words feels awkward.

PRODUCT	**OrangeCup Primary Package System**
DESIGN FIRM	Range
LOCATION	Dallas, TX
CLIENT	OrangeCup Frozen Yogurt

PRODUCT	**OrangeCup Grand Opening Package Set**
DESIGN FIRM	Range
LOCATION	Dallas, TX
CLIENT	OrangeCup Frozen Yogurt

RW So I get the rationale behind moving from the ultra-simple and iconic introductory identity to this more mainstream strategy, but did we have to lose so much of the signature color in the process? Certainly the geometric logo stands out more, and the wallpaper pattern and cup die cut are better referenced, but perhaps all of this could have better leveraged the ownable orange. Pardon the silly *SNL* reference, but, "I need more cowbell!"

SW Yes, this is a nice packaging system, but frankly, it's a bit of a letdown after the orange launch packaging. This system is much more expected. It feels a like a youthful, teen shop—a nice shop, but still a teen shop. I wouldn't love to reuse this bag (except if it contained frozen yogurt), but I would definitely reuse the orange launch bag. I'll have the orange bag, please.

!!! *The OrangeCup launch kit was created to promote the brand upon each store opening for one month*

RW Only a brand with a name this iconic could get away with this, so why not take full advantage?! Reminiscent of the UK cell phone company Orange, this identity indelibly carves out its ownership of the color spectrum. I appreciate the details, like the die-cut cup holder and the top of the bag that folds over so the inside also carries the signature brand color. Simple is often confused with easy. It's often much more challenging to sell an idea this elegant to a client. Bravo to the design team and the client who had faith in them!

SW Why, oh, why was this just for new store launches and only used for one month? Who developed the strategy for that? This is memorable, fun, and smart, and why would you take all that recognition away—and essentially have to start over again—after merely a month!? The clarity of "It is what it is" seems to be a strategy that could live longer than a month. This particular orange color has a nice depth that works well as a solid bleed, without being jarring or cheap-looking. The cup holder's asterisk-shaped die cut is interestingly sculptural.

PRODUCT	**Camilo Olive Oil**
DESIGN FIRM	Watts Design
LOCATION	South Melbourne, Australia
CLIENT	Camilo

MK The most attractive feature of this design is the landscape vignette. It is unusually violated by the brand identity, but that is exactly what is arresting about this design. The unusual hierarchy, however, calls for a more stylized product name and descriptor.

SW This olive oil has a historic, Old-World feel, but with a modern touch. The lino-cut illustration style is interestingly interrupted by the mortised white block-out with a modern typographic treatment of the brand name. The curve of the block-out is mirrored in the die-cut edge of the label—I can almost feel the olive trees swaying in the wind. I have only a couple hesitations with this design: The script font seems expected for olive oil; and the stacking and spacing of the words feels awkward.

PRODUCT	**OrangeCup Primary Package System**
DESIGN FIRM	Range
LOCATION	Dallas, TX
CLIENT	OrangeCup Frozen Yogurt

PRODUCT	**OrangeCup Grand Opening Package Set**
DESIGN FIRM	Range
LOCATION	Dallas, TX
CLIENT	OrangeCup Frozen Yogurt

RW So I get the rationale behind moving from the ultra-simple and iconic introductory identity to this more mainstream strategy, but did we have to lose so much of the signature color in the process? Certainly the geometric logo stands out more, and the wallpaper pattern and cup die cut are better referenced, but perhaps all of this could have better leveraged the ownable orange. Pardon the silly *SNL* reference, but, "I need more cowbell!"

SW Yes, this is a nice packaging system, but frankly, it's a bit of a letdown after the orange launch packaging. This system is much more expected. It feels a like a youthful, teen shop—a nice shop, but still a teen shop. I wouldn't love to reuse this bag (except if it contained frozen yogurt), but I would definitely reuse the orange launch bag. I'll have the orange bag, please.

!!! *The OrangeCup launch kit was created to promote the brand upon each store opening for one month*

RW Only a brand with a name this iconic could get away with this, so why not take full advantage?! Reminiscent of the UK cell phone company Orange, this identity indelibly carves out its ownership of the color spectrum. I appreciate the details, like the die-cut cup holder and the top of the bag that folds over so the inside also carries the signature brand color. Simple is often confused with easy. It's often much more challenging to sell an idea this elegant to a client. Bravo to the design team and the client who had faith in them!

SW Why, oh, why was this just for new store launches and only used for one month? Who developed the strategy for that? This is memorable, fun, and smart, and why would you take all that recognition away—and essentially have to start over again—after merely a month!? The clarity of "It is what it is" seems to be a strategy that could live longer than a month. This particular orange color has a nice depth that works well as a solid bleed, without being jarring or cheap-looking. The cup holder's asterisk-shaped die cut is interestingly sculptural.

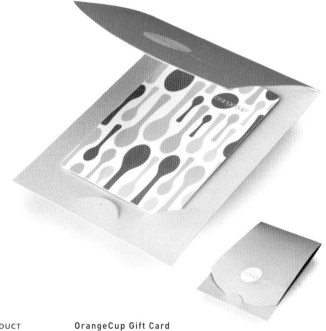

PRODUCT	**OrangeCup Gift Card**
DESIGN FIRM	Range
LOCATION	Dallas, TX
CLIENT	OrangeCup Frozen Yogurt

RW Again, I understand the brand's desire to stretch and be more expressive than what may be perceived as the too-restrictive (and perhaps boring?) all-orange architecture. But, here again, I'd move to see more of the signature brand color. I love the spoon, specifically in its incorporation into what I assume to be their sustainability-cause marketing. But what happened to the flowery icon from the cup-holder die cut and wallpaper? What's with the blue and green cards? I applaud the effort to make the identity more human with the photo, but this element could have come from the GAP or any other brand. Think Apple. Once you are on a horse, you need to ride it. You need to find a new, ownable, branded way to represent every consumer touchpoint and, to my mind, this one needs more orange.

PRODUCT	**Gourmet Condiments**		PRODUCT	**Heinz Deli Mayo**
DESIGN FIRM	Mucca Design		DESIGN FIRM	Cowan London
LOCATION	New York, NY		LOCATION	London, England
CLIENT	The Gracious Gourmet		CLIENT	Heinz

A fruity beauty, indeed! The intensity of the colors is the real strength of this design, juxtaposing the historic illustrations—with their punches of almost neon-colored block overlay—with the simple, sans serif branding that has an almost editiorial feel. The white band through the middle holds them together, giving it freshness, and keeping the colors from being too overpowering. Tasty!

The horticultural illustrations set among striking light-spectrum color strips immediately establish the visual character of these clear-sighted designs. The clean break of the background with a white band and matching color codes serves well not only to clearly communicate but as a resting place for the consumer's attention. Beautiful typographic lock-up and colors. Lovely, striking, and very desirable!

The brightly colored overlays give the botanical drawings a new life and a quirky, lighthearted, modern quality, which partners well with the product type treatments. The hierarchy of brand placement versus product name, with the opposing flush paragraphs, works well, at least for these product names, but I wonder if it will always stack so aesthetically.

Again, the Heinz keystone, an immovable lead weight, is cleverly transformed here into a great little idea, employing the language of New York deli. I really like the almost cartoonlike illustration style, with its brassy black outlines and the strong, careful typography that all sits neatly in the keystone. It really enhances the strength of this design. Quite fancy a bagel now....

A design that expresses the entertaining deli experience of orders being yelled out and others communicated quietly. The painterly quality of the vegetable illustrations and the use of the keystone as their speech bubble are both so appealing. I love how they call out to you. Kudos to Heinz once again for allowing the designer some flexibility with their brand. Although it probably was not part of the plan, an aging consumer population and the need to easily locate this product in the refrigerator makes the billboard typographic approach a welcome solution. Alternating the bold brand name and variety with an understated, retro, personalized script balances the communication aspects skillfully. The fine details have been resolved well, from the color-coded outline around the keystone to the tamper-evident label band. The declarations at the bottom of the labels epitomize a deli perfectly but are communicated ever so tastefully.

PRODUCT	**Waitrose Condiments**
DESIGN FIRM	Lewis Moberly
LOCATION	London, England
CLIENT	Waitrose Ltd.

 A simple and elegant way to communicate taste and premium cues, using a cleanly shot spoon to carry each variant, on a pared-down, simple background. The monochromatic backdrops and silver lids pull this refined range away from the cluttered shelf competition and make it easy to navigate.

  Love all but the seafood sauce—he looks like he bites! I love how the lime twist looks like it wants off the spoon. The beauty in this design is the earnestness of the silver spoon and its gesture, on a pure backdrop, with ingredients that are anything but serious.

RW Again, just a delight. It's relevant and appealing to every consumer segment, pedestrian, and epicurean alike. While their mustard identity's die-cut dollop shape (page 64) is more ownable than the silver spoon, and the startling background color shift to black is perhaps too strong a visual cue to separate sweet from savory condiments, this system still shines. I specifically appreciate the challenge of making this ingredient story work across all products— what's the signifying ingredient in tartar sauce? Thankfully, they added lime zest. I hope this strategy is as extendable for all their sauces.

SW Lewis Moberly does it again; always tasteful and beautiful. The silver spoon is not unique in packaging, but the presentation of this one is impeccable. The iconographic photography and minimal typography are all the difference this needs. I like the shift from black label with silver lid to white label with black lid.

PRODUCT	**Waitrose Mustards**
DESIGN FIRM	Lewis Moberly
LOCATION	London, England
CLIENT	Waitrose Ltd.

PRODUCT	**Lake Champlain Chocolates - Organic**
DESIGN FIRM	Optima Soulsight
LOCATION	Highland Park, IL
CLIENT	Lake Champlain Chocolates

 Simple and stylish, these do the very minimum to show the product—it's been done before—but the minimalism of the type and colors on the label keeps this fresh and timeless, allowing you to see the textures and rich color of the mustards.

 A fabulous die-cut of a dollop of mustard (a real tongue twister!) A smart solution enhanced by the product colors and simple type.

 This identity just makes me smile. While it's infinitely easier to achieve this level of simplicity with a specialty food than, say, the Wishbone brand, this architecture is still an accomplishment. This identity could have been so easily destroyed by one more superfluous element. The result is at the same time both unapologetic and unpretentious. Its approachable tone is relevant to the epicurean and the mass market alike. Super-simple, but still a far cry from being labeled as generic.

 Waitrose and Lewis Moberly do it yet again! The barest, most essential elements add up to an elegant, appetizing product presentation. I would be perfectly happy to live at a Waitrose.

In sharp contrast to some of the other cleaner, brighter, everyday chocolates reviewed, this system uses more of the expected category cues of chocolate— rich, indulgent color tones and cocoa ingredient cues. While I might buy the others as a gift to bring to a toney party, I'd buy this bar for myself! I very much like the rough wood cut and organic type, befitting its message. I like the high-contrast, dimensional overlapping label. Of course it would be much more effective, and perhaps not too much more expensive, to have this overlapping label printed on textured stock and applied over the matte, kraft-paper base wrap. Regardless, this strongly signals a decadent indulgence that appeals directly to my chocolate cravings.

PRODUCT	**Peace Cereal**
DESIGN FIRM	Hatch Design
LOCATION	San Francisco, CA
CLIENT	Peace Cereal

 Peace as a design concept in itself has so many visual interpretations and clichés, yet this version is nicely captured. Hatch's design, using a simple layout and construction, background illustration, and metallic ink, combine to enhance the overall experience. The design, layout, and color palette are particularly appealing in that the design does not spoon-feed the consumer with traditional category formats or color cues. I am particularly attracted to the appetite-appeal imagery that features hands cupping the bowl. This is a visual that sticks and is precisely what captures the story of a bowl that generates peace.

 This identity just screams, "I'm different!" without screaming at all. Sure, the product presentation is tiny. And yes, changing the brand color with each flavor is counterintuitive to great branding. But just imagine how strong this is at retail. Look how proudly it wears its cause-marketing badge. Notice how the label invites you to the side panel story to engage you further in the brand message. I am a bit bothered by the changing product perspectives and layouts in the photography. And while I might stay consistent with the background colors and illustration print techniques— and replace the metallic ink with a more earth-friendly, soy-based print solution—this identity brings a welcome moment of peace to the cacophony of the cereal aisle.

Product	**Tesco Tortillas**
DESIGN FIRM	P&W
LOCATION	London, England
CLIENT	Tesco

Does anyone remember the Frito Bandito? This is a delightful series, and this bandito is an equally memorable conversation piece, a funny and oh-so-simple use of everyday objects and styles as clues to the product variety. I love the portraiture style and how he sits there on a chair on a color-coded backdrop cloth. The use of white for the brand identity and his outfit create focus on two areas of importance. *¡Excelente!*

Again, I applaud the flexibility of Tesco's design regiment. It's usually quite difficult to effectively use people photography on pack. This strategy polarizes the brand by the gender and ethnic background of the people used. And because styles change so quickly and radically these days, people photography can quickly become dated. While the idea of the bandito character is certainly not new (remember the Frito Bandito?), this clearly tongue-in-cheek characterization is sure to make everyone smile, resulting in another relevant interruption in the noisy chip aisle.

I love the use of humor combined with the sophisticated design aesthetic. It's similar in approach to the Loseley ice cream package (page 79).

PRODUCT	Waitrose Cooks
DESIGN FIRM	Lewis Moberly
LOCATION	London, England
CLIENT	Waitrose Ltd.

BE I agree that the strength in this design is in the copywriting, throwing the pace and language of the kitchen into the branding. It evokes so much more than any product shot alone could. The typography is strong and singular, creating a very ownable look and style that works over a huge range of own-label products.

RW Without the whimsical copy, this would be another smart, organized, type-driven execution, and there's not too much that's wrong with that effective but over-proliferated strategy. Just the single, simple touch of real-world phrases warms this otherwise cold experience and makes it both more engaging and ownable for the brand. A tip of the hat to the team!

SW These Waitrose goodies strike a nice balance between the fresh colors of the foods and the labels that are primarily black and white. The product copy is strong; it takes this graphically bold design from what could be construed as industrial and cold and gives it a brand personality. The vessels for all the products are also just plain enough to further enhance the graphic quality—no fancy olive oil bottles here.

PRODUCT	**Provenance Honey**
DESIGN FIRM	Turner Duckworth
LOCATION	London, England and San Francisco, CA
CLIENT	Waitrose Ltd.

PRODUCT	**Indian Cooking Sauces**
DESIGN FIRM	Turner Duckworth
LOCATION	London, England and San Francisco, CA
CLIENT	Waitrose Ltd.

 This is very posh, and very twee; if Jane Austen were to partake of a slice of toast with honey, I can see her reaching for this bottle. It has that Victorian botanical-fascination style, with hand-written inky type and a feminine touch that's just the right side of being overly forced, resulting in a design quite charming in its execution.

 Another wonderful design solution from Waitrose. As an artist, I would love to have created these labels myself. The purity and richness of the hand-written product name, description, and colorful watercolor illustrations are absolutely inspiring.

 It's not a difficult challenge to evoke this homemade appeal with specialty products. In fact, the category almost calls out to be hand-crafted. And yet, this specific execution of a tried-and-true strategy is still noteworthy. The hand-scripted type and handmade watercolor illustrations scream, "Special occasion only!"—a break from the everyday jam. Sure, the type is hard to read, but it encourages a closer look. I imagine that the perception would be complete if the label were printed on watercolor-paper stock.

 Some of the most arresting designs are those that present themselves unobtrusively. The painterly palette and consecutive positioning around the label creates a harmonious line. The elegant use of colors holds the line together and distinguishes the product colors—not only can we practically smell the aroma of the products, but the consumer's palate is educated as well. The choice of a small stroke or ligature projecting from each product variety accents the product's cultural appearance nicely. The black closures smartly finish this family picture.

SW These are a handsome addition to the Waitrose brand. The small mounds of dried spices that make up the ingredients of the variety are lovely and add the graphic simplicity that is part of the Waitrose brand language. The beautiful, rich colors of the spices, balanced against the deeply colored backgrounds, take me to another world. The ligature aspect of the product flavor feels forced in some instances, but it is an interesting idea and overall, it adds the appropriate touch of authenticity.

PRODUCT	Chimes Ginger Chews
DESIGN FIRM	Sudduth Design Co.
LOCATION	Austin, TX
CLIENT	Roxy Trading Company

PRODUCT	Tesco Organics
DESIGN FIRM	Coley Porter Bell
LOCATION	London, England
CLIENT	Tesco

 An attractive design imbued with cultural ethnicity. Especially on the natural substrate, it feels very holistic, herbal, and medicinal. The silver tin adds liveliness, the line colors highlight important features, and the neon green highlights focus attention. But the face behind the logo on the tin is obscured by the four lines of copy, yet each line is too far apart. The lower "C" in the mismatched font is confusing, and the hanging particle on the "C" in "Chimes" is unsettling; it makes the viewer pause. Overall, though, a design with a charming appeal.

 I am immediately engaged by this concept, and I imagine it has killer impact in the confection case at checkout. Its overt mystique—reminiscent of an old Ouija Board (remember those?)—has a creepy weirdness and a defined message to a specific audience. The tin might have followed the pouch's kraft-paper background color and been more unified, but still the system works.

 These are such handsome packages that I want to explore all the nooks and crannies. They're kind of Chinese-medicine-shop-meets-Victorian-era, but I wish there were more interesting payoffs with the copy. The thin serif font in the subtext doesn't flow with the other type but doesn't nicely contrast it either. Many designers have tried this design aesthetic for products much less appropriate than ginger and, while not authentic, they are an interesting take on the authentic language of Chinese packaging. For the packaging alone, I would purchase this product.

 It's a challenge for any design to be flexible enough for a huge range; this is so carefully designed as to encompass anything (grass on dairy/meat, white on bakery, leaves on veggies.) Black communicates "premium" and throws forward the zingy greens, making them look fresh and tasty, developing a clearly ownable style that would hold its own across a vast supermarket environment.

 Out of context, it is hard to truly appreciate this organic line. This design firm has arranged these inter-related parts so they look sophisticated and effortless. The photography, enhanced by the background gradient, speaks to the consumer seeking first-rate, organic ingredients, products that deliver on taste, and chef-quality presentation.

 I'm normally not a fan of design architectures that segment the overall visual impression. Dividing the graphics into large blocks can sometimes make the package look smaller. Here is an exception. The dramatic close-up photography beautifully cues the organic nature of the brand. The black is an interesting choice for an organic line. It can feel very heavy, but here the bright, springlike side photo and the dramatic, spot-lit product shot offset that heavy feeling. The logo is a little expected—everyone's seen the vegetation inside the O before—and perhaps a bit undersized. However, the nutrition information block is clean and efficient and nicely incorporates the UPC. Overall, this is a most effective architecture; I can imagine it translates well across all product categories.

PRODUCT	Ode Oliva
DESIGN FIRM	DFraile
LOCATION	Murcia, Spain
CLIENT	Export Olive Oil

 BE The bottle is great—so solid, dense and simple—perfect for a quality olive oil product. I also love the matte finish on the glass; this gives it a lovely, premium feel. The graphics are minimal, stylish, and—particularly on the core product—the monochromatic starkness really oozes style. It's great that they've resisted cluttering up the design. Confident and strong—it has purity and class.

 MK The short, stocky personality of these dark, rich, opaque glass bottles pairs flawlessly with the thick, slab, serif (perhaps Claredon?) font. I am immediately drawn to the distinctive "O" identity in white—actually the entire typographic composition. Black-and-white or added color band—a sophisticated yet uncomplicated and appealing solution.

 SW Why is it that so much great packaging is "aimed at the European market"? Why not the U.S.? Oh, well, maybe that's a subject for another book. I love the stocky, dark bottle—such a nice departure from all those elegant, ultra-tall bottles. I don't understand the pharmaceutical reference the designer mentions, but no matter: Most people understand that olive oil is healthful, and these are beautiful as they are. The large "O" as the logo is a simple, smart solution to communicate the olive—it doesn't need anymore information than that. The color choices for coding the olive varietals on the nonorganic oils provide a nice palette. I would love to have the organic oils in the dense, matte-finish bottles in my kitchen.

PRODUCT	**Stanley Honey**
DESIGN FIRM	The Partners
LOCATION	London, England
CLIENT	Stanley Honey

 What a lovely idea to create something that encourages the product—planting flowers in your pot after use to keep the bees working! With this idea in mind, they've created an unusual structure and substrate that absolutely is a plant pot made of fired clay, with a really unusual cork fitted lid, all adding to the rustic garden feel. The type simply echoes this sentiment, screened-on in a considered unit that follows the structure, the little sign-off on the back giving it a classy touch. It's something to keep on the window-ledge for years to come.

 "Begin with the end in mind" is a mantra that I value. Far too few packaging designs are designed with reuse as a primary objective. This solution is just plain smart.

 This package commands immediate attention. I adore the combination of its earthy substrates, the reusable terra-cotta perfectly complemented by the renewable cork, both evoking a natural, hand-crafted artisan product. Contemporary typefaces bring twenty-first century sensibility to what otherwise could have been a dusty impression.

 I completely appreciate this design on many levels. The type is handled well, the copy makes me smile, but the best part of this design is its built-in reusability. Unlike some packages that claim to be "reusable," this is the real thing. And it would be fun to see a line of these on your window sill with herbs or flowers.

PRODUCT	**It's It Minis**
DESIGN FIRM	Sudduth Design Co.
LOCATION	Austin, TX
CLIENT	It's It

 The challenge of communicating from behind the doors of the freezer section cannot be overemphasized. Add to that the amount of information that needs to be conveyed on this product's packaging, and you realize why this solution is successful. The various communication elements are organized in a way that is effective, uncluttered, and does not feel like the box is screaming at the consumer. The major attraction of this design is in the details of snowflakes, bursts, sparkling graphic elements, and typographic highlights that make the packaging design shine. These details, combined with the icy gradient background and well-executed typography, is impactful. The product is well positioned in the spotlight and is clearly the coveted celebrity—a design that is modeled from the past but has a light-hearted, contemporary story.

PRODUCT	**Madres Salad Dressing**
DESIGN FIRM	Bungalow Creative
LOCATION	Kansas City, MO
CLIENT	Madres

 This design is stylishly modern and one that any youthful consumer would be proud to leave on the table. The neck label feels as though its influence is derived from the fashion designer Paul Smith. The visual landscape of the kitchen has changed drastically over the years, yet few products in this category have caught up to the new aesthetic. Consumers might eat more salad dressing (and proudly put the bottle on the table) if they had these bottles.

 This design exhibits strength in all its major elements. Strong type, strong colors, straightforward organization. As strong as these devices are, I'm even more attracted to the design's more subtle touches—the top label with its small "m" icon and the thin color band at the very bottom of the label, echoing the neck label's bolder color statement. All in all, a nicely balanced piece of work.

 As a whole, this is a completely appealing package. But the individual elements of the design seem vaguely like they've all been lifted from various "cool" designs and merged together. With that said, I do like most of the elements, with the exception of the large screened-back type and swirl detail—it takes away from an otherwise confidently modern, clean aesthetic.

PRODUCT	**BEEE**
DESIGN FIRM	DFraile
LOCATION	Murcia, Spain
CLIENT	BEEE

 Creating a design based on onomatopoeia (in Spanish, this animal says "bee," "bee") is both clever and amusing. This design statement is simple, fresh, and bold. I'm not sure which came first, the geometric figure of a goat with the brand identity dropped out, or the hexagon, but whichever the case, the goat works well housed in this form. I like how the structural form of the "B" and "Es" suit the shape of the side panels. The repetition of these letter forms, both around the box and when stacked, makes a strong graphic impact. The vivacious color choices boost this brand's appeal. Very different.

 This package makes me happy: the name; the silly udder; the bright colors that are skewed from primary just enough to be sophisticated; the octagonal shape; and most of all, the way the name wraps around the sides. It reads down; it reads up; it reads across. I am dying to see other BEEE goat dairy products. Smile.

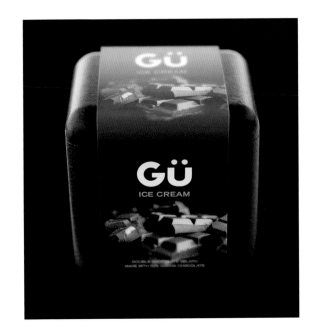

PRODUCT	**Gü Ice Cream**
DESIGN FIRM	Big Fish Design Limited
LOCATION	London, England
CLIENT	Gü Chocolate Puds

 BE Gorgeous, just gorgeous—where to start? First, structure: This is made out of black polystyrene, which is such a brilliantly different solution, nothing I've seen before in the frozen sector. It instantly stands out, looks so classy, and I have to say, after eating a few of these myself, it really does keep it colder, longer. The smoothed corners and intensity of the black give this pack such a unique look and feel, and the simple use of an outer sleeve lets the structure remain pure after opening. As for the graphics, the Gü logo itself is a lovely little observation. It's really neatly executed, complemented by the product shot on a dark black background, all adding to the luxurious and seriously delicious feel of this design.

 MK I would buy this, hide it, and never share it! Sinfully attractive.

 SW I am infatuated with this lovely little vessel. The soft shape and dark mystery of this container truly must hold the secrets to happiness! It's absolutely perfect on every level.

PRODUCT	**Heinz Farmers Market Soups**
DESIGN FIRM	Cowan London
LOCATION	London, England
CLIENT	Heinz

MK Love this close-up perspective—so hospitable, just as a farmers' market experience should be! The concept is so relevant. What's interesting is that the product is less the celebrity than the personalized chalkboard label. The farmer's crate makes sense for the case. The design is a fresh and imaginative departure from what is generally an unappealing, confusing, and cluttered aisle. Kudos to Heinz for tipping the keystone.

RW This design is so refreshing that it actually elevates the entire Heinz brand, an icon in America for its inescapable connection to ketchup. I'd love to see the brand launch these products and this design in the States! We currently consult with these folks. Perhaps this will be the topic of our next conversation!

SW I can almost smell the earthiness of the potatoes and the freshness of the peas. The crisp fullness of the photograph really says it all. By reinventing the Heinz keystone as the market sign, complete with script type, it feels authentic and fresh.

> **!!!** *As a start-up, Etiquette of Chocolate had a very limited budget. Mucca Design worked within these constraints by printing everything—various sized boxes, business cards, and belly bands, all on the same press sheet.*

PRODUCT	**Etiquette of Chocolate**
DESIGN FIRM	Mucca Design
LOCATION	New York, NY
CLIENT	Etiquette of Chocolate

 How delightful to find a chocolate box that isn't brown/black/dark and "intense"! This design is ultra-simplistic, slick, and modern. The gaping kerning and simple sans serif create the modern, clean logo, touched with the more decorative of breaking up the logo. The ribbons save it from what otherwise would be minimalism taken to dull, and the slivers of colors add elegance and a sense of gifting.

 Simple, unique, quietly elegant fashion statement. This design is reminiscent of the very hot Make-A-Wish jewelry and the popular tiny string bracelets. I like the type change for the "of" in the identity, I would love to see another small detail added—a knot, perhaps, or some other element of surprise—on perhaps one ribbon.

 This package speaks to the ultra-sophisticated, premium, special-occasion experience. I'm drawn to its white bakery-box credentials, a distinct departure from the velvety textures and rich, dark colors normally associated with chocolate. The idea of multiple colored lines signaling a wider variety of flavors, is interesting, but this will have to be discovered before it's appreciated.

 I am in love! I wish I had designed this simple, elegant package. I'm impressed with Mucca's resourcefulness in accommodating a start-up company's budget by getting creative with the printing. The line weight of the individual strings of emotions is thin and delicate but, as they build on each other, they create just the right amount of mass. The very open type treatment, with the crossed capital "I" and the small italic "of," is just the right amount of detail.

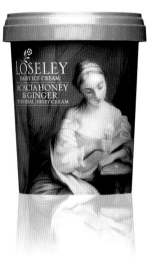

PRODUCT	**Loseley Ice Cream**
DESIGN FIRM	P&W
LOCATION	London, England
CLIENT	Hill Station

 What a great marriage of a traditional, heritage brand and a witty scoop of tongue-in-cheek! For those who don't know, Loseley House is a large English country estate. Each of the paintings on the front comes from the actual house itself, and popping the product within the frames makes me smile. Bring in the flavor variants to match the outfits, and you have a classy yet amusing pack that would melt any ice cream snob.

 Wouldn't the Queen just love this stunningly humorous ice cream brand? These historically rich portraits establish a personal relationship with the audience and then, instead of leaving it there, the humor added to the serious setting makes for an absolute showstopper. The painstaking attention to detail is flawless, from the precision of the typography, kerning, and leading to the painterly oil-color portraits. Focusing the gaze of the subject past the viewer is intriguing. The gold caps remind me of the traditional lights positioned above valuable artwork. The best of all, however, is the focus of the matter—ice cream—being skewered, dabbing the nose, dripping, and even being somewhat phallic that makes this a most memorable design solution.

 Brilliant!

PRODUCT	**DELADO Ice Cream**
DESIGN FIRM	DFraile
LOCATION	Murcia, Spain
CLIENT	DELADO

 The cups: Lovely, simple idea; tasty, relevant, and unusual. The identity builds successfully on the waffle texture whilst keeping this young and fresh. The typography is reminiscent of digital language aesthetic, again reinforcing the youthfulness of the overall brand without looking too tricksy. The sky blue has all the right connotations of summer freshness, and the punchy cyan is modern and eye-catching. Lastly, the fun and playful use of the waffle texture enhances the branding through the images on the side, simply and directly executed. They're positively mood-enhancing.

 Offbeat, irreverent, and with an unmistakably sexual undertone, this makes for a very avant-garde packaging design strategy. The graphic contrasts of black-and-white photography, the textural image of the waffle cone, and the use of positive and negative space against a visually stimulating neon background combine to make original artwork. The typography mirroring the grid of the waffle cone is simple, effective, and gives order to the overall style. The waffle cone cups are fun and save calories, too. Against an increasingly rational approach to design, this one breaks the mold.

 I've always loved the look, texture, and smell of waffle cones—I can almost feel the tiny crevices in my hand and smell the freshly made cones. The combination of black-and-white photography and the waffle pattern is a funny, almost Dada-like presentation, although I don't think the ice cream on top of the cone is aptly handled. The waffle cups are very clever and look tasty. The ice cream–cool blue background of the bag contrasts nicely with the waffle-brown cone and black-and-white photos.

PRODUCT	**Lake Champlain Chocolates - Winter**
DESIGN FIRM	Optima Soulsight
LOCATION	Highland Park, IL
CLIENT	Lake Champlain Chocolates

PRODUCT	**Casa Loreto Olive Oil**
DESIGN FIRM	The Partners
LOCATION	London, England
CLIENT	Casa Loreto

 Now what's happended here? I fully appreciate seasonal packaging and its need to appeal to a more festive and celebratory experience, but this execution has downplayed the brand essence so significantly that it could be anyone's product. As hand-crafted as the cut-paper illustrations are, they lack the warmth of the organic bar and the sophistication of the assortments. The retro typeface is playful at the expense of being premium. The loud and vibrating colors are festive at the expense of evoking a chocolatey richness. The overall impression stands in direct conflict with the remainder of the brand offerings. There's a way to balance seasonality with authenticity and this design goes too far toward the former.

BE Stunning. What is great about this design is that it breaks out of the packaging: It's gone from 2D to 3D through a simple and well-executed idea that glamourizes and glorifies the product in its simplest form. This would not work on a cluttered, ill-considered design, but again, giving the idea the space and platform to be the hero of this design creates a beautiful and elegant bottle.

MK I have never seen anything like this one. Beautiful, striking, and truly original.

 The 3D drip naturally leads the eye from the sculptured neck and shoulder, down the slender bottle structure, and directly to the sophisticated logo on its distinctive black label. This reminds me of the melting wax closure of Maker's Mark bourbon. The device not only lends a beautiful visual and tactile experience, it will become the core mnemonic by which consumers will remember the brand.

 I'm speechless. Casa Loreto is stunningly beautiful. The single gold droplet says it all. The simple black band carrying all the information is astutely handled and has just enough brand presence.

PRODUCT	**Belly Bars 2**
DESIGN FIRM	Sudduth Design Co.
LOCATION	Austin, TX
CLIENT	Nutrabella

BE This doesn't quite hit the mark with me; it ticks the boxes, yes, but it just seems a little lackluster, overly pastel, and so expected. Again, I agree there is an opportunity lost in the branding "B," which could have been amplified somehow to make it more of a branding equity.

MK Whimsical yet comforting for the mother-to-be. The "wallpaper" pattern, pastel colors, curves, and gentle brand identity say "joyful." The curved white band conveys goodness and purity. The belly-button on the "B" is a sweet touch. I would just like the stork to deliver the bundle in a less random location and the secondary type to be integrated into the design more effectively.

RW Hey, hey, Mama! What a cute way to signal this unique brand concept. The "pregnant B," pastel colors, and baby's-room background texture are sweet, the banners and oval architecture somewhat distinct. While the stork is a little juvenile, the flavor names unimaginative, and the appetite appeal severely lacking, the overall impression still fits the brand concept.

SW This design is competent enough, but it's all mother-to-be clichés: pastel color palette, stork illustration, and generic background patterns. What is appealing is the use of the "B" as the belly, which could have been more interestingly rendered. With the proliferation of this type of design in the baby and mother-to-be categories, I don't think this adds a unique or memorable voice.

PRODUCT	**Crumb Foods**
DESIGN FIRM	Folk Creative
LOCATION	London, England
CLIENT	Crumbs

 Crumbs! A nice spot of stacked retro typography, well executed and consistently applied. The brand name lends itself to a portion of tongue-in-cheek, so the humorous copy lifts this, the design allowing it to be the hero. The thorough and considered way in which this is applied makes this range hold together powerfully. Using a simple color palette to aid in flavor navigation also adds appetite and creates a bold, punchy brand that follows through with engaging copywriting.

The shapes, colors, and typographic formatting in this series of paperboard structures fit together like mosaic tiles, creating the sense that the possibilities and choices are endless. The letterforms become bold graphic blocks, and type hierarchy, scale, and weight make this slab-serif font communicate a friendly and approachable tone. Designers are psychoartisans—they use design to effect thought and action. This line is a prime example of the excellent results that can be achieved with clear marketing objectives.

PRODUCT	**Delectable**
DESIGN FIRM	Liquid Pixel Studio
LOCATION	Staten Island, NY
CLIENT	Delectable

 Impulse purchasing is a rather useful marketing tool and in that regard, these colorfully sweet striped canisters are definitely a strategic asset for a specialty café. It is estimated that as much as eighty percent of candy and sweets purchasing is unplanned; this eye-catching type built from colored stripes and fluorescent caps ought to attract some of those impulse buyers.

 Sure, this logo is almost impossible to read. Sure, there are no visuals of the product inside to help drive appetite appeal and assist in flavor differentiation. Yes, the colors are a bit jarring, But just look at the impact this generates. Just feel the spirit this brings the brand. This identity succeeds by breaking the rules. Yes, it could only work for a precious specialty product in a select retail environment, but from purely a visual perspective, wow!

PRODUCT	**Marmite Guinness**
DESIGN FIRM	Core
LOCATION	London, England
CLIENT	Unilever

PRODUCT	**Gusto Cheeses**
DESIGN FIRM	Pure Equator Ltd
LOCATION	Nottingham, England
CLIENT	Winterbotham Darby

 Well, love it or hate it, Marmite is an established treasure in the branding world, and few dare to meddle with its almost cultlike branding. So, tasked with combining this with yet another Goliath of the brand arena, this design succeeds in that you instantly know it's Marmite, and it's touched with the unmistakably Guinness monochrome. I happen to know it left the shelves at an alarming rate!

 As one who has not had a lifetime association with—or even an awareness of—this brand (in fact, I'm not even sure what this stuff is. Yeast extract??), I'm still struck by the brand's direct, in-your-face impact. Just check out the package shape alone. The super-wide mouth and short, squatty, almost circular shape is in itself a brand icon. Normally, a food product seeks to generate appetite appeal. Not so here. This is a stop sign for brand loyalists, and I bet those who actually like yeast extract are attracted!

 Nice idea here, pastiching the genre of cheese in its natural packaging—rind. This evokes the language of fine cheeses, of Italian delis, by simply emulating its authentic visual language without fussing or overworking it. Moving the product visuals to the side allows this to work to best effect, and gives both a clear area rather than trying to shoe-horn the two together (which probably would have ruined both.)

 The authentic stamps on Italian Parmigiano Reggiano cheese rounds are regulated by an Italian consortium. It's branding at its origin. Thus there is an obvious logic to its use on this grated form of the product that is also has a subtle wit. The photography certainly adds validity and appetite appeal but the sleeve would have been equally successful with a continuation of the cheese-round concept.

PRODUCT	Guston Cake Mixes
DESIGN FIRM	Pure Equator Ltd
LOCATION	Nottingham, England
CLIENT	Winterbotham Darby

PRODUCT	Halvors Tradisjonsfisk
DESIGN FIRM	Tank Design
LOCATION	Tromsoe, Norway
CLIENT	Halvors Tradisjonsfisk

 The shiny, vanilla-colored, flexible pouches ooze a rich-batter personality, while the visual language of the photography adds to the evocation of the delectable results of the product. Well-styled product photography is an art form. As exemplified in this image, the perception of taste, aroma, and even the environmental appeal are subconsciously altered by great photography. The label colors are appetizing and stylish and effectively project the communication hierarchy. This is an example of how the consistent design format allows room for typographic flexibility. Consumers appreciate slight variations in product lines, as it feels slightly less stock–design formula.

 I like the addition of the editorial preparation photography to this traditional, type-driven design architecture. One of the challenges of right-and-left-justified type block is that words of different lengths will have different emphasis in the communication hierarchy. For example, the generic product name "CAKE MIX" has more strength than the more important "VICTORIA SPONGE" flavor variant. I do like the drop-down brand logo and the gusset-bottomed pouch with its natural-colored substrate.

 A truly elegant pack. The simple structure makes it instantly recognizable and ownable, and doubles up neatly to divide the design elements. High-contrast marine imagery in crisp monochrome makes it feel modern, beautiful, timeless. The front continues this clean design with its vast white space, minimal branding (the crafted logo lends gravitas alone) and utilitarian, informative feel—almost editorial. It feels authentically fresh, stark and crisp—perfect for the product's Arctic provenance.

 The atmosphere set by the black-and-white snowy mountains/icy water imagery establishes the product's origin and freshness. There must be a cultural connotation to the humorous image of fish tails that is, sadly, lost in translation. Nonetheless, the typographic sensitivity, uncluttered layout, and innovative structure build a handsome line.

 This unique carton shape forces the consumer to consider the side panel as a complement to the simple, direct front. The high-contrast black-and-white photo of the Arctic Sea feels so very cold and so very remote that it adds a premium freshness to the brand experience. The product window and clear, straightforward flavor designator are effective, but could there have perhaps been different photo images to evoke the same Arctic source while differentiating between fish types?

PRODUCT	**Flours and Baked Goods**
DESIGN FIRM	Buddy
LOCATION	London, England
CLIENT	The Cornish Mill & Bakehouse

 Handsome, striking, and clever, this works brilliantly as a range because of its flexibility. The choice of typeface adds seriousness, while the communication at times is quite witty. The clever use of the Cornish flag to communicate each product message is a lovely idea, and the stark monochrome makes it premium, strong, and iconic.

 Buddy has created a visually stunning design solution that is both strong and simple. How fortunate to have the ideal icon, infused with so much symbolism and meaning, at the disposal of the design. The typeface, with its delicate serifs yet uppercase setting reads "time-honored." The scale and positioning of the elements rest perfectly within the slightly decorative sphere. The white cross functions cleverly as an ideogram and, when used to combine simple phrases, is very special. With the many structures and materials, the black and white palette serves well to tie the line together. The result is a solution that feels classic and yet strikingly modern.

 Stripping back all the nonessentials is often a great strategy, and this design system takes that strategy to the extreme, living on color + icon alone! Design is, and perhaps should always be, polarizing. The stark contrast that inspires me about this design may, to someone else, seem funereal and morbid. That's okay. While this identity probably works well in specialty shops, it will obviously require a lot more information in the mass class of trade. Adding more stuff to this architecture might ruin it, and therefore the system may be a bit limiting. However, the design aptly fits its market, and I'm sure it leaves a lasting impression.

 Handsome and smart: What more could you want? It's perfect!

PRODUCT	Jordans Cereals
DESIGN FIRM	Pearlfisher
LOCATION	London, England
CLIENT	Jordans

PRODUCT	MAISE
DESIGN FIRM	Diseño Dos Asociados
LOCATION	San Andrés Cholula, Mexico
CLIENT	MAISE

 It's refreshing to see a new trend that pares the brand right down to the basics, the Jordans logo almost stamped onto a simple, rustic yet modern, illustrative pack. A full third of the pack is actually dedicated to the logo, which makes this a powerfully recognizable brand without allowing the logo to overwhelm the pack. Creating provenance through the heritage silhouette brings a believability to what could feel stark. The carefully designed type around the window adds a sense of care, and the product reveal reassures consumers. This no-nonsense, straight-talking pack clearly differentiates with color and simplicity, but its lack of depth may compromise its longevity.

 Visual contrast lends bold richness to this design. The use of illustration, photography, and actual product in a window; the white background breaking to a solid color; the black arced stencil type and the bold sans serif typefaces; text positioned centered, flush left, justified, rag right, and even curved; and an open top layout opposite a full bottom make for a knockout strategy. The intensity of this design that makes me want to fully participate in the experience.

 The cultural legacy of this brand identity is beautifully executed. The colors and the design elements convey authenticity with a modern ambiance and visually establish this tortilleria as a fashionable gourmet destination. The use of unbleached paper expresses a place that is sensitive to the environment and to the past. The simple and clever use of tints and drop-out type make the design appear to be more than a two-color job.

The I have to agree with the prior comments: A perfect balance of authenticity and contemporaneity. To me, it's also the unexpected contrasts that make this identity notable. The octagonal shape of the pack structure is nicely contrasted by the striped pattern. The somewhat heavy-handed brand logo and icon are nicely married to the hand-scripted typeface. The earthy textures are an unexpected match to the fresh, vibrant colors. Both premium and approachable.

PRODUCT	**Bangras**
DESIGN FIRM	The Partners
LOCATION	London, England
CLIENT	Mr Singh's Bangras

 !!! *Sold in Great Britian, Mr. Singh's Bangras are literally the product and the packaging. Each sausage has a henna pattern, specific to the flavor, which is applied using a food grade polypropylene stamp and natural, edible ink.*

BE This is a by-the-book example of how to elevate the product to the most special-looking sausage this world has seen! Starkly shot on a black background, this is classic dramatic photography made punchy and fresh by the contemporary colors in the logo and top face that aid flavor navigation. This bucks the genre with gusto; it's bold and manages to look tasty and premium. The nice little touch however, is the grilled henna patterns that differentiate and add a touch of authenticity.

 MK There is a world of people addicted to ink that would drool over this product. I have to admit it's an incredibly fascinating concept. Its positioning as the smokin' hero on a silver fork is perhaps an understatement; against a stark background, this is hot!

 RW Straightforward and super-premium—a heroic presentation of the product. I was originally interested by the henna pattern on the product itself, assuming it was applied in retouching specifically for the packaging and flavor differentiation. Now knowing that these graphics are actually applied to the sausages, I'm not quite sure how I feel about the product. I'm not sure I want printed graphics on my food, edible ink or not. Still, the identity is noteworthy.

PRODUCT	Little Bug Baby Food
DESIGN FIRM	Brand Engine
LOCATION	Sausalito, CA
CLIENT	Little Bug, Inc.

PRODUCT	Clearspring Organic Oils
DESIGN FIRM	Mayday
LOCATION	London, England
CLIENT	Clearspring

 There is something so pure about this design—the name, the simplicity, the colors—I just wish I had a better idea of what is inside the box.

 This is sweet without all the syrupy clichés of baby products. There are small clues that this is a product for babies: the type treatment, the tiny ladybug, and of course the name. The wrap-around label has a bold impact at retail and appears to also serve as the "tamper evident" seal. I would be tempted to give this a try myself; I wonder if strained peas would tempt me as well.

 These are almost identical to the Minale Tattersfield olive oils of the 1970s, and it's true that a good idea is timeless, as this pack demonstrates. I like the way the top of the label dips in sympathetically, enhancing the drop movement.

 The brand mark goes beyond establishing immediate visual equity for this product; it creates a stunning sensory experience. Not sure about the color-coding or typographical hierarchy, but the die cut is really special.

 I simply can't take my eyes off this icon; it's literally a stop sign-like visual vampire that just steals your attention. In addition to the unmistakable drop, the die-cut wave interrupts the top of the label. My obvious concern is that the dark bottle color makes the drop look more like crude oil than anything I'd want to consume. I imagine that the design firm explored lighter, more natural-colored glass which would have assisted in flavor differentiation and added much-needed appetite appeal. Regardless, this is a most impressive solution, which would have been complete if they could only have modified the Clearspring logo to match it!

PRODUCT	Waitrose Cheese
DESIGN FIRM	Lewis Moberly
LOCATION	London, England
CLIENT	Waitrose Ltd.

 BE I really like this simplicity. As an own-label range these are easy to spot, refreshingly simple, and have a vibrant color range, all on a white canvas to let them breathe. Keeping the type in a considered, condensed block keeps the design clean and uncluttered, nicely highlighted by the country shapes. It's also interesting to easily see where each variant originates, which I'm sure hooks the cheese enthusiasts. Cracking!

 MK This approach is modern and original in a product category that can be either intimidatingly stuffy or dumbed down. The way each white, waxed paper–wrapped cheese expresses its locality is informative and intriguing. The justified text using weights, scale, and point size, layered on top of tinted silhouettes of the country with transparent, full-color dots to show the specific point of origin is striking. The visual and verbal information are literally layered and scaled so that the perception of depth creates informational hierarchy. The Waitrose logo, positioned in a different place on each design, makes a bold statement by a brand confident of its positioning.

 SW I love this solution. The butcher-paper wrap conjures up a purchase from a local cheese shop. The flavor-descriptive copy guides the non-cheese expert—again as if you were in a cheese shop with the head cheese-maker lovingly describing the piece of cheese he's just wrapped up for you. The beautiful color of each package has a stunning retail presence. The system of defining the cheese-making province is brilliant. This is worlds apart from cheese in plastic wrap.

belve

ABSOLUT®
Country of Sweden
RUBY RED

...merse yourself in the refreshing
...of zesty grapefruit, blended with
...ka distilled from grain grown
...e rich fields of southern Sweden.
...distilling and flavoring of vodka
...an age-old Swedish tradition
...ing back more than 400 years.
...ka has been sold under the name
...Absolut since 1879.

40% ALC./VOL. (80 PROOF) 1 LITER
IMPORTED
GRAPEFRUIT FLAVORED VODKA

OLUT®
Sweden
RED

...in the refreshing
...it, blended with
...grain grown
...outhern Sweden.
...oring of vodka
...dish tradition
...an 400 years.

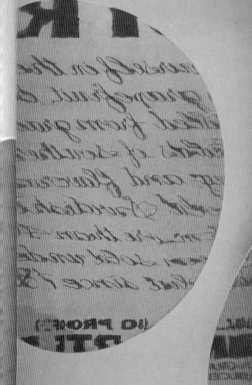

CHAPTER 2

rages

"Absolut is the Coca-Cola of spirits branding."

— Rob Wallace, page 129

PRODUCT	ONI Double Cross Vodka
DESIGN FIRM	Capsule
LOCATION	Minneapolis, MN
CLIENT	Old Nassau Imports

BE Structurally, this design is striking—strong, linear, intimidating—and yet premium, with its heavy base and slick silver cap. I agree with Rob below, though, that the design distracts from, rather than enhances, the beauty of it. I love the little "TT" on the cap. The script font that sits at the back is beautiful in its own right, but because of its composition, it gets lost behind the slick, modern "TT" logo. It would benefit from one or the other, rather than both. The branding down the side is an unusual touch, though, and the over-sticker adds a level of luxury, making this a heavyweight vodka brand to be contended with.

RW There is a lot going on here. The architectural bottle and square cap, the double-cross icon, the embossed logo on both sides, and the thin side label are all quite striking. And while the overall visual impression is effective, I find that the hand-scripted back label graphics are overdone and detract from the clean and powerful brand presence. Like fine artists, designers need to know when to stop. In my opinion, this design is a case of one element too many.

PRODUCT	Chivas 25-Year-Old Original
DESIGN FIRM	Coley Porter Bell
LOCATION	London, England
CLIENT	Chivas Brothers

BE The "Most Prestigious Whisky" certainly has pulled out every available stop. This is a finishings feast: embossed glass; foils; etchings; a wealth of metallics; and intricate detailing, all held together with the mother of heraldic branding. It's posh; it knows it; and I don't know many other whiskys that can pull off this level of heavyweight, super-premium prestige with such aplomb.

RW Stunning. Kudos to Coley Porter Bell's ability to incorporate premium whisky category cues with a revitalization of the brand's rather dusty core mnemonics. The result is at the same time nostalgic and contemporary; familiar and unexpected. Great design lives in the details, and this identity embraces that in the opulent graphics, the embossed label area and neck treatments, and the authoritative pedestal.

PRODUCT	**Midnight Moon**
DESIGN FIRM	Airtype Studio
LOCATION	Winston-Salem, NC
CLIENT	Piedmont Distillers, Inc

PRODUCT	**p.i.n.k. Vodka**
DESIGN FIRM	Bailey Brand Consulting
LOCATION	Plymouth Meeting, PA
CLIENT	The p.i.n.k Spirits Company

 The structure is great; the solid, extra-heavy base and simplified glass bottle make it seem sturdy. The graphics themselves, ironically or not, look like they just hopped off a Greyhound in front of a 1940s chrome diner in South Carolina. The type seems a little unworked, but the dynamic label shape, great car illustration, the name, and the pastiche give a glamorous nod to the bootleg era and make this design delightfully, unashamedly retro, but not too kitsch. It's a cool addition to anyone's cocktail cabinet.

 A combination of 1950s-retro, hot-rod speedway graphics, and moonshine—very nostalgic and very Americana. Since moonshine was produced illegally at night, the lock-up of the brand identity with the black-and-white graphics emits a radiant, polished personality. I'm not keen on setting this script font on a curve, and the Midnight Moon typography should be more ownable. Actually, I feel that different typefaces might complement the design better.

 As a consumer who shops "pink" (for my daughter), hears Pink, and sees pink everywhere, I know that pink—as a design, a name, and a personality—is not only a fashion trend but also a personal statement. Pink, in today's culture, has meanings well beyond the interpretations of the past (soft, demure, innocent). Pink is now the passionate, rebellious, wild child. This glowing design would appeal to the youthful, club-going generation which seeks an alternative to liquor bottles with a manly design.

 The brand name obviously drives the key design element here—its unique, blushing color. With the hyper-proliferation of flavored vodkas, one might assume that this product has a sweet, fruity infusion. As a result, the overall impression is most definitely female. I can't see a guy ordering this at a bar or bringing it to a party. This is an interesting choice for a caffeinated vodka. However, in the testosterone-driven vodka category, being approachable to women is perhaps a bonus. I'm also curious about the periods between the letters of the logo. It almost suggests that PINK is an acronym for some evocative message.

PRODUCT	**Akvinta Vodka**
DESIGN FIRM	Lewis Moberly
LOCATION	London, England
CLIENT	Adriatic Distillers

PRODUCT	**Tableaux Wine**
DESIGN FIRM	PhilippeBecker
LOCATION	San Francisco, CA
CLIENT	Artisan Wine Group

BE Sumptuous touch of red on the base. Lovely little silver emblem; looks like it's debossed into the glass, giving it gravitas. The way it contains all the crafting detail contrasts nicely with the expressive and spontaneous script font that crawls up the bottle.

MK Imagine this bottle frosty, and you get a beautiful aesthetic from all angles. The rough pen-and-ink signature conveys "authentic," "personalized," and "premium" with a "V" that becomes an ownable mark. The red foil neck and cap and the subtle hint of red in the base are curious but certainly command attention. An applied gold-seal medallion communicates trust and confidence in quality and brings the consumer into the Akvinta Vodka story.

BE The strong use of yellow here works well. The unusual die cut is impressively complex; it certainly helps make this bottle stand out on the shelf.

MK This label applies the art form of silhouette in a clever way to position the product in a social, unpretentious, imaginative scene. The consumer can almost foresee himself or herself enjoying the wine among friends. The conventional hierarchy and graphic elements add an earnest quality to the overall perception.

RW I like this design for its unexpected imagery and brighter-than-bright color. But I specifically applaud the design firm for walking the talk. I imagine that designing the package was among the easiest tasks in the complex process of bringing this brand to market. I bet the lessons learned through this process will give this firm great empathy for their clients. And I bet it will make them a better partner.

!!! *The folks at PhilippeBecker like wine (a lot). So they created their own brand. Tableaux launched in 298 stores.*

PRODUCT	Jack Daniel's Outer Gift Packaging
DESIGN FIRM	Mayday
LOCATION	London, England
CLIENT	Brown Forman

PRODUCT	Dry Port Wine
DESIGN FIRM	Risedesign
LOCATION	Zibo, China
CLIENT	Tiancun Group

 Jack Daniels, a veteran of crafted labels, has been given a modern twist, using the iconic bottle shape as a masking device. This works brilliantly, as Jack Daniels is so established that, even cropped to just "JA," it's instantly recognizable. The unusual cropping highlights the existing label to full effect, forcing us to look afresh at its intricacies, and using the die cut instead of printing straight onto the carton adds a premium feel. Continuing the bottle-shape device for the type on the reverse side makes this box feel beautifully considered, crafted, and unusual. I'll be looking out for one!

 This brand is so iconic that it would not be difficult for the average consumer to visualize the glass bottle and label graphics. It really makes a statement when 80 percent of the brand identity can be covered by placing it inside a die cut of the contoured glass bottle and still be completely recognizable. Love the signature, placed as though the artist signed the masterpiece, and the way the well-engineered box unsnaps from behind, unfolding forward to reveal the trophy inside.

 This is stunning, smart, handsome and—more importantly— not over the top. It takes a strong, iconic bottle and label and uses them to build and enhance the brand, rather than adding more stuff. Beautiful typography. I'm not sure what the button in the back does, but who cares? I would buy this!

 This design is rich and typical of Eastern class and style. I love the rich, Indian-blue gradient from which the decorative characters sing out, and the unusual positioning and smaller-size branding make this box striking.

This is an example where the cultural nuances of design can be lost on a foreign audience. The radiant blue structure with the white symbols and gold Chinese characters is quite appealing, but clearly, the overall authenticity of the products is the component of the design that will resonate with the consumer.

PRODUCT	**Coca-Cola Aluminum Bottle**
DESIGN FIRM	Turner Duckworth
LOCATION	London, England and San Francisco, CA
CLIENT	The Coca-Cola Company, North America

 BE Charged with the redesign of the world's most iconic brand, this team has achieved what so many designers have longed to do—taken Coca-Cola back to its iconic roots. This is one example where "make the logo bigger" is actually a welcome directive, and the resulting, confident use of an oversized, no-fuss logo has managed to make Coke fresh, clean, and strikingly strong again. It's back to what it's best at...how refreshing.

 RW Only Coke could get away with this. But when you absolutely own a color, a shape, and a typestyle, what else do you need? Anything more would be superfluous. While the logo's rather large size prevents it from being read in its entirety from any angle, every consumer knows at a glance exactly what's in this bottle. Bravo to Turner Duckworth for resisting the urge to gild the lily. Bravo to Coca-Cola for their brand-building zealotry, providing this absolutely unique opportunity.

 SW There really isn't anything else to say; it's perfect! But since this is a book about explaining packaging: They've taken three of the most recognizable elements of the brand (really, of any brand) which are known the world over—the Coca-Cola bottle shape, red, and the script—and boldly let them speak. The bottles look great all together as they complete the name. Was this really produced? Where is all the legal stuff? I'm thirsty.

PRODUCT	Selfridges
DESIGN FIRM	Lewis Moberly
LOCATION	London, England
CLIENT	Selfridges & Co

PRODUCT	St. Urbain Rousse
DESIGN FIRM	Nolin Branding & Design
LOCATION	Montreal, Canada
CLIENT	Labatt Breweries Inc.

BE This is just a little sneaky preview of a huge range that this design covers within Selfridges and, for such an enormous task, this design is pure class. The unusual color choice stands out a mile from the branded competition, and the considered, restrained type and luxury finishes all deliver a seriously premium product line. I particularly love the gothic *S* die cut; it makes the design iconic, strong, and modern, yet still exudes gravitas.

MK Out of the context of this notable retail establishment, it is difficult to truly appreciate the value of design for this line of products. Selfridges says "fashion" and this line beautifully expresses that dictum. Each packaging reflects attention to detail. The elaborate gathered fabric, holly-decorated cover, hinged book box, bottleneck collar, die-cut over-wrap, the contrast of soft, matte textures with foil stamping, and the die-cut *S* are all symbols of distinction.

RW Just look at the combination of colors and textures. Check out the details of the crimped fabric and the box pull. Lush. And while its overall impression is just a little bit cold and perhaps overtly sophisticated (if not snobbish), I'd still be proud to bring this entire line of products to Christmas dinner. Although my family might consider the packaging too nice to open!

BE The understated, well-executed idea in the logo itself—effortlessly hijacking a street sign—still plays true to the traditions of beer branding. The simplicity of the color palette supports the rustic, homegrown attitude, but the simplicity of the type keeps it modern. It's unfussy, quaint, and evokes nostalgia without dwelling too heavily on it.

RW I would love to have seen the brief on this project to discover the significance of the delivery peddler's wagon. Nevertheless, great design tells a story, and this street-sign label tells all: Local, hand-brewed, and custom-delivered only to places within biking distance of the brewery. If, in fact, this is the brand's authentic story, this design is an apt visual testament to it.

SW This will become a classic—that is, if the product lives up to the package. This is true to the beer category but takes it to a more refined and elegant place. The typography is impeccable, and the quaint illustration adds a bit of whimsy. I wonder if the designers tried something besides the oval label shape? Although it fits comfortably in the category—too comfortably—it could be mistaken for a competitor.

PRODUCT	**Kilo Kai**
DESIGN FIRM	Turner Duckworth
LOCATION	London, England and San Francisco, CA
CLIENT	Apostrophe Brands

BE Simplicity is this design's best attribute in a category that's overwhelmingly fussed. It certainly rejuvenates a stuffy genre, and the reference to pirates is a softly witty idea that works well.

MK The intriguing modern twist on a skull and crossbones—which historically represents the warning of danger (as in poisonous substances)—and the stereotypical pirate flag (pirates got drunk on rum, right?) combined with uppercase sharp serifs and wide-open kerning create a memorably mischievous brand identity. The shelf appeal—beyond the intriguing name and identity—is enhanced by the amber bottle and an ACL white identity. The well-formatted black-and-white label with the red signature has a classic, premium sensibility.

RW It's hard not to be impressed with how Turner Duckworth combined a rather cumbersome brand name with a cliché icon and transformed them into an ownable and relevant brandmark. The elegant neck label balances the masculine symbol, making the brand at the same time more premium and more approachable. The bottom label organizes all the additional information, underscoring this simple and effective identity.

SW The matte-finished bottle is a great canvas for this intriguing icon and product name. It feels like a spiced rum without falling into all the trappings of the category—pirates, parrots, etc. The skull and crossbones winks at the iconography but does it in an ownable and memorable way. The limited color palette is bold and provides good shelf presence in a back-bar situation. My only negative comment is the kerning on "Handcrafted" on the neck band.

PRODUCT	essn
DESIGN FIRM	Brand Engine
LOCATION	Sausalito, CA
CLIENT	SkylarHaley

 The copy is the hero here. It's the short, sharp syntax that gives this design its edge, a nice change from the saccharine-sweet marketing copy that's flooded the market in the UK. The design itself is simple, organized, contemporary in its minimalism, with a no-nonsense approach, but it doesn't especially move me.

 A layout that breaks away from conventions. Few designs position the body copy above the brand identity, but this positioning seems to communicate the story behind the brand—literally—almost as if the label was slid down the can to reveal the text. Clean and organized, the use of color and the silver of the aluminum can read sparkling and flavorful. The graphic illustrations of the Minneola tangerine, Fuji apple, Meyer lemon, and blood orange and cranberry within the silver circles appear as a window into the cans' contents. I find this design refreshing.

 It's not enough to be simple. Simplicity at the expense of personality can quickly skew generic. It can leave most people cold, and the drink world is already overcrowded with stripped-down design. While this identity follows that general trend, there's something about the all-lowercase logo, considered color palette, unexpected layout, sardonic copy, and in-your-face icon style that brings a smile into this all-too-austere category.

 A simple design for a relatively simple product—fruit juice. How novel! The composition with the upside-down hierarchy of information (the product description at the top) is just enough of a twist to give these products an ownable personality and look.

PRODUCT	**Lanjaron Mineral Water**
DESIGN FIRM	Tridimage	Grupo Berro
LOCATION	Buenos Aires, Argentina
CLIENT	Danone Spain

 The structure of this design works beautifully: It has a great idea, well executed. It challenges the existing constraints of PET with a beautiful result. The mountain looks pure, clean, and has just enough detail. The graphics, however, don't seem to be in the same league (don't get me started on that logo) but are thankfully confined to the top part, allowing the structure to be the hero.

 The punt is definitely the strongest asset of this design. Not only does this feature form the literal and geographical base for this design but its sheer presence communicates the quality and exclusivity often seen in sparkling wines, hand-blown bottles, or the art of Steuben Glass. The Lanjaron brand identity hovers above the mountains as a vision in the atmosphere.

 I'll gladly forgive the somewhat expected logo and mountaintop graphic for the slender shape of this bottle, its thin label, its embossing and, of course, its decorated punt. Having had some experience with creating an icon in the bottom of a glass bottle, I can tell you it's not at all easy to create an embossing of this depth, size, and dimension and make it look good. I understand the production mandates that prevented the decorated bottom from looking a bit more sleek and detailed. Still, this execution generates a great presence for the brand.

PRODUCT	**Hammer + Sickle Vodka**
DESIGN FIRM	Monahan & Rhee
LOCATION	New York, NY
CLIENT	Hammer + Sickle Vodka

BE The bottle design is impressive: It's bristling with Soviet minimalism, unashamedly masculine, yet graceful. The combination of finishes on the linear structure make it elegant. I like the way the liquid it contains is held in a rounded bottom, contrasting with the angled exterior.

MK A great monument—a dominant fortress of a bottle. The strength, independence and pre-eminence of this brand are beautifully captured. Amazing how the structural design—with its imposing, magnificent, chiseled form—combined with the hammer and sickle, appropriately positioned, can perfectly capture Russian heritage and nationality. This design projects authority.

RW I heard one of our designers rave about this package well before I saw this image. It lives up to the hype. This is a nice tip of the hat to Russian deconstructivism—those iconic, angular, illustrated posters of hard-working laborers and the like. The chiseled facets, the square neck, the flat cap, the glossy red enamel, and the dramatic taper create a towering architectural impact. Traditionally, this bottle would be rather top-heavy and therefore hard to manage during filling and distribution. I'm glad to see that they overcame these issues and invested in this stunning result.

SW This is a beautiful, monumental, architectural bottle, and the designer should be applauded for keeping the design so simple. This is clearly a case for less.

PRODUCT	Aroma Ragusea
DESIGN FIRM	Laboratorium
LOCATION	Zagreb, Croatia
CLIENT	Aroma Raguesea

PRODUCT	Fluid
DESIGN FIRM	Tank Design
LOCATION	Tromsoe, Norway
CLIENT	Mack Bryggerier

BE This plays by all the rules of premium packaging: Black, black, black; minimal type; a bit of detailing; and a confidently luxurious use of space. Allowing the product to show through adds a touch of natural color, which the black accentuates. It's over-packaged, luxurious, and hedonistic, but it still looks sleek, refined, and desirable.

MK Nothing is more authentic than images of pure, aromatic products on beautifully crafted packaging. The mono-chromatic palette lets the products stand out and yet, where the product is not revealed, the illustration tells the story. White on black, classy, elegant, and simple, these are gift-worthy.

SW This is a lovely presentation. The beautifully simple type on black is handsome and lets the colors of the herbs and fruits take center stage.

MK This is a look that definitely appeals to a young generation that views traditional category cues as dated and old-fashioned. I read recently that consumers who make spontaneous inferences about a product are more likely to make a purchase. In this case, the creative aesthetic drives consumer appeal. Design for design's sake, with branding that literally wraps itself into the image.

SW I'm stuck on these. I'm not sure what to say, but I'll try. They are lovely packages, but I don't get any sense of beer. The brief stated, "Development of name and design of a modern beer concept to appeal to a target group who do not traditionally prefer beer," but these look more like lemonade. So how do you utilize some of the iconography that says "beer" and still make it appealing to those who don't like beer? I think this package misses on that point altogether. But as a package for an energy drink or soda pop, I think this is a beautiful design solution.

PRODUCT	**Bloom**
DESIGN FIRM	CBX
LOCATION	New York, NY
CLIENT	Del Monte Foods

PRODUCT	**Will & Jamie's Fresh Yogurt Drinks**
DESIGN FIRM	Designers Anonymous
LOCATION	London, England
CLIENT	Will & Jamie's Fresh Yoghurt Drinks

 I'm not a big fan of the type used here, but one thing this design has in abundance is serious shelf standout. In a traditionally masculine energy drink market, it's a nice take that packs a punch without overstating it—especially impressive for a brand historically wedded to its boring, big-fruit photography. The colors and flavors are clearly differentiated with the strong iconic composition, and they've managed to get the fruit on there without being predictable. Not an easy task for such a monolithic brand!

 In the hierarchy of human perception, we recognize and emotionally respond to graphics more quickly and more viscerally than to words. (Funny how every design assignment is initiated by the words in a brief or positioning statement that consumers never see.) Color is the first and foremost visual cue, followed by shape. Here the brand seeks to own a recognized and relevant shape, or more accurately, a symbol. Owning the exclamation point is an interesting strategy. The logotype is somewhat expected, and the verbose product story in the background gets in the way of what would otherwise be a smart, simple design. Still, this design is noteworthy just for its attempt to own this unique and relevant symbol!

 The success of this design is all in the great little idea in the logo, the main feature on the label. It's quirky and fun, and using the udders to describe the variants makes this a lighthearted take on a category already crowded with home-made, natural design. Simple, strong, fresh, and focused, it lets the flavor itself come right through the bottle.

 The simple, black-and-white, children's-book illustration style of this spotted cow with a great poser personality is made even more memorable with the hysterically funny color-coded udder! A great example of my principle that if a packaging design is not visually compelling in black and white, it may not be powerful at all. The bottle structures complement the simplicity of this solution.

 This design is refreshingly simple. It takes the category of yogurt and gives it a friendly, personable spin that both kids and adults can relate to. It's funny—the uncluttered design of this product actually makes it appear to be made by people rather than by a corporation. The strict two-color application adds a perfect boldness for retail impact, and the touch of flavor-color works well and isn't overwhelmingly sweet.

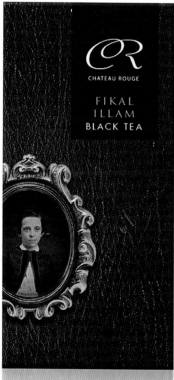

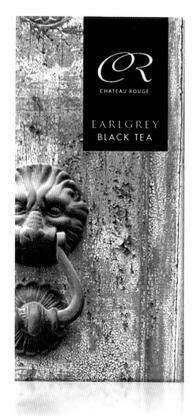

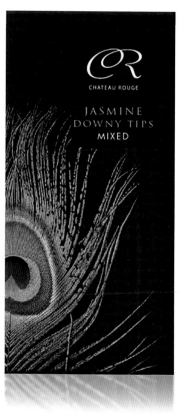

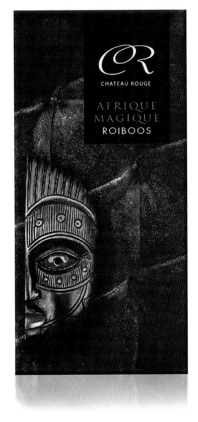

PRODUCT	Chateau Rouge
DESIGN FIRM	Brandhouse
LOCATION	London, England
CLIENT	Chateau Rouge

 A captivating and richly cultural story—and some artifacts that maybe a little too eerily make eye contact—make for an interesting collection. Their positioning—well balanced by the upper-right orientation of brand identity and flavor variety—focused lighting, and rich, textural backgrounds set a luxurious yet tailored tone for this brand.

 Great brands all have a great story. What a beautiful story these textural photos tell about this brand! I can imagine the visceral and visual impact that these packages have at the point of sale, specifically when several of these products are merchandised together. Each photo is so unexpected and at the same time so relevant to each flavor. I am also pleasantly impressed with the fluid "CR" logo and the black banner that contains all the branding information. Brilliant.

PRODUCT	**Sero2**
DESIGN FIRM	Curious Design
LOCATION	Auckland, New Zealand
CLIENT	NZ Aquaceuticals

BE In a market saturated with both water and supplement drinks, it's a breath of fresh air to see a design without a) dew-ridden fruit, b) splashing liquids, c) leaping yoga freaks, or—worst of all—d) power swooshes [shudder]. Trendy, minimal design can be really boring and personality-free, but this design manages to stay fresh, clean, and energetic with a simple graphic that hints at science with a touch of nature. Simple, modern, uncluttered type and a single aqua color palette help keep it thoroughly refreshing.

MK A number of elements make this design successful. From the top down, the design choices work to make it eye-catching and appealing. The silver screw cap adds sparkle and sense of purity; a white screw cap would have been monotonous. The vertical positioning of "serotonin naturally" subtly brings the eye downward to the graphics that begin on the bottle's shoulders, then to the positive cerulean diamond shape within the starburst, pointing directly to the brand identity. Notice how each successive diamond within the starburst brings your eye around the graphics while pointing to the brand identity and secondary copy. The starburst graphic itself hangs like a piece of jewelry around the bottle's neck. The overall impression is of a fresh, modern, dynamic, softly sparkling spring water.

RW I agree with Bronwen's comments: A refreshing perspective on an over-proliferated category. This design has an eye-catching radiance that is hard to achieve with this cool color palette. I specifically like the fashionable and cascading shoulder line contrasted with the vertical type coming down from the neck. The design is simultaneously revitalizing and soothing.

110

PRODUCT	**Safeway Fruit-Flavored Sodas**
DESIGN FIRM	Anthem Worldwide
LOCATION	San Francisco, CA
CLIENT	Safeway Inc.

BE These certainly work brilliantly as a range. To me they look quite young, but they're fun, colorful, and have a pop-art quality that's crisp and bold. The bright colors sing out on the shelf, and the circular, focused area creates a clear and recognizable navigational unit that's functional yet playful, a refreshing change from the bubbles and swooshes that usually adorn the category.

MK It's not easy for private-label beverages to get the customer's attention, but with their undemanding and good-humored shelf presence, this line strikes a chord. These symbols, held within what feel like parentheses—as punctuation marks that want to emphasize what is within—create unique, instantly recognizable identities that position the brand and visually articulate the beverages as a version of the Mac iChat icons. This reference, combined with a refreshing family of colors, communicates a user-friendly, engaging beverage experience.

SW These private-label fruit sodas give new direction to generic brands. They're fun and smart and they look premium without the premium price tag. I would definitely try these once, and I'd be so happy if they tasted good, since it would give me great joy to buy them regularly.

PRODUCT	This Water
DESIGN FIRM	Pearlfisher
LOCATION	London, England
CLIENT	Innocent Drinks

 These encapsulate the current trend for the cutesy, friendly, homemade design that is Innocent's core attribute. The illustration style fits perfectly, and the lowercase logo enhances this. The copywriting is what really gives this brand its amusing twist; it's quirky and pokes fun at the serious conventions of the water category. It's a shame there isn't more of an idea to the little illustrations, but overall it feels fresh, frivolous, and fun.

 I was in a retail establishment in London recently and this brand absolutely caught my attention! What initially stopped me as a consumer was the unexpected choice of illustrations, along with their colors, positioning, and execution style. The combination of a strong, dark, lowercase, flush-left, traditional serif font (perhaps Antique Ultra) married to a savory-colored, unconventionally arranged, hand-written font is well designed and well executed. The addition of good-humored copy reveals a smart design sense and an even smarter client.

 This brand cuts through the clutter and gets to the core of the product. It's got a great name that is unique in its almost-stupid straightforwardness! I can easily picture this name being interpreted in a sterile and cool package, but the designers executed the concept playfully—and with the right dose of humor and intelligence—for broader appeal. Congratulations to the client for having the guts to believe in the irony of the name.

PRODUCT	**World Market Sparkling Soda**
DESIGN FIRM	PhilippeBecker
LOCATION	San Francisco, CA
CLIENT	Cost Plus World Market

PRODUCT	**Fat Bastard**
DESIGN FIRM	Turner Duckworth
LOCATION	London, England and San Francisco, CA
CLIENT	Click Wine Group

 I applaud trying to get an idea in, especially with a name that begs for it, but somehow this feels a little too forced and pedantic. I'd like it to be a little rougher and more spontaneous; it's a little too restrained, the illustrations a little too twee. They could have die-cut the label to have stamp edging, or at least positioned the origin stamp in a different place on each variant just to liven this up a bit. It's a shame, as the idea is there, but the execution isn't, quite.

 The layered elements team up to express the brand's positioning. Specifically, the use of a simulated DOC (Denominazione di Origine Controllata, or Original Location Certified) imprint, a quality assurance label found on many Italian wines; the tariff stamp; the "Italy" brand; and the simulated sepia-tone background harken back to an older world market story.

 A name like that is a great starting point, and the design has been tastefully and elegantly executed, with the rotund little hippo cleverly using the label itself as its prop. Understated design playing to traditional wine cues carries off this rather interesting name with a wink and a smile and quietly witty class.

 I can't tell you how many people I know—wine connoisseurs and beyond—who have purchased this wine and told me about it. From that unscientific survey alone, I think this brand is a successful consumer magnet. Perhaps, in a retail environment that too often conveys an air of superiority, this label design is a spoof on the French origins of both wine and the epithet. I recognize this label as a more engaging redesign. The fat hippo now sits well, making the right point (or in this case, dent) and the typographic elements now flow well.

 With a name like this, in less confident hands, this could have gone so wrong! But the simple white label with the beautifully elegant, understated typography is the perfect prop for this cute, rotund hippo. It's one of those designs I wish I had thought of. It will haunt me for years.

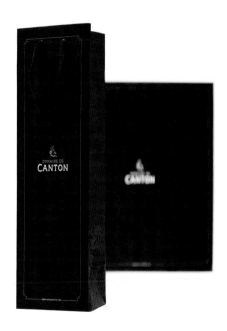

PRODUCT	**Domaine de Canton**
DESIGN FIRM	Mucca Design
LOCATION	New York, NY
CLIENT	Domaine de Canton

 This bottle of ginger liqueur is structurally stunning: It's elegant, refined, and beautifully evokes Colonial Indochina, the liquid itself almost glowing through the paper-lamp shape. The simple black lines enhance the concept yet still feel delicate and refined, and the type has a French Colonial ambience without being overcomplicated or archaic. The gift box and bag exude luxury. The simple foliage illustration as a subtle black-on-black extension complements the lightness of the bottle, allowing it to shine.

 Impeccably conceived and executed. A genuine treasure—artful, sensitive, and fragrantly seductive. The design reads like a beautiful story unfolding. What more can be said?

 Here is a fitting tribute to cocktail culture. Imagine this bottle glowing on the back bar. Imagine it at retail. Imagine it in your home, on your sideboard. In every environment, this primary package makes an indelible impression. Why hide this most elegant of sculptures in a gift box? Even if they were needed, the box and bag seem rather heavy and funereal. Both could better reference the beauty and elegant translucence of the bottle design.

 This is a stunning system. The balance of the Chinese lantern–shaped bottle and the thoughtful, French aesthetic of the label typography is perfect. They've managed to successfully create a historical perspective presented in a contemporary design. The additional details on the support material—the pattern, the limited color palette, the refined borders—further enhance this brand story.

PRODUCT	**Terras do Foro**
DESIGN FIRM	Bürocratik Design
LOCATION	Coimbra, Portugal
CLIENT	Terras do Foro

 I'm always a fan of black on black, but it seems a little unnecessary here, as the logo is so refined. However, I actually prefer the back of the bottle: The bold and unexpected use of the single red strip on the back, where some designs get lazy. This design was considered as a whole, and the back is graphic and stylish in its own right.

 Lovely typographic execution of "FORO." Black-on-black spot matte varnish characteristically says high quality. The hierarchy of the label reads perfectly, with a warm final resting place for the variety.

 What a fine marriage of type, texture and composition. The bold logo and its lyric icon are beautifully contrasted by the matte, patterned texture. I specifically like the thin red back label as an elegant staging area for supportive type. Dramatic and authentic. The only build I might suggest is to have the grape-leaves icon emanate from the background illustration, tying together the logo and background as one contiguous image.

 The typography is elegant, beautiful, and befits the wine category. I wish the designer had let the logotype hold the design; the matte varnish details seem cluttered and unnecessary. I like the single red graphic strip and how it contrasts the organic logotype. Unfortunately, if this were to be imported into the U.S., the designer would be forced to clutter up this design with regulatory information. So sad.

PRODUCT	Pixie Maté Ready-to-Drink Tea
DESIGN FIRM	Brand Engine
LOCATION	Sausalito, CA
CLIENT	Pixie Maté

PRODUCT	London Tea
DESIGN FIRM	Cowan London
LOCATION	London, England
CLIENT	London Tea

 BE I have to admit, this design is not to my taste; however, one has to admire the simplified, easy-to-navigate branding that clearly differentiates the flavors, and its clear, circular logo clearly holds the range together.

 MK Soda-pop packaging of the 1960s often consisted of simple, bold, graphic shapes with novelty display type and subdued colors. Pixie strikes that chord as it subconsciously references the good old days when products were not over-branded and life was less complicated. The added bonus is the twinkle, which creates a nice exchange between the consumer and the product.

 RW It can be a fine line between retro and dusty. As mentioned elsewhere, the geometric architecture, rounded typefaces, sparkle graphic, and even the name Pixie harkens back to an earlier, simpler time when everything was organic. Yet the balanced layout, sophisticated secondary colors, and whimsical cap copy make it relevant to contemporary tastes.

SW These bottles have a beautifully simple aesthetic which, along with the loose-tea bag packaging, makes a nice brand system. It doesn't need Photoshop tricks and gimmicks.

 MK This is (obviously) an extensive category in its native retail marketplace, hence the need to make a clean break from quintessential English stereotypes. The pleasure of informal afternoon tea is nicely depicted; the use of white focuses your attention effectively; and the organic emanations from the cup draw you into the experience. The people's body language is a bit anxious; perhaps they could connect to the product and the experience a bit more.

 RW It's usually quite difficult to incorporate people into an identity without immediately dating the brand. This is a nice exception. The people become as iconic as the "L" and "T." A welcome breath of fresh thinking in what can be a stuffy category—specifically for a brand with the austere name, The London Tea Company.

 SW In my opinion, these packages are already dated-looking, from the inclusion of the rather stiff and awkward-looking people to the now-overused floating flourishes. I don't know the price point of these products, but they look inexpensive. I do think the spots of white highlights (brand name and cup) work well to guide the eye. And the "L" and "T" as table and chair is interesting, however, I can't get beyond how uncomfortable the figure looks interacting with it.

PRODUCT	**Williams-Sonoma Bar Ingredients**
DESIGN FIRM	PhilippeBecker
LOCATION	San Francisco, CA
CLIENT	Williams-Sonoma

 Designs that emulate a retro style can go so wrong when done sloppily, but, through the sheer detailing and crafting of these labels, the designers at PhilippeBecker have created something that looks genuinely timeless. The care and consideration that's gone into these complex labels speaks volumes about the quality of the product, and a nice, simple glass adds class. They've recreated something which could be sitting on a saloon shelf in the nineteenth century, and although they've not created anything challenging or innovative, this certainly is an example of how it's done!

 These labels are clearly reminiscent of the packaging graphics, label shapes, and printing technologies of the late 1800s. In particular, the gold medals on the Spanish Olive Brine are reminiscent of the awards given to new food products in competitions at international exhibition halls throughout Europe back in the day. Even then, these medals were used in packaging design as valuable marketing tools. Although consumers do not connect these dots, these label designs reflect traditional values and thus evoke craftsmanship and quality. It's not hard to visualize this family in its retail space and in a marketing environment that uses retro design to appeal to consumers on a deeply emotional level.

 This is a nice series of individual products that works even better when viewed as a collection. I specifically like the balance of consistent elements—the neck labels and bottle structure—combined with the distinct personality of the die-cut labels and nostalgic type styles. The faded, classic colors and gold leaf filigree are timeless.

 The attention to detail on these well-crafted labels is impeccable. However, I would have liked to see a twist in the vintage liquor label and bottle shape, which could have made these feel like a new take on the vintage language.

PRODUCT	Fortnum & Mason Teas
DESIGN FIRM	Pearlfisher
LOCATION	London, England
CLIENT	Fortnum & Mason

 BE Fortnum & Mason is such a British establishment, I doubt the designers had much chance to meddle with it. These products provide differentiation in a vast product range. The subtle tin colors and delicate embossing add a touch of class and save this design from being a tad dull.

 MK Classic, collectible storage tins with a discreetly ornate embossment. The angle of the embossments—top right, bottom left—take the overall design out of the ordinary, as do the tin tints and label colors. Yet the typographic hierarchy, fonts, and crest follow the traditional British label designs of the early nineteenth century, which endows the brand with credibility.

RW Creating elegantly precious tea tins is some designer's dream project. There's nothing really special about the graphics: strong, appropriate type; interesting colors. To me, it's the embossing that makes this concept work. I'm drawn to touch it. I imagine a tiny sense of delight each time I hold the tin to open it. And that's enough.

PRODUCT	Lotus Vodka Bottles
DESIGN FIRM	Cahan & Associates
LOCATION	San Francisco, CA
CLIENT	Delicious Brands

BE Simplicity is the strength of this design, which is aimed at the young, urban, hip crowd. It certainly has a strong icon, easily spotted from the other side of the bar when slightly inebriated! The strong blue, white, and silver add to the standout; it's fairly utilitarian but fits the target audience to a tee.

MK There is seductiveness to this austere brand—that's its cachet. Bold and straightforward, the design has the exclusivity of a young, trendy, urban lounge that only the few may enter.

PRODUCT	Frederick Miller Lager
DESIGN FIRM	Optima Soulsight
LOCATION	Highland Park, IL
CLIENT	Miller Brewing Co.

MK So much to talk about with this limited-release packaging design. The luxurious color palette, shimmering graphic elements, metallic foil, gold seal, and signature are eye-catching. These elements are great attention-getters in retail. The flush-right orientation for the carrier is unexpected and breaks away from stereotype in this category. The background pattern reflects a fashionable design style. Lush, rich, and alluring, this brand positions itself as one for the aficionado.

RW Almost everything about this identity—from its high-walled outer container to its off-center layout to its lush typefaces and cigar-bar color palette—speaks to the delicious, chocolaty smoothness of this brand's essence. This sort of craftsmanship might be somewhat expected for a tiny micro-brew, but when Miller Brewing adopts this aesthetic, it speaks even more eloquently. I'm curious about the "2006 Edition" choice. It's neither modern nor traditional. Wouldn't "1890 Edition" seem more credible?

PRODUCT   **Boris Cherry Cans**
DESIGN FIRM   lg2boutique
LOCATION   Montreal, Canada
CLIENT   Brasserie Licorne Québec

PRODUCT   **Boris Cherry 4 Pack**
DESIGN FIRM   lg2boutique
LOCATION   Montreal, Canada
CLIENT   Brasserie Licorne Québec

BE Boris again, and this time he's replaced with a giant, splattered cherry, which certainly looks like it packs a punch! The red/black/silver graphic style combined with the rough, uncut way the cherry has been represented gives it real pace and refreshing bluntness. It's true to its comrades in the range—a striking, strong, unfussed, and confident design that's graphic, has attitude, and sticks a finger up at traditional beer branding.

MK Flavor comes across loud and clear: a mouthful of sweet, effervescent beverage. The bold red graphic on the black can—very Pop Art. The graphics place this product in the moment—the rebirth of the '60s phenomenon with the younger generation. I can't make it out, but I hope the silver text tells a wonderfully adventurous story. I love how you hold the can and the cherry is bursting onto your fingers, and then you turn the can over and pour the cherry into your mouth.

SW I'm not familiar with Boris Beer—and I'm not certain I would like a cherry beer—but this package would make me stop and at least consider trying one. The strong graphic quality of the red-on-black splattered cherry is appealing, if a bit '80s. It has a rock'n'roll aesthetic. I'm not sure what the white script is saying, but visually it takes away from the strength of the rest of the design.

SW This is a nice relationship of the outer carton to the can design. It takes the real estate and explodes the cherry even larger than it is on the can. It has a strong balance.

PRODUCT	Castel 330ml Beer Bottle
DESIGN FIRM	Tsikolia Design R&D LTD.
LOCATION	Tbilisi, Georgia
CLIENT	Castel

PRODUCT	Incanto
DESIGN FIRM	Bruketa&Zinic OM
LOCATION	Zagreb, Croatia
CLIENT	Fructus

BE The brief to make this bottle radically different but keep the dimensions the same could not have been more of a challenge, and I applaud the solution: It is innovative, different, and the result is a very sleek bottle with delicate touches. Confining the graphics to the neck area makes the bottle unusual and striking. I'm not particularly moved by the design on the label; it doesn't have the same modernity and style that the bottle conveys. But keeping the branding so small at the top is a brave move that allows the bottle's shape to shine unhindered.

MK A glass beer bottle that breaks away from the stereotypical form elevates the perception of quality and distinctiveness for this brand. What appears to be the brand identity embossed on the sides of the bottle makes for a tactile grip—the consumer is literally holding the brand. As described in the brief, this design succeeds in the challenge of making this brand refreshingly palatable.

BE This is lovely. The black really pings out the colorful, refined, typographic fruits to maximum effect, using a glossy black label that blends visually into the glass bottle. I can't actually read the type that masks the fruit image, but I imagine it has relevance to the taste, cunningly holding all the secondary information. It's a different take on an ingredient-led design, and the understated foil branding combined with all that considered space gives this a premium and elegant finish.

MK Oh, how I wish I could read this language! What a striking concept—the beauty is in the details, from the shading of the type to create highlights to the stems of type curving off the typographic fruits that so delightfully identify this brand. The brand identity, with its beautifully locked-up typography and delicate silver foil stamp, is positioned perfectly, but with artwork that captivating, the name is almost immaterial.

SW This design is intriguing—I would love to have designed this. The way the color plays off the type to create the fruit shapes is well done. The optical illusion of the shapes appearing and disappearing makes me want to spend time with this package. Placing the brand name near the bottom gives the fruit room to breathe.

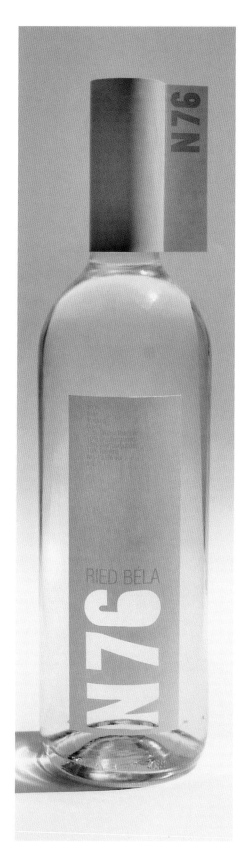

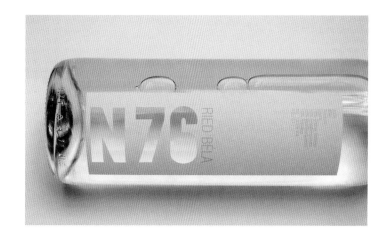

PRODUCT	**N76**
DESIGN FIRM	Alexander Egger, Lisa Vrabec
LOCATION	Vienna, Austria
CLIENT	N76

 There's something rather striking about the simplicity of this design, with its ultra-typographic solution and simple white paper stock. The unusual neck label saves it from being another minimal design solution without personality—it looks great! Not sure what happens when it's opened, but with the heavy die cut making it look sleek, understated, and sophisticated, it certainly stands out on the shelf.

 The simplicity of this bottle is stunning. The flag on the neck wrap is an interesting and unusual touch. I'm not sure why the center of the "6" is removed on the bottle but it's still there on the neck wrap. If it is the brand identity, I would like it to be consistent. The monochromatic color of white on the light liquid works well.

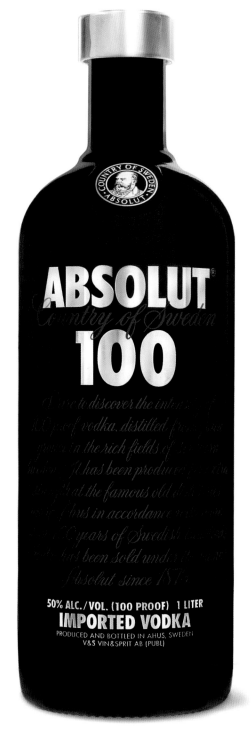

PRODUCT	Absolut 100
DESIGN FIRM	Pearlfisher
LOCATION	London, England
CLIENT	Absolut Vodka

BE Absolut is such a recognizable brand that it must be difficult to differentiate a new family member from the existing range. This scarily alcoholic version (100 proof/50 percent alcohol by volume) is successful in that it absolutely conforms to the family image, yet it's definitely the bigger, tougher brother. Heavy black with silver chrome contrast exudes strength in this seriously masculine design. It is not to be messed with, and certainly the black sheep of the family!

MK Absolut's packaging designs never fail to capture the essence and spirit (no pun intended) of their contents. This one nails it! As dramatic and edgy as an icon can get. This *fashionista* black-and-silver bottle sets a new standard in the category. Goth, urban, Hell's Angels, and yet smart, sexy and powerful, Absolut 100 is clearly the rebel of the Absolut brand family, and this rebel has a captivating personality.

RW Black sheep, indeed! In fact, it's the black glass that concerns me. It's important that this high-test brand offering immediately stands out from the rest of the family. However, if the brand's essence is quality and purity, the black is perhaps too strong and a bit off-brand. A semi-opaque silver might have evoked that same masculine strength, with more of a nod to brand equities and premium vodka credentials. Nothing too special about the type here, but with this brand's truly iconic shape-driven equities, what more do you need?

PRODUCT	**Coca-Cola Holiday 2007**
DESIGN FIRM	Hatch Design
LOCATION	San Francisco, CA
CLIENT	The Coca-Cola Company

 Ignoring the one on the left—no comment necessary—I like the 1950s retro feel of the illustration style. It's difficult to work with a monolithic brand such as Coke and effectively decorate it without it looking throwaway, but I feel this Christmas decoration has style. The retro feel harks back to the golden age of Coke, and keeping the colors true to the brand and using the silver can as a finish works cohesively. The subtle hint at bells and baubles reins this away from all the chintzy horrors that Christmas can coax out.

 The Museum of Modern Art is renowned for their award-winning holiday card selection. It would not be surprising if these cans found their inspiration from that impeccably designed artwork. I imagine that the appearance of a simple application of color and the perception of multiple transparencies can be a technological challenge, but the beauty in these designs is the facade of effortlessness. I wonder if Hatch Design creates cards for MoMA....

 Although I think the Classic Coke can on the left is a perfectly appropriate answer to the problem of creating a holiday theme package, the other two are far more interesting and fresh. The modern patterns are intriguing and the balance of tones keeps the essence of each of the brands. The size of "Zero" could have been smaller, relative to "Coca-Cola."

PRODUCT	**Blossa Annual Edition**
DESIGN FIRM	BVD
LOCATION	Stockholm, Sweden
CLIENT	V&S Group

 This is true Scandinavian class: Beautiful typography on a simple, elegant backdrop that allows for a new variant that's totally different, yet still unmistakably Blossa. This is achieved through a unique, recognizable bottle, with its unusual cork closure, and an ascending numerical system that is always the hero of the design. The result is so collectible and iconic, I can see this going for decades!

 So handsome! Short, stocky, broad shoulders, a long neck, and great coloring convey—at least in this case—a classic, sexy strength. Perhaps this wonderful typographic execution was inspired by the German typomaniac Erik Spiekermann. However it was conceived, it sets the tone for the year perfectly. I would enjoy hearing the analysis for each font. Too bad it's an annual edition, as the entire line would make for a stunning billboard on shelf.

 I can immediately see these bottles lined up against a bar back, encouraging the liberating experience of taste-testing each vintage. The bottles work as well as individual statements as they do collectively. Collectibility would encourage you to add each year's new product and replenish the past year's stock—what a great marketing strategy.

 As a group, these are stunning—I want to own them all. Individually, there are some that are visually more appealing than others. I love the simplicity of just the numeric year, sans additional decoration, which makes "05" less successful in my mind. This is an unusual-shaped bottle for wine—it communicates a brown goods spirit to me, like a whiskey or maybe a port—but I do like the shape and the large graphic surface.

PRODUCT	Belvoir Cordials Range
DESIGN FIRM	Big Fish Design Ltd
LOCATION	London, England
CLIENT	Belvoir

 MK There is a loving appeal to the lost communication form of handwritten correspondence. The illustrative penmanship and the perfect lockup of type and illustration on this beautiful label hark back to traditional packaging design and the value of quality and regional appeal. The deckle edge and angled placement of the label and neck-band add to the authenticity of the design. The color-coding is stunning and not only functions to convey the flavorful essence of the products but brings a modern flair to the line. The bottle structures with the embossed logo enhance the handcrafted, ownable style. This line is breathtakingly beautiful.

 SW This line of packaging has an effortless appeal that is difficult to achieve and yet manages to maintain its sophistication. The full range of colors across all the flavors would make for lovely merchandising. Generally, this much script on a label is difficult to read and I would not suggest it in less adept hands, but Big Fish has managed to pull it off with great success.

PRODUCT	Absolut Ruby Red
DESIGN FIRM	BVD
LOCATION	Stockholm, Sweden
CLIENT	V&S Absolut Spirits

PRODUCT	Garagiste Wines
DESIGN FIRM	Emdoubleyu Design
LOCATION	Vancouver, Canada
CLIENT	Garagiste Wines

 It's not just the stunning production technique of the red transparent circles on the etched glass but the freeness of these modern, geometric forms floating in space. A superbly imaginative solution that brings a nice levity to this line.

 Here's a brand that has so effectively owned its bottle shape that it's become one of the leading icons of our industry—the Coca-Cola of spirits branding. And here, again, they use shape and color in concert to decorate their iconic bottle, proudly signaling this new flavor. I love the combination of frosted glass and transparent ink that allows you to see through the bottle with a rosy tint. And oh, by the way, with a little tonic and lime, the product itself is absolutely (pun intended) delicious!

 It's a gift of a brief, but there is a touching simplicity to these, a rough-and-ready yet quietly elegant feel. To me, it's almost too easy, but adding the grape is a nice solution, giving it a sense of care and precision, and the unusual format and casually stuck-on type helps neatly tie in with the garage idea.

 Tools and a label taped onto the bottle—great imagery in a wine store; just this side of irreverent. It will really turn on the shopper's radar. Greasy—or grapey—fingerprints on the label would add so much to the storytelling. Perhaps the tape is too perfectly cut and positioned; it feels like it should be ripped. The elements definitely evoke a clean garage and a well-organized process.

 This is a great concept for a garage-made wine. I love the idea that these tools were utilized in the making of this wine—it definitely makes me curious enough to want to try it. The label strips—although an oft-overused design device—seem nicely functional here, an inventive way of customizing the year and adding a textural, hand-done element.

PRODUCT	**96 Degrees Coffee**
DESIGN FIRM	The Partners
LOCATION	London, England
CLIENT	96 Degrees

 MK If I drank coffee I would want to try this one, as I find it to be intelligent, interesting, and attractive. There is an intensity in this design; it communicates a sense of impeccable standards.

RW Everything about this package reinvents coffee category convention. The cylindric package structure counters traditional tins or pouched bags. The interchangeable double-ended opening is a revolution. The brand name is informative to the proper product brewing temperature. Its iconic logo, able to be read in both orientations, is also unique. I even like the editorial photo inset with its testimonial copy, adding a bit of personality and authenticity. A striking contrast in all expectations, this package promises a truly extraordinary product.

 SW Beautiful, innovative, and smart—what more could you ask of a package? The revolutionary concept of two sealed compartments, one on each end, to provide maximum fresh coffee is a genius innovation. Pairing that with the "96" that reads from either end is smart, and the intensely dark color paired with the red is handsome and communicates a dark, rich coffee. I only wish they hadn't included the postage-stamp photograph; it seems fussy and unnecessary and—most importantly—it takes away from the ambigram.

PRODUCT	**Java Republic Organic Loose Tea**
DESIGN FIRM	Design Tactics
LOCATION	Dublin, Ireland
CLIENT	Java Republic

MK An educational experience—for me and most likely for the majority of the consumer population—as I have never seen tea pickers before. This brand conveys reality, and these images definitely personalize the product.

 RW Great design often evokes an authentic sense of place, a location from which the brand is truly derived. Fewer designs have made this strategy more palpable, more real. No smiling models here. No Hollywood costumes. There is a realness in these tea farmers' faces. You see the pride of their work in their eyes. I was originally concerned by the copper-colored sky; it struck me as not real (and perhaps foreboding), but it does contribute to a visual consistency across the overall line.

PRODUCT	Tropicana Pure
DESIGN FIRM	Sterling Brands
LOCATION	New York, NY
CLIENT	PepsiCo

PRODUCT	Pescaia Wine Labels
DESIGN FIRM	Giorgio Davanzo Design
LOCATION	Seattle, WA
CLIENT	Facelli Winery

 This is an example of how a brand breaks out of its comfort zone. With new form, as in the ergonomic PET structure, comes a new perception about a brand. The premium brand positioning comes through from a variety of touchpoints. The gold shrink cap and typography, the invisible labeling, the rectilinear format, and the Van Gogh–style illustrations. Ultimately the thick, rich, and deliciously appealing product colors serve as the canvas for the brand's premium identity. A successful way to break through category clutter.

 I adore this structure and graphic identity for the super-premium juice category. I love the slender bottle shape and how well it transitions between sizes. I love the crafted illustrations and the secondary flavor labels that immediately communicate this variant without disrupting the brand block. But I am missing the connection to the Tropicana base brand. Please know that I am not at all a fan of the new base Tropicana redesign. More than enough has been said about its generic look, its confusing pulp designators and its reckless abandon of the straw-and-orange visual mnemonic. I certainly understand why these super-premium products want to look different from the base, but they could just as easily come from a different company. A great design architecture finds that appropriate balance between value tiers. By disregarding the core brand identity, this beautiful work misses the opportunity to elevate the entire brand perception.

 Mmm...every designer loves a bit of letterpress, and this wine label showcases it with a subtle, harmonious color palette, rustic feel, and solid condensed font. Its strength is in its simplicity. The nonfussy approach to the logo—the main feature, all caps—is perfect for revealing the beautiful effects you get from letterpress. Keeping the label no bigger than it needs to be, making it a bit unconventional, and allowing the colors to harmonize with the wine itself (particularly on the red) all work beautifully.

 These labels feel like pieces of art. I love the beautiful simplicity of the warm color combinations, the imperfectly hand-printed characters on the irregularly textured background with a white border, and how the letters sit together on the table. The subtlety of this design is how it conveys the gratifying experience of working with one's hands to create a beautiful outcome. One cannot overlook the debt this design owes to a great relationship between a good designer and a quality printer.

 Hand-picked, hand-sorted wines deserve this hand-crafted identity. I like the block letterforms and the choice of different contrasting colors within each. I like how the type color palette changes between reds and whites but the background colors just swap top-to-bottom. The label stock has an indulgent texture that complements the small-batch perception. And, yes, the letterpress printing completes the sensory experience.

PRODUCT	**Bootleg**
DESIGN FIRM	Turner Duckworth
LOCATION	London England and San Francisco, CA
CLIENT	Click Wine Group

 The humble wine label has been somewhat reinvented over the past five years or so, and this frivolous example is a contemporary take on the fusty world of wines. Both the idea and the execution are simple and striking, and using the zipper in almost-neon colors as a simple differentiator between the wines makes it easy to navigate. The restrained touch of branding on a label keeps the concept pure, modern, and just a little bit sexy.

 A great name and a show-stopper. Wikipedia states that bootleg "refers to making, transporting, and/or selling illegal alcohol...". The intelligent play on this concept is not completely lost. I would love to see the fashionista who unzips her leather jacket to reveal this bootlegged bottle, or a catwalk of models carrying this brand down a runway. This design asserts personality and shocks the category.

 Although I did not immediately make the connection between the zipper and a boot—nor between Italy's boot shape as an inspiration for the brand name—I do very much like this concept. Great design changes the experience. This identity's fashionista whimsy is a refreshing departure from the expected deadpan authenticity. The full-wrap label and spartan hand-tag graphics extend the shelf height and must make this package sing at retail.

 I, too, didn't make the link between the product name Bootleg and Italy—but I am certain I would not have wanted to see the shape of Italy on yet another label. I am intrigued by the design and, at point-of-sale, that's more than half the battle. In the photograph, the illusion of the tight wrap and the zipper are so real—it takes this type of super-realism to pull off a concept like this.

PRODUCT	**maDIKwe**
DESIGN FIRM	Sayles Graphic Design
LOCATION	Des Moines, IA
CLIENT	maDIKwe

PRODUCT	**U'Luvka Gift Pack & Bottle Labelling**
DESIGN FIRM	Aloof
LOCATION	Lewes, England
CLIENT	The Brand Distillery

 The vivacious colors and—frankly—the overall confusion of this design certainly make you stop to look. The fact that the name is hard to read (and even harder to pronounce) makes you want to grab the bottle, turn it on its side, study it. Conceivably, that's the catch, since 85 percent of what is handled by the consumer in the marketplace ends up in the shopping basket. Although I am not a fan of (a) a PDP that has type placed vertically as well as horizontally, (b) the use of so much copy overall, or (c) the use of so many typefaces, there is nevertheless something intriguing here that catches the eye and pulls you in.

 It's so over the top you just want to stare at it. Overall, this is a fun and interesting design from three feet away, but up close, the details are clunky and don't flow together. The stances of the elephant and lion are at odds with the crest shape and with each other. The serif font on the side bands feels more "Old West" than exotic, and it has an Asian feel as well. It's hard to tell what kind of "adult cane beverage" this is—rum, perhaps—or is it fruity? All in all, it communicates several mixed messages.

 It's a shame we can't see the bottle on its own here, as it's beautiful. It totally breaks all the category norms of refined, symmetrical bottles, creating an organic droplet of molten glass that's totally unique. Its imperfection, combined with the slightly pagan symbol on the front, makes for a little bit odd, bizarrely different brand, and thank goodness Aloof hasn't plastered that unusual shape with unnecessary graphics. As for the outer box, it's slick and almost textural, black on black contrasting beautifully with the purity of the bottle.

 This mysterious and obscure design has an unusually engaging quality. The contrast between the foreign name and the subtext of friendship, love, and pleasure evokes a captivating story. The spot-varnish, painterly pattern combined with the hieroglyphic symbol is provocative. The bottle structure has a distorted, surreal fluidity, appearing as either a hand-blown decanter or a melted glass vessel—both alluring interpretations.

PRODUCT	**Coca-Cola Classic Packaging**
DESIGN FIRM	Turner Duckworth
LOCATION	London, England and San Francisco, CA
CLIENT	The Coca-Cola Company

PRODUCT	**Sprite**
DESIGN FIRM	Collins
LOCATION	New York, NY
CLIENT	The Coca-Cola Company

BE As I mentioned with the bottles, this design achieves what so many designers have longed to do: It takes Coca-Cola back to its iconic roots. It's successful in that it peels off all the unnecessary fuss that Coke has accessorized with over the years, allowing it to play to its true strength—that logo that's universally recognizable at 100 yards (in the dark.)

MK How do you redesign a classic? The enhanced red background is as clear and bright as ever. With this new approach, the transparency of the metallic can is now hidden from sight, allowing the white identity and the white wave to pop. Simple and pure, quietly reinforcing the classic.

SW I'm not exactly sure what the designers did here. This package is exactly as I think Coca-Cola always has been; it looks exactly as it should. If it hasn't always been this way, then kudos to the designer for vision and restraint. It's perfectly classic.

MK This limited-edition design fits strategically in a youthful design trend. As a matter of fact, it reminds me of a great iTunes ad. The wallpaper pattern of silhouettes over the split fountain printing technique of Sprite colors—layered with effervescence dots and repeating signature-script logos—hits the target market perfectly. Obviously, part of the appeal of this design is that it does not have the stereotypical hallmarks of a mass brand.

RW I like the branding strategy of limited-edition specialty packaging. But it takes widely recognized and highly proprietary brand mnemonics to be able to pull this off. Sprite's blue-to-green blend and bright yellow accent colors are such powerful brand equities that all else can be modified to this degree and the brand still survives. The logo is tiny, and its hand-lettered quality is a departure from the base brand identity, but it's so often repeated that it still has impact.

SW I love that large brands are starting to realize that one brand face cannot always appeal to everyone. This limited-edition Sprite packaging was designed specifically for a young audience that may not have thought to purchase Sprite. It's cool, with a fun, sophisticated edge. The slim can speaks to an energy-drink culture. This is a very trend-driven design that is a bit post-peak, which I am certain was the idea behind the limited-edition direction.

PRODUCT	**Tapio Beverages**
DESIGN FIRM	Transfer Studio
LOCATION	London, England
CLIENT	Tapio Ventures Ltd

PRODUCT	**Pixie Maté Boxes**
DESIGN FIRM	Brand Engine
LOCATION	Sausalito, CA
CLIENT	Pixie Maté

BE Screen printing usually demands a certain simplicity, which this design builds on. It's light, refreshing, and communicates naturalness through a simplified illustration, all nicely tied in with the logo. I particularly like the way the bottle lets the product color do most of the work in differentiation, allowing the branding to be super-simple.

MK The structure of the Tapio typeface fits the bottle shape, as does the overall positioning of the graphics. I would prefer the line weights of the leaves to be consistent with the type weights rather than varying from them. The secondary copy is tucked nicely under the leaves—perhaps a sans serif typeface would tie in with the young, naive personality of this design.

RW I celebrate brand identities that use their logo as their primary graphic (think Coca-Cola, Apple, BP, for example). Here the logo reflects the product's natural ingredients and the corporation's green ethos. The overall impression feels a bit sweet, which may or may not accurately reflect the product. It also appeals to a younger adult drinking audience without being too juvenile. This identity requires that the product color itself must act as the primary flavor differentiator. This could be hard to sustain if the brand grows and has, for instance, several red-colored products.

MK You have to admire the subtleties of this design. The colors used to convey nostalgia—as in the softness of the tea-stain-colored backgrounds balanced with the vintage shades of the softly curved base—trigger just the right emotional response. Add to that the dynamic graphic of the brand identity, the just-so-slightly stylized novelty type, and the well-balanced hierarchy, and you have a brand that signals its positioning in a cultural framework that feels warm and comforting. Just a little picky—I would like the organic text on the top to feel more connected to the overall design sensibilities.

RW A design system this simple can be polarizing. Some view the sans serif, all-cap type, geometric shapes, and one-dimensional layout as clean and contemporary. Others see it as generic. This architecture, however, is beyond question. In fact, my design team has used it as an example of clarity, balance, and impact.

SW The simple design aesthetic and lack of gradient swoops and textures that are prevalent within the category will definitely make these tea packages stand out on the retail shelf. The hierarchy of information (brand/flavor/description) is fairly basic and communicates well to consumers. Together they make a nice system, and the playful copy is a bonus to label readers everywhere.

PRODUCT	**Feel Good Drinks**
DESIGN FIRM	Turner Duckworth
LOCATION	London, England and San Francisco, CA
CLIENT	The Feel Good Drinks Company, Ltd.

 MK There's a vibrancy to this line. I like the boastful description, the handwritten recipe style on the smaller juices, and the fun application of text color that creates a quieter or louder exclamation. The photorealistic rendering of the leaf with stem and the way its drop shadow creates a sense of layers make this design particularly eye-catching. I am not sure why this distinguishing element was not carried throughout the rest of the line. The brand identity's typography is fun, fresh, and positive. The yoga man's posture conveys feel good but his illustration style says insecurity. The product colors nicely complement the graphics colors. The label curvature and bottle structures add to the lighthearted, approachable character of this brand.

 SW At first glance, I found this design interesting, and I really liked the shape of the larger bottles. But after really looking at it more closely, it's sort of a mess, which, admittedly, I sometimes like. Rather than making me feel calm, though—as I suspect the Yoga pose is meant to do—it makes me anxious. The hand-wrought typeset font and the sort of '70s mod treatment of Feel Good don't work together, yet they're not different enough to complement each other; they both feel contrived. The variety of bottle shapes— each nice individually— adds to the disconnect for me. Honestly, it feels like a big brand trying to be a mom-and-pop small brand.

PRODUCT	**JAQK Cellars Wine Bottles**
DESIGN FIRM	Hatch Design
LOCATION	San Francisco, CA
CLIENT	JAQK Cellars

 I would put all my money on the table for this exciting line! I am enthralled and energized by the individuality of each of these flawlessly designed bottles. Each design is executed with absolute precision and the family is held together by the consistency of the neck label. I believe that in the game of cards players should always keep their emotions under control and avoid giving unsolicited advice...so all I can say is WOW!

 When seen as a system, these bottles are a fun and interesting take on playing-card language. I would love to own all of them. I wonder, however, if they hang together as a brand when they are separated into the various varietals in a busy retail environment? Would a consumer immediately see these as coming from the same vineyard, since the looks are so distinctly different? Many wine consumers buy a wine because of the look of the package and/or because they've had another of the company's wines; will JAQK lose some of these sales? The shippers work well as point of sale, creating a large billboard when stacked high and wide. I might be forced to buy a case just to have the shipper box. Nice job—can't wait to see them at my liquor store.

hom
gar

"This structure quite literally creates the form of a house, which is a perfect message for this company."

— Marianne Klimchuk, page 166

CHAPTER 3

CHARLES LUCK
STONE CENTER

Purveyors of Fine Stone and Building Knowledge

www.CHARLESLUCK.com

PRODUCT	Random Acts Of Summer: Outdoor Grill
DESIGN FIRM	Wink
LOCATION	Minneapolis, MN
CLIENT	Target

PRODUCT	Random Acts Of Summer: Tablecloth
DESIGN FIRM	Wink
LOCATION	Minneapolis, MN
CLIENT	Target

BE This is fun and frivolous. It feels like it's straight out of the '50s! It certainly has color and charm in a category that's normally dull and functional, with a logo that's gloriously rammed with color and movement. Let's just hope the weather holds! (Or is that for just us Brits...?)

RW Admittedly there is a whole lot going on here, perhaps way too much. The hyperactive logo mark; the animated, illustrated, and photographic images overlapping one another; the multiple textures and colors are all a lot of visual noise that on first blush can look rather—well—random. However, there is an inherent spirit here that overrides the chatter. It makes for a joyous brand experience that somehow is as relevant for pool toys as it is for grills and tablecloths. I can just imagine the backyard party.

MK The header on the tablecloth packaging demonstrates the true power of iconic imagery. These small graphics build the brand, and it is purely through these carefully selected images that the story is effectively imbedded into the consumer's mind. It's important to note that the success of this design is in the broad cultural meanings of the imagery. Interesting, witty, and fun, but smart as well. Even the mismatch of the tablecloth fabric pattern and the header graphics works in a wacky retro style.

SW I still remember this seasonal campaign in Target. The logotype and the bright colors felt like summer. It translated well from signage to packaging and on to products. The color simplicity of the barbecue grills and the overall scale of the package work well with the segmented, icon-based graphics. These graphics add personality to an otherwise common product. Unfortunately, the designs of the tablecloths don't have this same strength. They work when you see them in the context of the full campaign, but as a single package, the patterns and colors of the tablecloths fight with the busy details and colors of the small labels. This is always a challenge when you're trying to create a system for such a diversity of products and create an overall, exciting seasonal theme.

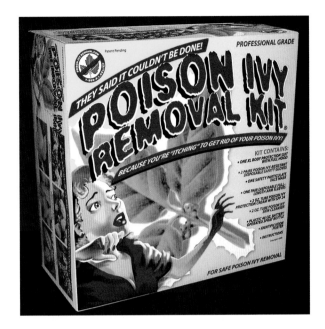

 Poison Ivy Removal needed an attention-grabbing mockup for a trade show. This packaging was conceived, designed, and created in one week.

PRODUCT	**Poison Ivy Home Removal Kit**
DESIGN FIRM	YOE! Studio
LOCATION	Peekskill, NY
CLIENT	Poison Ivy Removal

 I'm searching for the ACME logo and can't seem to locate it! Glorious indulgence in 1950s horror-movie pastiche, even down to the claims of the subsidiary copy ("They said it couldn't be done!") and the gratuitous use of puns. Laudable, tongue-in-cheek creativity in a category usually festooned with scientific language and dull imagery. The typography seems rather hastily and haphazardly applied, however. With more time, I'm sure this could have been considered to better effect.

 Wowey, Zowie, Batman! Marvel Comics meet pulp fiction in this whimsical look at a serious concern. The vivid graphics and in-your-face font and color palettes generate immediate impact, even if the package is cluttered with way too much copy. The Little Shop of Horrors plant icon is balanced on the side panel with photographic representations of the real thing. Overall, this is just a lot of fun in an overtly serious (read, "boring") product category.

 This would immediately catch your eye in a busy retail environment, but then what? The parody is apparent, but the overall design lacks the finesse of the details. The spooky, hovering type is a clunky, disjointed element. The woman's hand is almost as scary as the poison ivy itself. The bulleted, right-justified text is awkward to read, especially as there is so much of it. Given the one-week window, this is a good start, but with a little more time it could be fantastic.

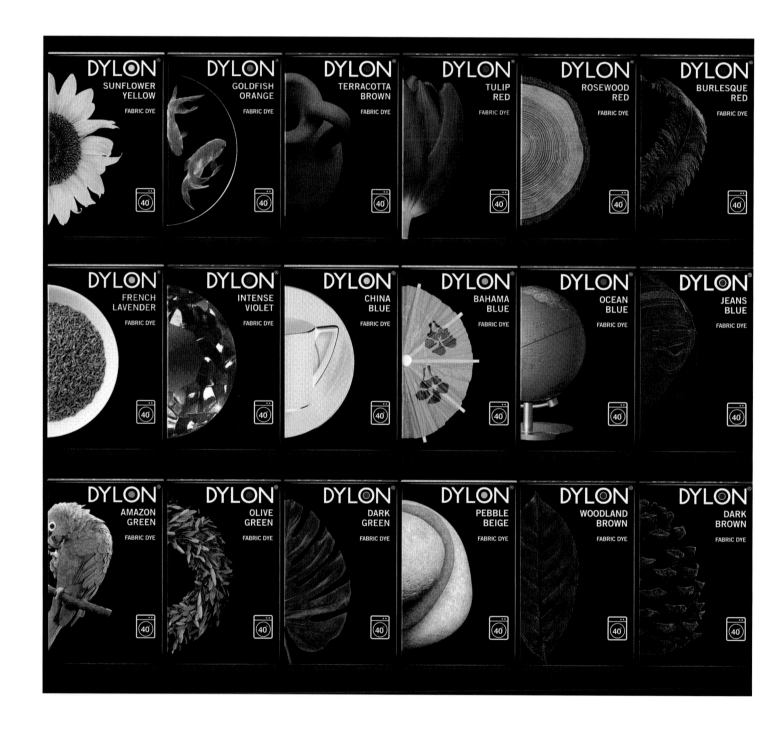

PRODUCT	**DYLON Fabric Dyes**
DESIGN FIRM	Coley Porter Bell
LOCATION	London, England
CLIENT	DYLON International

BE The flexibility created by using a semi-circle of color and content against black instantly pulls this vast, colorful, and vibrant range together. With a few lovely little thoughts thrown in for good measure, it works a treat! Who'd have thought fabric dye could look so glamorous?

MK Call me odd, but this line evokes a very Zen, sensory experience. If we had these beautiful designs here in the U.S., we would all be dyeing our clothes! These boxes could have a second life as tools to teach school children colors and the names of objects, and to stir their creative juices. A striking design!

RW I thought that fabric dye kits went the way of my old Grateful Dead T-shirts. Here the artisan is reintroduced to fabric dyes in a sophisticated and attractive way. The black background is a nice contrast for all product colors, making them strong and vibrant. I love how the colors are represented as natural items, encouraging creative self-expression that's a far cry from my old tie-dyed tees.

SW Due to the way this was submitted, it's difficult to assess the overall package form and material. But it's refreshing to see the chic update on this very outdated category. The color-cued imagery consistently coming in from the left on the black background makes a very handsome system. I especially appreciate the somewhat obscure color-referenced imagery; it gives the brand depth and an international scope. The color dot inside the "O" of "DYLON" clarifies any confusion over the exact color. This is a stunning system.

145

PRODUCT	**Flawless Paint**
DESIGN FIRM	Turner Duckworth
LOCATION	London, England and San Francisco, CA
CLIENT	Homebase, Ltd.

BE Nice, simple idea, elegantly executed, no frills or fuss, just a clear and cohesive range that does what it says on the tin. Works a treat.

MK Turner Duckworth does it again! A concept that seems so obvious yet is stunningly original. The name matches the design—there are no imperfections here. The design projects a confident assurance that the product will make any paint job successful. There is a quality to the finish on the label that is simply magnetic—I want to reach out and touch it (ah, the temptation of touching paint that has not dried!). Impeccable.

RW "Make the product the hero." As a designer, you hear this again and again as a key objective, and yet it is often a difficult thing to do well. This strategy is worth imitating. The huge product swatch boldly signals the product color and finish. The matte black background allows every color (except black, perhaps) to shine. Owning the brush as a brand mnemonic is a brilliant coup, making the process of painting more tangible and appropriate for do-it-yourselfers and pros alike. The silver area that holds the logo creates a strong brand billboard at retail. The system transfers well to smaller sizes. For all these reasons and more, this is one of my candidates for best in class.

SW Is it possible? Finally, an answer to everyone's painting nightmares? Gone are the stacks of dusty paint cans in a storage room with obscure names and no clue as to the actual color. This is brilliant. The graphics are iconographically simple and sophisticated. From the elegant typography and straightforward information hierarchy to the simple, flat, colored paint shape on the brush, this is a timeless, flawless package design.

PRODUCT	**Bloomscape**
DESIGN FIRM	People Design Inc
LOCATION	Grand Rapids, MI
CLIENT	Bloomscape

 I think I may be missing something; this leaves me a little nonplussed. It's strong and clear however, and the simplicity of it certainly means you won't be missing the brand identity!

 An uncomplicated yet memorable brand identity design. There is a wonderful subtlety in the visual of the brand floating above the grass and the sense of bliss it conveys. The feeling of great happiness when this box is delivered at your doorstep is a clear message. I can imagine my own exclamation— *Aahhh!*—upon delivery, so I love that the design captures that expression.

 I am enamored with this design strategy for two prime reasons. First, I love the iconic "b" and leaf as an example of what P&G calls an "extractable branding unit," a design element that can be extracted and used in any consumer touchpoint. Second, I also am a fan of graphics that wrap around the pack, encouraging consumers to further explore the full 360-degree experience. This wraparound logo works only because this package does not have to meet the rigors of the shelf environment; otherwise it would have told only half the brand story. Last, I like how the package "talks." Adding the quote, "I contain live plants. Please keep me upright" gives the brand a personality and charm that completes the experience.

 This box makes me smile. I would be happy to see the courier drop this off at my door. It's perfect. The client should give the designers a hug, and so should the mail couriers.

PRODUCT	**Get Clean**
DESIGN FIRM	Turner Duckworth
LOCATION	London, England and San Francisco, CA
CLIENT	Shaklee

 Again, a lovely idea: Bringing the outdoors in by combining the product activity with natural elements in a simple way that works well across the range. The fresh, light colors and simple, clear information unit make for a refreshingly upbeat and quite delicate brand feel. I'm particularly relieved to see a total lack of bubbles, sparkles, swooshes, or ingredients; now that's cleaning up the category!

 There's a little bit of René Magritte in these stunning concepts. I prefer the transporting color, imagery, and fade of the dishwasher, fresh laundry, and soft fabric packaging, their sense of illusion. One can practically smell these products. Such a smart concept—why shouldn't consumers feel like they are on holiday as they clean? This fresh, inviting line definitely has a competitive advantage.

 Light and breezy. This is the immediate impression created by this effective identity. The translucent substrate allows just enough of the light-colored product to show through. The understated graphics and wispy illustration generate a soft-to-the-touch perception that makes this brand stand out in contrast to its bold competition.

 This package design is a refreshing solution for an environmentally kind product. It gives cleaning-category cues yet manages to avoid the swooshes and tornado graphic treatments around the cleaning aisle. The color and imagery palette is lovely, and I trust these products smell as fresh and clean as they look. Given the variety of products in the category, the amount of content can vary greatly, and the information is laid out so that there is adequate flexibility amongst all the products, yet it maintains a strong, consistent format.

PRODUCT	**Harrods Duvet Packaging**	
DESIGN FIRM	Paul Cartwright Branding	
LOCATION	Ramsgate, England	
CLIENT	Harrods	

PRODUCT	**Home Fragrance**
DESIGN FIRM	lg2boutique
LOCATION	Montreal, Canada
CLIENT	Fruits & Passion

 Harrods is usually so archaic and decorative in its design, so these are refreshingly modern in the macro photographic black-and-white style. It definitely speaks volumes about the softness and quality of the product.

 Feather teasers tickle and excite, and this subliminal allusion does just that. There is nothing like climbing into bed and pulling up a luxurious down duvet. The artful, high-contrast, perfectly cropped photography sensuously captures the attention and brings the viewer into a distinctly ephemeral experience. The beauty of each image is in the way it conveys lightness. Of course, the front-and-center brand identity speaks volumes, but I kind of wish it didn't obstruct my view so much.

 This redesigned luxury packaging befits its luxury retailer. The ethereal black-and-white photography says just enough to suggest the various grades and fabric content of the duvets. The central placement of the logo and the center-stacked type give the packages an elegant finish.

 The rounded bottle and elegant neck, the translucent film label, even the brand name all borrow from the conventions of the high-end personal fragrance category and still make this brand most relevant for your home. I love the illustrated patterns and how they work with the colors to differentiate fragrances. I like the matte silver cap and the brand name running vertically to even further elongate the elegant neck. The controlled copy completes the experience.

PRODUCT	**Method O-Mop Refill**
DESIGN FIRM	Method / Amcor (collaboration)
LOCATION	Manchester, MI
CLIENT	Method

 Method strikes again with yet another stunning structure—so innovative, slick, refined, and different— allowing the product color and clarity to be the hero, and keeping the graphic-design elements minimal and unobtrusive. Cracking!

 Not only is the graphic structure of this bottle design stunning, it becomes another instant icon for a brand with a long line of iconic forms. Everything about this feels right, and I imagine this feels great to hold. I imagine that the product is proud to be in this bottle. When a PET bottle is this well designed, I can't envision why a consumer would want to discard it. Kudos.

 Form following function, this shape allows you to grip and squeeze the liquid into the O-mop reservoir. The graphics are direct and functional. Cushioning the label within the bottle's deep central depression focuses your attention on it while keeping it nice and clean on the shelf—nothing can scratch it up or get it dirty. There is nothing at all special about the aperture, but then again, a custom cap might have been just window-dressing. All in all, it's what we've come to expect from a brand that embraces design as its primary consumer benefit.

 Method has done an amazing job, rising to the top (at least visually) in the cleaning-products category. They have consistently done this due in large part to the packaging. And this is another instance of a very simple product that manages to stand apart yet clearly communicate its attributes. And functionality was not without thought— the bottle is easy to hold in one hand even if it's wet.

PRODUCT	**Fertilizer Compost**
DESIGN FIRM	Blok Design
LOCATION	Mexico DF, Mexico
CLIENT	ICC

 An entirely appropriate structure for its immediate communication value. The stitched-seam closure and simple, illustrated labeling with garden tools set on the vegetation or textural background communicate the hand craft of plant care. This personality is built further by the no-frills branding and copy which complete the message of a product that is humble, unpretentious, and clearly environmentally focused.

 Here is an identity that I would not be surprised to find in an artisan-foods grocery store. The organic paper stock is matched by the hand-drawn graphics and sans serif type. The gusset-bottom bag is a nice distinction from traditional fertilizer's flat, lay-down bags. Although this lacks the visual impact of the competitive category, I still believe that it will stand out from the screaming crowd. As natural and understated as compost should be.

PRODUCT	**Preserve Kitchen**
DESIGN FIRM	In-House Design Department
LOCATION	Waltham, MA
CLIENT	Preserve by Recycline

 Bravo to the in-house creative team for successfully convincing the boss that a simple, clean design aesthetic would engage their consumers. (Why should the consultancies have all the fun!?) While the slightly stylized logo and synthesized brand messaging support a simple, intuitive brand message, I'm missing the "green" message that the brand apparently stands for. Still, it's another good example of knowing when to stop. Anything more would have overburdened this design.

 This is a simple labeling solution, done well. The strength of the Preserve type choice and strong color blocking make the system hang together. No matter what shape label, the bowls and colander are particularly challenging. It has just enough detail to make it interesting and fun—not generic, but not cluttered. It would have been a nice detail, but admittedly more expensive, to see the flower petals diecut to let the product color show through.

PRODUCT	**Lawnseed**
DESIGN FIRM	Turner Duckworth
LOCATION	London, England and San Francisco, CA
CLIENT	Homebase, Ltd.

 Simple idea? √ ... Elegant solution? √... Utterly relevant? √.... Yep, Turner Duckworth whips off another lovely solution in a category usually highly cluttered and ill-considered. It's direct, easy to decode, and builds strong consistency across the range. Lovely.

 So unconventional! These symbols of dissected grass with a reveal of earth below the surface are completely original. The black typography with a few call-outs of product specifications is straightforward and uncomplicated. The little bits of dirt and the football add a lighthearted approach so needed in this category. The grass is a great example of how symbols are charged with inherent meaning.

 The heart and cross symbols work so well in designating the specific use for each of these grass seeds that I wish this iconic system would work just as well for the fast-growing family grass. However, I did not immediately recognize the sphere as a ball, nor did I connect it back to families. When you embrace a strategy like this, you have to ensure it will work for all current and future brand proliferations. I'm not sure that this design system does. Regardless, it is yet another thought-provoking and elegant design strategy from our friends at Turner Duckworth.

 This is a great solution to an often-mundane, always-confusing product. The use of icons made from turf to distinguish between the variety of seeds is at once informative, humorous, and graphically strong. The information hierarchy is clear and doesn't look cluttered, even with all the mandatory industry icons. The products should stand out in a big box store environment and might even make buying lawn-care products fun.

PRODUCT	**Nortene Garden Products Solar Lighting**
DESIGN FIRM	HTDL
LOCATION	Henley in Arden, England
CLIENT	Solus Garden & Leisure

 Substance of imagery, when used effectively, says it all, and the consumer can practically feel the glow of the lights and the aura of the environment. I would imagine that the emotional message of "ambient" helped to perfectly craft the design direction. I am drawn to this design like a moth (pun intended). The black band serves this graphic format well as it allows the lighting to shine, and the crisp, well-balanced typography speaks to a high-quality product.

 Having appreciated the design aesthetic of the other Nortene products, I'm surprised that this line of garden lighting does not follow some of the branded graphic architecture. Where is the living green? Where is the color system? Why the heavy black banner? Somehow the floral inset does not seem quite as relevant here. Still, considering the heavy-handedness of the competitive category, this is perhaps more effective than the norm. It's a shame, however, that more of the garden-equipment architecture could not be leveraged.

PRODUCT	**Nortene Garden Products Range Rebrand**
DESIGN FIRM	HTDL
LOCATION	Henley in Arden, England
CLIENT	Solus Garden & Leisure

 The architecture of this design is well structured and builds nicely to a crescendo that features the product. There is an immediate attraction to the extremely close, textural, vibrant green-leaf background that initially sets the tone. Element by element, from top to bottom, the graphic bands communicate in a clear, organized layout with colors and imagery giving a sense of something that is full of life. A well-conceived experience that would create great shelf impact.

 The living green background and the inset floral photo are welcome emotional touches in this product feature—driven category. The contrasting color bands also quickly differentiate products and create a unifying staging area for all product information. The product photography smartly steers away from the artificial setup common to product catalogs and instead uses natural light in a real environment, giving this brand a true sense of place.

PRODUCT	R~Earth Plant Food
DESIGN FIRM	Blok Design
LOCATION	Mexico DF, Mexico
CLIENT	ICC

MK This is a winner—a definite impulse purchase for me! There is something about the all-over pattern of ferns and growth and the color contrasts that are particularly alluring. Whoever thought plant food could look so desirable?

RW The compost brand architecture is nicely carried over to the liquid plant food. The controlled brand block, all-cap and all-lowercase font family, and living green background texture all provide a fervent experience. Caution your little ones; this almost looks good enough for human consumption!

SW This package has brand authority—as a consumer, I believe this is a re-searched and tested product and that it would do the job well. Sometimes when products of this kind—based on chemistry and science—are overly designed, they can appear to be all about marketing flash and very little about performance. R-Earth does an excellent job of bridging both through the technical-feeling logotype and the clean, center-stacked, sans serif font.

PRODUCT	**Slice Kitchen Tools**
DESIGN FIRM	Liquid Agency
LOCATION	San Jose, CA
CLIENT	Slice

 The highly animated quality of this Karim Rashid product rests perfectly within the progressive personality of the blister packaging. It's fitting that there are no sharp edges and that the graphics and type are simple yet descriptive. Perhaps it's the influence of Japanese animation, but yes, Sharon, I see the wide-open mouth and the nose pointing up on this screaming blob, too!

 There is much to like about this simple, clean design. The "sliced" logo makes the otherwise nondescript brand mark more proprietary. Karim's signature adds a nice human touch—designer as brand! The vibrant colors contrast and yet complement the bright product color. The magenta violator is a little harsh, however, both violating and perhaps detracting from the overall look and feel. I'm not as big of a fan of the clamshell structure. All too often, you need a tool to "slice" this kind of package open. Perhaps a back-panel perforation would allow easy access to the product to complete the simple and intuitive brand experience.

 The soft oval shape of the package is a nice platform for the sculptural peeler. I just wish this didn't utilize a clamshell package; it can turn what could be a pleasant experience—opening something new—into a frustrating brand experience. The sliced-off logotype gives a word picture that is really smart: simple, yet strong. Does anyone else see an alien in this peeler shape?

PRODUCT	**Brown's Birdseed**
DESIGN FIRM	Stephan and Herr
LOCATION	Marietta, PA
CLIENT	F. M. Brown's Sons

PRODUCT	**InSinkErator Hot Water Dispensers**
DESIGN FIRM	Design North
LOCATION	Racine, WI
CLIENT	InSinkErator

 I really enjoy this endearingly playful concept of a civilized serving of quality food for wild birds. The kraft bag is the logical choice for nature. The yellow highlight of the server's beak effectively directs attention. The attention to detail in the layout, type kerning, and overall architecture, along with the clear color-coding, adds to the appeal.

 How much fun is this? A whimsical borrowing of the artisan-foods aesthetic gives this product a premium look and feel. The flat four-color printing and brown bag speak to sustainability, a key concern, I'd imagine, of bird lovers worldwide. I specifically like the in-your-face good/better/best product designators. I'd be curious to learn the sales and margins of each. Are there enough bird enthusiasts to warrant a three-tiered brand offering? If so, this architecture does a nice job of adding personality to a dire and emotionless category.

 The flowing graphic and warm color palette evoke the product's core benefit. The descriptive product photo and circular, inset images all visually communicate the brand's many uses. I am attracted to how the graphics wrap around the side panels, further engaging consumers with more end-benefit visuals to help close the sale.

PRODUCT	**Daub & Bauble**
DESIGN FIRM	Wink
LOCATION	Minneapolis, MN
CLIENT	Daub & Bauble

 There is a trend for silhouetted Victorian-style wallpaper at the moment—Cowshed, Liberties, etc.—which certainly looks elegant and refined. This simple color palette elevates these to adorn any bathroom with style.

 There is an unmistakable style to these packaging designs. The bold graphics and repeating patterns, perhaps inspired by the sophisticated interior-design patterns of another era, are an oasis in a sea of uninspired personal-care products. Such a wonderfully fashionable attire for stock bottles! The elegant typography is meticulously formatted, from the brand identity and detailed monogram to the body copy. The vertical orientation is a surprisingly fresh contrast. The bar code becomes an aesthetic element that adds interest to the overall design.

 Here's an interesting brand name—not quite sure if these are family names or contrived. The graphics are equally a bit quirky, marrying the ultra-simple, sometimes one-color texture with the brand block. Again, here is a paragraph of type that few will read and perhaps fewer will care about. Wouldn't it be nice if the brand label could be peeled off so as to leave a nonbranded message in the bath? Still, a nice piece of work, bringing Victoriana into the twenty-first century.

 May I have all of these, please? This strong identity and mark feel modern and at the same time communicate a history, which is appropriate with the vintage wallpaper patterns. The ornate ampersand and serif font are a refreshing change from all the sans serif type prevalent in current luxury products. Restricting all the copy and the UPC to the one face is amazing and actually looks as good as the beautiful wallpaper. Nice work.

PRODUCT	**Aerogarden 3**
DESIGN FIRM	EBD
LOCATION	Denver, CO
CLIENT	Aerogrow

PRODUCT	**Attitude Packaging**
DESIGN FIRM	lg2boutique
LOCATION	Montreal, Canada
CLIENT	Bio Spectra

 The clean lines, half-moon die cut, and crisp product presentation speak well of this brand's unique experience—fresh-grown herbs without the dirt! The side- and back-panel architecture is just as effective. Bold color blocks, organized type, and descriptive photos tell the brand story without words. A visualist's delight!

 I can't help but think, "if only the Chia pet had such a lovely package." The clean white surface is striking and allows the herbs to take center stage.

 It's a bold move to go black and white in a category dominated by splashes of intense color. It gives it a more premium feel, a little dirty perhaps, but this modern photographic route is brought into freshness by the swath of vibrant color at the bottom that differentiates and livens up this rather sophisticated range. Having all the ingredients on the front is also a brave move, but it builds on the brand idea confidently, and the almost editorial feel links this range together.

 I'm trying to figure out what exactly about this design articulates Attitude, but it definitely does. (I visualize a design studio with Patti LaBelle's *New Attitude* reverberating—hey, maybe a great idea for a commercial!) From head to toe, the black bottle caps, the posture of each structure, the typographic story and hierarchy—uppercase, bold, flush-left—the environmental signs, the black-and-white duotone graphics and then the splash of color—definitely a bold assertiveness that is a force to compete with. A for Attitude.

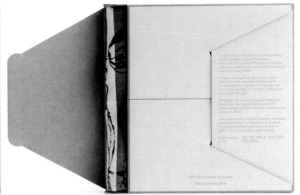

PRODUCT	**Lucienne & Robin Day Re-issued Classics**
DESIGN FIRM	Aloof
LOCATION	Lewes, England
CLIENT	twentytwentyone

MK A design solution that captures the essence of these twentieth-century design pioneers, who were known for using new materials and creating vibrant textiles to develop inexpensive furniture. This economical paperboard box with two-color screened graphics and structural opening speaks to their sensibilities. The die-cut window serves not only to reveal the enclosed product and contribute to the color story, but the white background and the signature below nicely frame the work of the designer. I like that the box is opened from the bottom and that the underside tells the narrative.

SW Of course I love the work of Lucienne and Robin Day, so I was particularly interested in this packaging. I think the designers handled the design with restraint, letting the die-cut hole do most of the selling. The opaque white screen print has a nice, flat, tactile quality on the corrugate. The biography and portrait on opposing flaps add to the experience of opening the box.

PRODUCT	**Method Dish Soap**
DESIGN FIRM	Method / Amcor (collaboration)
LOCATION	Manchester, MI
CLIENT	Method

BE The elegant structures, minimal graphics, and slick, considered design are a winner once more.

MK If asked to structurally communicate fluidity, this PET bottle design would do it. The perfect marriage of cap and bottle completes this streamlined elegance. A prime example of the outstanding results that occur when design, engineering, and manufacturing collaborate.

RW The designer's favorite! How many times have you referred this brand to your clients as one of their perceptual mentors? How many mood boards does this show up on? In the early days, Method's inverted packages had some messy issues with their closures. No measure of beautiful package design will compensate for leaking soap. Great packaging is not great unless it achieves every one of its basic functions, like dispensing the product. As far as I know, all of those issues have now been resolved. What I find most interesting about this newest streamlined, fluid design is how functional it is. In real use, I am surprised to find how well it fits my hand, how it does not slip out of soapy hands, and how it allows me to deliver just the right amount of soap directly to where I want it. Form following function with an elegant result—what a concept!

SW Method does it again, only better: It doesn't leak! This brand is defined by custom bottle shapes and elegantly minimal branding. I love how the streamlined over-cap continues the lines of the bottle; this must have been tricky.

PRODUCT	**White Picket Paint Brushes**
DESIGN FIRM	Mig Reyes
LOCATION	Wheaton, IL
CLIENT	White Picket

 The product name symbolizes the traditional perception of the perfect suburban lifestyle. Therefore, the success of this solution is the imaginary value immediately evoked by this well-designed identity. Perfectly positioned as an arched entry gate for the brush, the design has just the right amount of formality, with colors that exude charm.

 The beauty of this identity lies in its name and branded icon. Sure, the information is well organized. The colors and striped and dotted textures add interest and value. And the back panel is self-explanatory. However, it's linking this brand to an all-American icon of home that makes it work. Great brands use all of their attributes in concert with each other: brand name supports the graphics; graphics support the structure; all of these elements support the experience. This is a good example of that practice put to use.

 Who doesn't love a freshly painted white picket fence? And this identity and package capture all the charm and serenity that a white picket fence represents. I can almost hear the birds chirping and the kids playing. The way the information is laid out on the front and back is clear and uncluttered; it has just enough design sensibility to look thoughtful but not overworked. The choice of the blue color against the dark bristles is appealing and would have nice impact when merchandised.

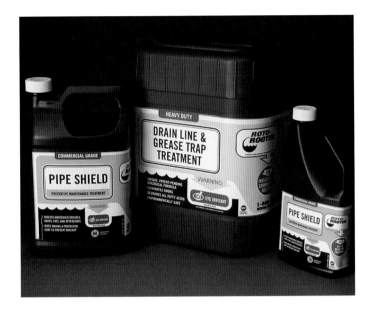

PRODUCT	**RotoRooter Plumbing Chemicals**
DESIGN FIRM	Sayles Graphic Design
LOCATION	Des Moines, IA
CLIENT	RotoRooter

PRODUCT	**Heal's Candles**
DESIGN FIRM	Aloof
LOCATION	Lewes, England
CLIENT	Heal's

 This category is predictably abysmal, so it is refreshing to see a design that breaks away from the pack. Playing off the intense array of labels, symbols, and regulatory requirements mandated in the communication of hazardous chemicals, this design brings levity and simplicity to what is frequently intimidating, off-putting communication. Well-organized graphics, bold typography, and contemporary, less-industrial colors. It's difficult to clearly define the function of the background graphic forms; nonetheless, this solution communicates effectively and its pictorial style serves this reputable brand well.

 An incredibly difficult category, usually toxically ugly, this manages to look good and still fit the plumbing category, which is important. When consumers are facing an aisle of products, you want them to immediately find what they need with no confusion. Using the industrial visual vocabulary of bold arrows, bold sans serif type, and industrial blue containers and mixing it with turquoise, red, and yellow and the interesting, positive/negative play of shapes, this transcends the product category. I like how the designers incorporated the wave of the RotoRooter logo on the front label face. The information is surprisingly easy to navigate, as they've developed a language: Each type of information has its own placement, color, and shape, which is consistent on every package.

 Another refined, simple, and gorgeous design from Aloof, using structure and texture to create a sense of luxury and indulgence.

 There is virtue in pure forms, simply adorned. The type, tucked neatly to the left and dropped out of a simple gold metallic shape, is graceful. The inner structure that blossoms open to reveal the candle set in a gold environment adds to the pleasure of receiving this present.

 Every detail of this small box is perfect. It had to be to work this well. The structure is beautiful when closed, but when opened it's as if it blooms. The flame reflects off the gold interior, creating a lovely, warm glow.

Charles Luck, a high-end stone retailer, often sends their clients home with samples of their stone products, and needed a way to transport them safely while still showing them off.

PRODUCT	**Exposed Stone Carrier**
DESIGN FIRM	WORK Labs
LOCATION	Richmond, VA
CLIENT	Charles Luck Stone Center

 Sometimes the simplest solutions are the best. This solution takes the mundane, frames it, and elevates the product to the star of the show. The earthy color and restrained, refined graphics are footnotes that set it all off simply, and the effective structural engineering contributes to a highly successful design.

I love the pure utilitarianism of this vehicle for transporting stone samples. The structure quite literally creates the form of a house, which is a perfect message for both the company and the products' carrier.

 Branding brings value to the most commodious of items. We once branded lumber for Home Depot, allowing them to increase the price of their commodity product over the identical nonbranded stuff from the lumberyard. Here, the stonecutter lends his name, credibility, and craftsmanship to the fruits of his labor. The package structure is an interesting piece of architecture, beautifully displaying a half dozen paving stone samples that consumers can carry home and use like paint swatches in making their home décor design decisions. My guess? Charles (don't call him Chuck) Luck commands a nice premium for his stones, selling them for a whole lot more than the nonbranded guys from the quarry!

 A feat of structural engineering, allowing the weight of the stone to create tension on the corrugate to keep the stone in place. Nice work!

PRODUCT	**Focus McKeller Power Tools**
DESIGN FIRM	P&W
LOCATION	London, England
CLIENT	FOCUS

 There is an immediacy and straightforwardness to this design that is commanding. With the combination of black and yellow–which instinctively represents caution–how can one not stop and take notice? The tools, poised for action, practically speak to the consumer. Lester Beall, the great twentieth-century graphic designer, said the designer "must work with one goal in mind—to integrate the elements in such a manner that they will combine to produce a result that will convey not merely a static commercial message, but an emotional reaction as well. If we can produce the kind of art which harnesses the power of the human instinct for that harmony of form, beauty, and cleanness that seems inevitable when you see it, then I think we may be doing a job for clients." This design most definitely does its job.

 The packaging is appropriately well designed for the category, the silhouetted tools against the solid-colored backgrounds are bold and immediate. The icon system is a good strategy for communicating product attributes for this type of product. However, this design very much reminds me of the well-known power tool brand, Black and Decker. I have a difficult time understanding why a new brand would choose to so closely mimic an existing brand.

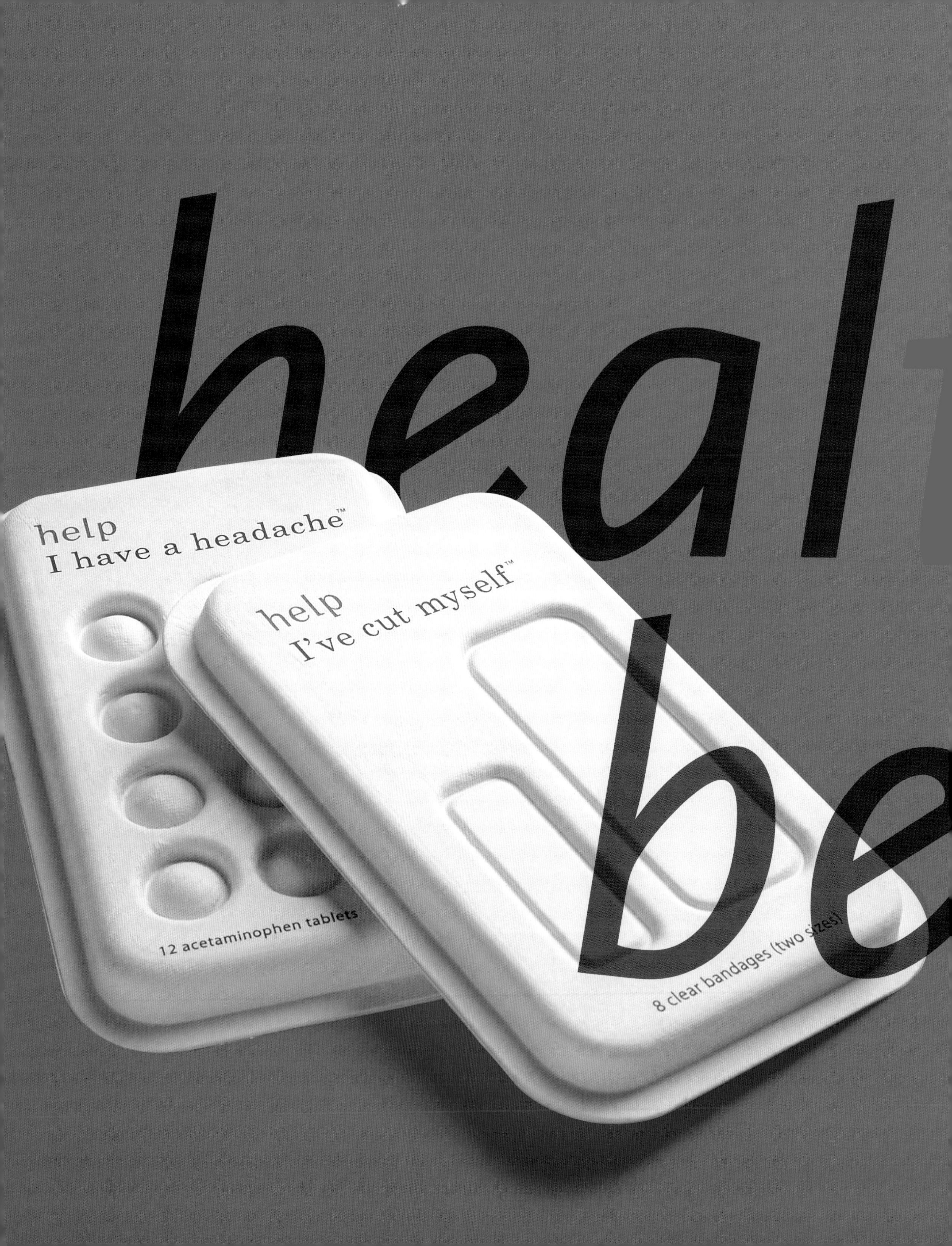

health be

help
I have a headache™

help
I've cut myself™

12 acetaminophen tablets

8 clear bandages (two sizes)

CHAPTER 4

"*I wish I had designed this.*"

— *Sharon Werner, page 199*

PRODUCT	**Dashing Diva**
DESIGN FIRM	Beyondesign
LOCATION	Bombay, India
CLIENT	Dashing Diva

PRODUCT	**Paqit**
DESIGN FIRM	Toast Marketing & Design
LOCATION	New York, NY
CLIENT	Paqit, LLC

 BE Singular, strong, vibrant colors combined with the unusual cropping of the dynamic watercolor imagery pack a punch. The strong differentiation through color, framed by the clean, pure, white background makes this fresh and fruity. The simple logo—predictably sans serif but redeemed by the clever way in which the typographic information is contained and held together using the color in the logo to help with differentiation—pulls it all together in unison.

RW There is much to like about this identity. I like the name, first and foremost, and how the color of the "Sin" changes to signal the form and fragrance. I like the subtle facets in the package structure, married by the soft shoulders, which are both echoed from the bottles to the two-piece, lidded carton. The super-close-up photography nicely reflects the fragrance cues. And, although no one will read the tiny, supportive type, this does suggest that the product has a credible brand story.

SW The brand starts with an intriguing name, carries through the design, and is paid off in the witty copy. The vibrant colors and soft edges of the watercolor paintings contrast the faceted structures of the bottles, making the packages more dynamic. The logotype reading vertically obviously allows it to be larger and creates a natural location for the brand message. Overall, this is a nice system; however, I don't think it's as successful on the handled case.

BE Achingly modern, these are stripped down to the very bare essentials. Two simple, strong swaths of fresh, pure color plus white give pace to what is essentially an extremely simple, utilitarian design. Allowing the substrate to show through, the lovely metallic finished with gloss and matte inks, elevates this to a premium feel, and the simple logo that has just a touch of personality helps it to avoid becoming sterile.

 MK In their purest form, graphic shapes can be effectively engaging. The interaction of the vertical and horizontal forms visually connects the copy, and the subtle colors and printing techniques project a high-quality persona. Of course, the "i" that pops up from the identity serves to reinforce the personal nature of this product.

 SW Pure, clean, modern, these are handsome paqits. It's difficult to bridge the gender gap with beauty products, and this towelette package does it perfectly. The colors with silver and charcoal gray are masculine, yet pretty. The logotype is distinctive but not fussy and puts an emphasis on the personal with an *i*.

PRODUCT	**Oxygen Plus**
DESIGN FIRM	Spunk Design Machine
LOCATION	Minneapolis, MN
CLIENT	Oxygen Plus

PRODUCT	**CND Brisa**
DESIGN FIRM	MiresBall
LOCATION	San Diego, CA
CLIENT	CND

 With this line of copy, atmospheric imagery, and effervescent graphics, who would not have the urge to open this structure?

 Selling air—will it be the next bottled water? If so, O+ will definitely lead the pack. The package is as intriguing as the product itself, from the tag line, "the energy crisis is over" to the simple, clean, distinctive logotypes. Is it my imagination, or is the product applicator a bit phallic? Intentional? Since it's called the O-stick? I also appreciated the wavy-haired guy on what is usually a very intentionally generic demonstration diagram. Nice touch.

 Gorgeous. The bold, expressive imagery here—a dynamic, textural splash of color with consistent composition that holds the range together—utterly heroes the beauty of the product itself. Not sure I like the logo, but the overall look is modern, beautiful, stylish, and striking, the modern typographic treatment in simple white allowing the imagery to be the star.

 Highlights, vibrancy, and depth are communicated by the texture, smear, and color of the paint. What makes this design so smart is that it projects an image of artistry and professional skill. A stylish solution.

PRODUCT	**Method Body Marine Naturals Body Wash**
DESIGN FIRM	Method/Amcor (collaboration)
LOCATION	Manchester, MI
CLIENT	Method

 Great structure here, almost like a droplet of water poised to drop, holding on to that simple cap that crowns the structure elegantly. This design allows the color of the product to be the hero, with its simple branding unit that sits neatly in the middle, minimally containing all the information needed. A little idea in the die-cutting rescues it from being a bit dull.

 An impressive extension to the wide array of stunningly individualistic structures within this brand. What makes this structural design work so beautifully is that, with its restrained simplicity and fluidly slow curves, the experience is visceral and visually sensory. I am sure the bottle feels great to hold. The graphics don't completely complement the form, however, the overall presence feels clean, fresh-smelling, and inviting. Well done.

 I have been watching this design-driven brand evolve and wondering how its minimalist graphic design architecture would adapt to the increasing demands of differentiating the many products within this mega-brand. I'm happy to see that a distinctive and proprietary structure still leads the way. The graphics are more involved but still true to the Method brand. Keep it growing!

 This lovely bottle shape feels like Man Ray's photo of the nude, *Le Violon d'Ingres*, with its elegant curves. How perfect for a body wash! The pale color of the product doesn't communicate an overly strong scent; darker colors might have looked cheap.

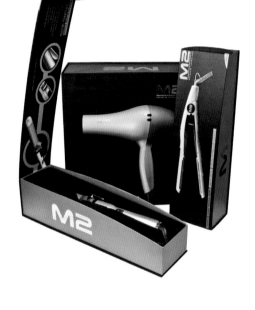

PRODUCT	**April Rain Skin Science**
DESIGN FIRM	ImagineDesign
LOCATION	Gainesville, VA
CLIENT	April Rain Skin Science

BE This structure lives up to expectations—with a name like that, it would have been a crime not to—and the clear acrylic with color on the inside gives it a luxurious translucency. The graphics seem a little like an afterthought, but at least they are applied minimally, allowing the form to soak up the limelight.

MK A sensuous form. The typographic design falls short of completing the brand essence, but we can excuse this since the physical structure has such a graceful and understated elegance.

SW This luxurious jar with its beautiful shape and luminescent color reminds me of vintage beauty products that were designed to be displayed on a pretty vanity. I would have liked the branding and product message to be even more minimal on the jar, maybe relegated to the bottom surface, but alas, branding needs to be seen. A girl can dream, can't she? The Skin Science type choice—or maybe it's the setting on a curve—looks awkward and stiff, detracting from the smooth slope of the lid.

PRODUCT	**M2 Packaging**
DESIGN FIRM	Version-X Design
LOCATION	Burbank, CA
CLIENT	M2

MK Good-looking is what these set-up box structures convey—which is an exacting message for a discriminating consumer. The steely colors are high-tech fashion. The beauty and simplicity of the matte black combined with the metallic-blue-and-silver-foil brand identity beautifully complement the product photography. First impressions are important, and this line was well worth its investment: The design delivers a great first impression.

RW The technical brand name and authoritative identity give these products a professional appeal. This elegant product-as-hero visual strategy requires, of course, that the product design is exceptional, and these products are somewhat ordinary. Still, the architectural pack shape, with its elongated opening and iconic brand story on its inside lid, sets up an effective product presentation. The graphite-and-metallic color palette is right on trend, even if the typeface is just a bit expected. Can't wait to see what M3 will bring.

SW These packages would make me think I've made a wise investment. These are THE TOOLS. The structure of the boxes feels sturdy, strong, and authoritative—and that impression is transferred to the product. The packages are very masculine, due to the color and the logotype, but when buying a tool—whether it's for my hair or my car—I'm much more comfortable if it leans to the masculine instead of the feminine.

PRODUCT	**Sanitas Skin Care Line**
DESIGN FIRM	Hatch Design
LOCATION	San Francisco, CA
CLIENT	Sanitas

BE Another minimal, minimal cosmetic packaging solution where the structure and graphics combine in their stark simplicity to create a slick, utilitarian look. The structure is beautifully streamlined and unfussy, helping make it look luxurious and slightly masculine. The graphics clearly help with range differentiation with a simple but effective two-box system—one for the branding, the other for the item description—simple enough to carry a large palette of colors for the variants. The colors themselves sit in harmony with the unique matte, metallic substrate color and feel clean and refreshing.

MK What this design has going for it is its modern, geometric architecture. The two squares—one being a tint of the other—indirectly convey change, an appropriate message for a skin-care line. With its elimination of fussy details, a decorator color palette, and carefully positioned type, this design beckons to the consumer looking for a product with high style and classic sensibilities.

RW Owning a brand color is normally an important objective. This identity is so simply strong that it lets this complementary palette of brand colors work for it. When an identity is this stripped back, it needs to walk a fine line between clean and stark, between engaging and ascetic. This clean and engaging identity strides that fine line with a bold yet approachable confidence.

SW Lovely. I would try this; I'd perk up seeing these first thing in the morning (and that isn't an easy task). It looks authoritative, clean, and healthy. I love the color palette with the warmer silver metallic.

PRODUCT	Sprunk-Jansen
DESIGN FIRM	Ping-Pong Design
LOCATION	Rotterdam, The Netherlands
CLIENT	Sprunk-Jansen

PRODUCT	Sprunk-Jansen
DESIGN FIRM	Ping-Pong Design
LOCATION	Rotterdam, The Netherlands
CLIENT	Sprunk-Jansen

 As a window of communication, the butterfly works elegantly across a wide range of products. I particularly like the blue one; with its lines and rich color, it really draws your eye in to the center of the pack. Dynamic and fresh.

 I find a peculiar eeriness to the form of this butterfly. However, the vivid, bold form with captivating graphic markings communicates a transitional, transporting experience. The colorful creature is striking against the white background, and the typographic style and hierarchy speak to an efficacious product line. I like the little messages on the inner tuck of the folding cartons. Perhaps my perception of this insect is a cultural nuance, but if the wings were softly curved, this design would feel more approachable.

 It's a pleasure to see how effectively this icon transforms between product offerings. What is rawly sexual for the male and female "performance" products works equally well for these more natural skin-care remedies. The background visual is mirrored on each side of the butterfly icon, accurate to nature and at the same time strikingly alluring. The contemporary color palette and organized type are clear and authoritative. Overall, a most effective brand identity architecture.

 The iconic butterfly symbol certainly grabs your attention with its slightly surreal nature. I'm not entirely sure what it is intended to portray, but it's certainly different. Its depth and richness draw you in, and it's very feminine, which draws me to the point that I am not sure whether it would appeal to a male audience. For me, the two should have been treated differently. The stacked information works well across the range, it's clear and concise, and the deep color inside is an indulgent finish.

RW Talk about your latent power of symbols! Rorschach and his ink blots would have a field day with this one. The butterfly is a visual and visceral vampire that aggressively grabs your attention and will not let go. It exudes sexuality, working quite well for the feminine skew. I'm not at all sure if it effectively evokes "Masculine Performance", but who cares? It most certainly gets its message across. The organization of type, the balance of visual elements, the colored carton interior with the playful sayings on the opening tab all support the icon and work quite well. Not that I need it but, ummmm, where do they sell this stuff??

PRODUCT	**Pretty Polly Skincare**
DESIGN FIRM	Brandhouse
LOCATION	London, England
CLIENT	Pretty Polly

This design was inspired by Busby Berkeley's 1930 choreography.

 I loved water ballet! Its beauty, grace, and harmony are flawlessly captured here, not only in the symmetry and style of the swimmers but in the way they seemingly float around the tubes. The sense that these images are movie-screen captures is perfect. The varying viewpoints, technicolor choices, and '50s-style ligature monogram greatly enhance this pleasurable experience.

 What a beautiful reinvention and contemporization of a nostalgic convention! Silver-screen glamour is brought back to vibrant life with opulent photography and contemporary colors. The scripted flourish that links the double "P" brand mark is nicely reflected in the supportive type styles. Normally, I'm not a big fan of using multiple typefaces, but here the script and sans serif faces effectively differentiate product form and function.

PRODUCT	**Beautao Skincare**
DESIGN FIRM	Miller Creative LLC
LOCATION	Lakewood, NJ
CLIENT	Dermapeutics Corp.

 Again, the Victorian–silhouette ornament style is scattered across design at the moment, but this has more virtue, with its botanical ingredients. The riot of colors, so confidently used, takes it up a level and instantly makes this fun, impactful, and modern. The simple white label which contains the information holds the range together simply and cleanly. The overall effect is a punchy and beautiful range.

 Brand wallpaper, or the silhouetted pattern aesthetic, has been used so broadly of late that it can almost be considered a visual cliché. Yet here, it still works. I think it's the combination of brash colors that helps carry this off. Imagine this in a drugstore. The gable-top bag and the specialty store/spa/salon graphic sensibilities both work hard as meaningful differentiators from the other skin-care products in the mass class of trade.

 The bold color combinations really make these packages special. The high-contrast, flourishy, organic illustrations are fun, while the asymmetrical layout gives the packages an edge. I was somewhat disappointed to see a screened back flourish repeated on the right side—balancing the design—as I felt it was more powerful off-kilter and in bolder color. I would love to take away the oval before the Beautao brand; it feels like a blemish. Overall, this is a striking package system.

PRODUCT	**THERE Bath Luxuries**
DESIGN FIRM	PhilippeBecker
LOCATION	San Francisco, CA
CLIENT	Cost Plus World Market

PRODUCT	**THERE Bath Luxuries Family**
DESIGN FIRM	PhilippeBecker
LOCATION	San Francisco, CA
CLIENT	Cost Plus World Market

 I am intrigued by the use of dark banding and white graph-ics with customized cultural icons; these elements function beautifully as the entry point to wherever *"THERE"* is. The subtle secondary line supports this appropriately indefinite personality. The architectural format of the color band (with a well-designed typographic format) and the vertical photo-graphic imagery nicely enhance the story of a richly fragrant and culturally transporting line of products. The cap labels add a nice detail to the narrative.

 The *"THERE"* logo works nicely as the navigation point to wherever "there" is. These packages tell a distinct story for each of the fragrances while managing to work well as a system. The intense, unified color of the toned photographic images help the labels to flow and not look disjointed even though they are compartmentalized. The dark brown tempers and balances the bright colors, which could have looked too sweet-smelling and cheap.

 I often am concerned by design elements so strong that they detract from the unified brand impression. The dominant black banner literally cuts this package in half. However, this overbearing element is nicely offset with the interesting colors, beautiful floral cues, and images of brand origin. Again, I like breaking the branding rules with the differing icons modifying the logo. I like the thin labels that wrap around the bottom of the bottle caps and draw your eye downward and away from the black brand banner.

PRODUCT	**DOLCE & GABBANA the one**
DESIGN FIRM	NiCE LTD
LOCATION	New York, NY
CLIENT	Procter&Gamble

PRODUCT	**No Frizz**
DESIGN FIRM	Wolff Olins
LOCATION	New York, NY
CLIENT	Living Proof

BE Trust D&G to produce an opulent, classic perfume bottle that is refreshingly simple in the category. It's certainly luxurious and has a timeless quality through that strong, minimal structure, with no expense spared on the finish.

MK Gold represents wealth, beauty, and purchasing power. Perhaps the divas who buy this stunning gold structure believe they will absorb its magic. It certainly looks like it's worth its weight.

SW This package becomes a touchstone in a woman's purse. The cool, smooth surfaces, the sharp corners and debossed branding make you want to hold it in your hand and feel the weight like a gold bullion. This package definitely lives up to the elegance of the Dolce & Gabbana brand.

BE Three things really work on this design: Firstly, the original and striking structure. I can't envisage how the lids open, but they break the mold, so to speak, giving the brand a unique and innovative feel. Secondly, that lovely logo—such a simple idea, confidently left to do its work uncluttered by the utilitarian and clear subsidiary copy—using a serif typeface to buck the slightly soulless, modern typographic solutions that usually adorn this category. And lastly, the unusual warm concrete color, which—again—stands out in a category that is prolific with intense, saturated colors. It's almost architectural in its overall feel, brilliantly suitable for its purpose, and makes a strong statement on shelf.

MK The grammatical style of this design is well conceived and well executed. The structures are distinctive. The color system and the lowercase body text make perfect sense and build this brand's character. The positioning of "Living Proof" smartly represents authorship. An example of discipline and restraint. A real success story.

SW The sensual forms, matte finish, and gentle curves are beautiful. As the product line grows, the horizontal division of color lining up between the packages will have a strong, elegant impact at retail. The serif typeface gives these modern shapes a warmth and approachability unique within this product category.

PRODUCT	**Spiezia Organics Body Care**
DESIGN FIRM	jkr
LOCATION	London, England
CLIENT	Spiezia Organics

 The interplay between the sculpted carton structure and the graphic icon is what makes this identity noteworthy. The deep die-cut depressions at both top and bottom of the carton seem to highlight the branding area as if it were onstage. I, too, like the bottle label with its drop-like shape, but I am curious about the choice of the deep green glass color. This seems out of place with the soothing, silvery blues and whites of the outer carton. I'm also concerned that the versioning does not immediately differentiate between the product offerings. Still, the carton structure and icon drive appropriate attention for this brand.

 This is a case where the form carries the design. The green matte glass bottle and the interesting water-drop-shaped label work well together; it feels like the sea. I wonder if it needed the outer package? The paperboard package is an interesting form as well, but it's not as elegant as the bottle itself.

PRODUCT	**Neil George Salon Hair Care Products**
DESIGN FIRM	meat and potatoes, inc.
LOCATION	Burbank, CA
CLIENT	Neil George Salon

 Simple and strong, the elegant choice of typeface and subtle color palette all combine to create a monolithic range that's clear and consistent, and the stacked logo takes a traditional typeface and creates a modern feel.

 I love Bodoni and I am certain that Giambattista Bodoni would have loved this enormously successful application of his elegant typeface. The sheer simplicity of both the clear tube with the graduated-color letters and the beautiful drop-out letters on the colored box is what makes this classic design feel so desirable.

 This package isn't breaking any new ground in the salon packaging category, but Neil George still manages to be distinctive, with its use of gradient color palette and the large brand name in an always-lovely Bodoni. It's too bad they didn't have more faith in the consumer's ability to read the brand name broken apart, that they felt the need to repeat it underneath. I suspect this may have been a client request?

PRODUCT	**DermaQuest Collateral & Packaging**
DESIGN FIRM	Vyant
LOCATION	Thousand Oaks, CA
CLIENT	DermaQuest

PRODUCT	**CleanWell Hand Sanitizer**
DESIGN FIRM	PhilippeBecker
LOCATION	San Francisco, CA
CLIENT	CleanWell

 A huge part of great packaging design is its ability to be consistently leveraged to every brand touchpoint. As a product's primary branding tool (the one that consumers engage first and far more often than any other), packaging needs to be the cornerstone of an integrated communications architecture. From the sell-in program, to the media kits, to the Web presence, to the advertising, merchandising, and sales promotion activities, the brand must speak with one visual voice. Here is a nice attempt at this synergy. I specifically like the asymmetrical die cut of the media kit. It's reflected as an icon on the ads and website. I do miss it, though, on the primary and secondary packaging. The cartons, for example, could have been much more engaging if they also reflected this interesting structural detail.

 This package is yet another skin-care line that isn't raising the bar on design within its category. It feels completely comfortable and acceptable, but it is nice just the same. I like the chemical structure to reference that this product has been extensively researched and tested—it's not just another beauty product. This is reinforced by the clean type and clear information hierarchy across the system.

 This looks hygienic. I like the simplicity of the leaf mark with the balance of the words *"clean"* and *"well"* and the ownable, small leaf element. The typographical hierarchy and efficacious white backdrop assert "safe," "straightforward," and "effective." The little stem growing from the base of the wipes adds a friendly, approachable touch.

 I love the crisp, clean, and direct logo. No swooshes or gradients—yeah!! The intensity of the green against the white, with highlights of yellow, says "clean." It's interesting how the lids break through the logo, allowing the logo to be as large as possible—this works since the containers are oval.

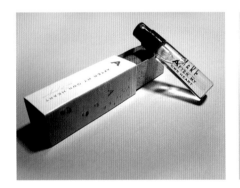

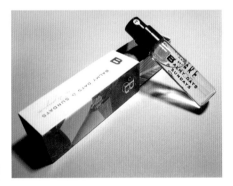

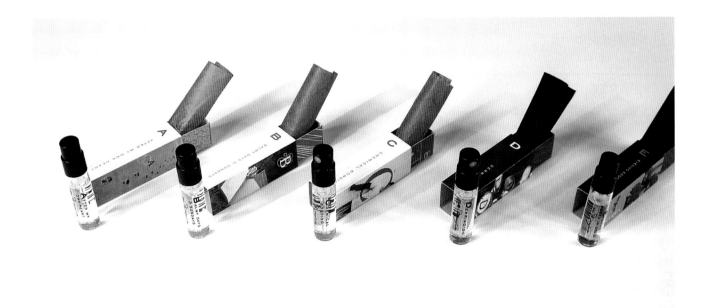

PRODUCT	**Ineke Deluxe Sample Collection Package**
DESIGN FIRM	Helena Seo Design
LOCATION	Sunnyvale, CA
CLIENT	Ineke, LLC

 Luxurious outer gift packaging: tactile black varnish on black illustrative calligraphy, contrasted with the modern typographic treatment of the descriptor. It makes for a classy and refined pack that would certainly impress potential buyers with a sense of discovery, luxury, and indulgence. I particularly like the way the color and illustrations on each product have been kept to the sides, so that on opening the outer package you are presented with a striking monochrome, and the color is a secondary experience.

 I am always drawn to black-on-black spot-varnished packaging, so this one is no exception. Although I wish the lovely pen-and-ink–style script were mirrored on the alphabet incorporated on the small inner structures, the overall picture is aesthetically pleasing. Perhaps a bit over-packaged, nonetheless the inner structures reflect an upscale, artisan style.

 These are lovely, from the matte black exterior box to the scroll of brightly colored paper on the inside. The long, telescoping, horizontal package and the extended type font contrasted with the calligraphic alphabet in shiny black foil elegantly scream sophistication and style. The single letters "A–E" on the small boxes and vials are an interesting method of identification. I wish the design of the small boxes would either have been simplified or gone completely over the top to complement the striking starkness of the exterior sleeve.

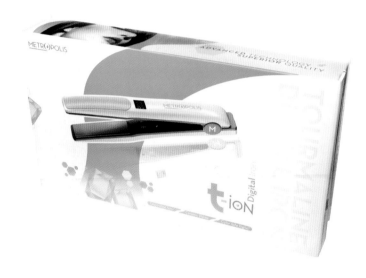

PRODUCT	**Metropolis T-Ion Digital Iron Packaging**
DESIGN FIRM	Version-X Design
LOCATION	Burbank, CA
CLIENT	Metropolis Technology

 It's clearly the opening device of this pack that makes it most noteworthy. I like how the inside of the front panel continues the branding message and how the open carton acts as a stage to highlight the product inside it. However, you don't get that experience until you open the box. I wonder if they could have eliminated the front panel, added a transparent blister, and allowed the product itself to be the brand's primary icon. In this age of sustainability, this product seems over-packaged. What if the pack was smaller and had an after-use as a carrying case while traveling?

PRODUCT	**Fair Trade Skin Care**
DESIGN FIRM	Emdoubleyu Design
LOCATION	Vancouver, Canada
CLIENT	African Fair Trade Society

BE The ethnicity of these products shows in the unique treatment of the imagery and the rough, unhewn typography. It reminds me of stamp designs, a motif which is echoed in the border on the type areas. The lack of a logo—using only typography and the cream holding area—is brave and builds on the locally produced, rustic, ethical pull for the consumer.

MK The pinking-sheared, postage-stamp-edge label with the typewriter-chic text communicates a discriminating and skillful handcraft. The Gauguin-like, Impressionistic illustrations of figures in primitive settings make a personal connection. I particularly like how the illustrations are not completely dense but establish open space for the eye to rest. It feels both welcoming and genuine.

RW Hand-craftsmanship is a desired brand position, and authenticity is hard to come by. The rudimentary fine-art paintings eloquently evoke an authentic sense of place. The typewriter type style and cut-paper labels make it real. The stock containers and caps are generic but most appropriate. You just get the feeling that the artisan who creates these products is being directly compensated, completing the Fair Trade mission.

SW I first saw these as a consumer in a retail environment, and they screamed to be picked up. So already it's successful. The paintings have the character of a color copy and an unusual hand-labeled quality that usually requires hand-drawn typography. Instead, these find a fresh, honest way to communicate. I believe there is passion behind this brand promise, not just a ploy to sell more product. Plus, I'm a sucker for typewriter fonts.

PRODUCT	**Lizhara**
DESIGN FIRM	Tridimage
LOCATION	Buenos Aires, Argentina
CLIENT	Laboratorios Firenze

PRODUCT	**Fruitée Gift Set**
DESIGN FIRM	lg2boutique
LOCATION	Montreal, Canada
CLIENT	Fruits & Passion

 I believe a customized form of the masterfully crafted typeface Didot is used for many magazine mastheads. This skin-care line clearly leverages the cues from the fashion world to establish a high-style personality for the brand.

 There is often a fine line between the therapeutic skin-care category and prestige fragrances and cosmetics. They share the same place on a woman's vanity; why can't they be inspired by the same aesthetic principles? This well-considered logotype seems borrowed from the image-driven cosmetics or even the high-fashion category. The brand name itself, Lizhara, also has, for me, cosmetics/fragrance overtones. A well-designed logo is really all that is required. Anything else would have been superfluous.

 Giftability is a key purchase incentive for high-end personal indulgence products. Here, the client made a significant investment in the tooled leather carrying case. And the design team made the most of this investment by keeping the branding on a removable banner. Counterposing the base line of "Orange" and "Cantaloup" and flushing both words off the top of the type unit is a smart way to address a rather long brand name. The involving background pattern and effervescent colors are nicely leveraged from the brand banner to the shrink seal on bottle tops to complete the visually refreshing experience.

 The removable label on this boxed set is a definite added value to this giftable set. The intense orange case is lovely and would catch your eye from across the store. Its mixed orientation of the fragrance copy is interesting and works unexpectedly well—I'm not exactly sure why this was done, but I like it. The gold background of the wrap helps to give the other colors a celebratory feel which would have a tendency to look summery rather than Christmas. Overall, the colors are bit heavy for my taste—I associate the heavy color with heavily fragranced products.

PRODUCT	**CND Liquid Starter Pack**
DESIGN FIRM	MiresBall
LOCATION	San Diego, CA
CLIENT	CND

 This looks straight off the catwalk, and the unusual way in which the imagery has been masked off makes for a contemporary design that's colorful and fresh. I would have liked to have seen different shots across the variants, but they certainly hold strong as a range.

 What could have been a fairly straightforward concept of photography and color-coding is significantly enhanced by the inventive application of a tile grid. The idea of putting the pieces together with this starter pack is subtly communicated and creates a nice opening for well-formatted typography. Her eyes, well-hidden by the shadows, redirect the focus and enable the viewer to check out her other striking features. The fashion-forward color palette adds to the positioning.

PRODUCT	me
DESIGN FIRM	united* dsn
LOCATION	New York, NY
CLIENT	{me}zhgan

 BE Elegant brand mark here, feminine, a little idea in the twist, with a crafted and modern feel.

 RW This identity transcends all its applications. From the outer carton to the tin to the product inscription—even to the inside of the carton—the unifying brand color and texture both work well across all consumer touchpoints. The brand emblem, with its playful capital and lowercase typefaces, is equally appealing. I like how the naming architecture calls out each brand feature and attributes it directly to the consumer's every mood—flawless me, glowing me, sultry me. I specifically like how the {me} is set apart by brackets, drawing even more attention to the user. After all, at the end of the day, it really is all about me.

PRODUCT	**Sainsbury's Active Naturals Toiletries**
DESIGN FIRM	Paul Cartwright Branding
LOCATION	Ramsgate, England
CLIENT	Sainsbury's PLC

PRODUCT	**Pout Plump: Gold Glitz**
DESIGN FIRM	Wrapology
LOCATION	London, England
CLIENT	Pout

BE This certainly borrows from the food market to create an almost edible sense of ingredients, amplified by the really narrow-depth photography on the fresh white background. The silver caps top it off with a credibly luxuriant finish, and the super-simple range descriptors work without distracting.

MK When close-up product photography is perfectly stylized and the image fades softly into a white background, the results are pure and crisp. Although this is a well-established aesthetic, its use in this design feels authentic and grabs consumer attention. Straightforward type, colors that you can practically smell—what else is there?

RW This design system is simply delectable. Taking its cues from the fresh-food category, the luscious ingredient photography most certainly delivers the fragrance message. Stripping everything else back to just the simple essentials allows the one visual element to shine. Of course, this requires that all the ingredients are in fact attractive to look at. I have a little trouble reading the Olive & Bamboo type. The photo could have blended to white much sooner so as to be readable and consistent with the other fragrances.

SW I want to eat these. This information hierarchy is surprisingly simple and pared down. The controlled color of the photographs helps to unify the packages yet clearly define the fragrance.

BE Marvelous idea here: Plumped lips demand a plumped packaging solution! It's rather extravagant but adds a playful and highly original branded feel. The graphics seem a little like an afterthought, just replicating the illustrations on the inner product, but the overall result is an enjoyably girly, cheeky pack that makes me smile.

MK Risqué. Black lace, gold glitter, and accenting graphic devices that take their cues from sexy lingerie certainly form a subconscious stimulus. A bit overdone and over-packaged, but fits the target market. The plump packaging serves well in subliminal seduction. The totality of this design shouts of a product that is ready for action.

PRODUCT	**Natura Dermatology JAM Product Line**
DESIGN FIRM	Pumpkinfish
LOCATION	Ft. Lauderdale, FL
CLIENT	Natura Dermatology

PRODUCT	**Sanity Package**
DESIGN FIRM	Diseño Dos Asociados
LOCATION	San Andrés Cholula, Mexico
CLIENT	Sanity

 This design plays to all the norms of the category: minimal, utilitarian graphics; slick, refined structure; finishing to the hilt, but I somehow like the way these look like pure bars of aluminum. They are so utilitarian they wouldn't be out of place on a building site, and the combination of shiny versus brushed aluminum has been handled quite effectively here. Not sure if I would like to smear Skin Jam on me, however... but I'm sure this appeals to a metrosexual male market that retains an element of rawness I rather admire.

 The warning with a highly reflective substrate is that it will pick up the ambient light and color of its environment. Put it next to a pink package and it will look pink. Put it anywhere but on the topmost shelf and it will look dark and dreary and lose all its luster. As a result, designers often use high-gloss metallics only in very careful measure. Not this time! Damn the torpedos. This brand makes a statement as bold and brash as its in-your-face names. I'm not so sure what I am to do with Neck Jam (kinda sounds like a rugby injury) but then again, nothing is as sexy as confidence, and this brand abounds with it.

 A challenging category, but this design is resolved so well that it raises the bar. This line has all the right elements: comforting color hues, confident yet approachable brand identity, subtle graphic elements that communicate quality (the stitching), reassurance (the photographic imagery), and personal (the small icons). There is a soft subtlety to this design. The attention to detail, down to the rounded-cornered die-cut window, works well to present a quality product. A creative, uncomplicated, and beautifully harmonious design strategy.

The angels are in the details and this identity has them. In addition to the supple forms and the approachable photography, I specifically like the natural, nongeometric, organic blue brand icon and how its soft dimensionality is highlighted by the die cut. I like the three off-white icons at the very bottom and how they reinforce each product's target audience. I am curious why the hot-water bottle does not follow the architecture with the human touch that the beautiful people-photography brings—an important detail that the angels may have overlooked.

PRODUCT	Nude Skincare
DESIGN FIRM	Pearlfisher
LOCATION	London, England
CLIENT	Nude Skincare

PRODUCT	Gage For Men
DESIGN FIRM	Route 8 Design
LOCATION	Louisville, KY
CLIENT	Gage For Men

 The structure does all the hard work here, elegant and pared back to its minimum, living up to its name. It's almost a shame there had to be so much on the front, but the soft, sophisticated colors matched with the simplistic branding make for a refined and delicate range.

 Smooth, sensuous, minimalist...what more is there to say? (Perhaps, I wish they were wearing even less.)

 In generating shelf impact and relevant differentiation, you have two choices: You can scream a common brand message louder than anyone else, or you can whisper a new story. Far from retreating on shelf, this identity stands out and speaks loudly, almost without speaking at all. Reflecting its name, this architecture is stripped bare, allowing the eye to appreciate the curves of its unique structure and Mondrian logo. Running the supportive copy vertically elongates the already-elegant cylinders. The stacked copy on the square structures reflects this structure's geometry.

 My compliments to the designers in letting the structure be the star. Just a small bit of type and of course the logo-type that mimics the shape of the bottle—done. Pencils down. Finished.

 The beauty of this logogram is that it has the simplicity, elegance, and classic style of an old-fashioned typewriter key. With a whole generation of consumers who have never seen a typewriter, this iconic image becomes fresh and original. The lowercase character projects a very personal identity. The white icons against the black circular closure with white have the strength and intrinsic beauty of a hockey puck. The clean organization of type on the label adds to a design that is both recognizable and memorable.

 This concept is smart, masculine, sophisticated, flexible, adaptable, recognizable, and effective. I imagine if a consumer had a great experience with one of these products, the package would encourage him to try them all—a fully matched, precision set. And you can't ask for anything more than that from your brand identity architecture.

PRODUCT	**on10® Cosmetics**
DESIGN FIRM	Alternatives
LOCATION	New York, NY
CLIENT	on10®

 Vintage design has enormous consumer impact when well utilized. The graphic masters that helped shape early forms of mass communication (Alphonse Mucha, Jules Cheret, among others) captured the zeitgeist and culture of the times. This line replicates the essence of that appeal with stylized typography, bold lithographic replicas, attention-grabbing illustrations, and structures that add collectibility.

 What a delightfully kitsch repurposing of existing brand imagery! What soft drinks have to do with cosmetics, I just cannot imagine. I'm concerned that the on10 branding is almost an afterthought, a contemporary "violator" forced onto the retro visual palette. I am curious to learn if the Dr Pepper/7UP company has given permission for on10 to employ their beautifully elaborate intellectual property. But as long as those who own the visual assets have approved this (and are being adequately compensated) and these visuals add value to both the soft drinks and the cosmetics brands, then I'm all for it.

 This brand is competing in the same world as Benefit makeup and skin care that has been smartly utilizing this retro-kitsch direction successfully for many years. These designs as they are don't seem to bring anything new to the retro language of these brands. The addition of the black band violator with the modern "on 10" logotype is distracting. In addition to Benefit, there are numerous other companies taking this spin on beauty; is there room for one more?

PRODUCT	**Herbal Supplements**	**PRODUCT**	**Pomology**
DESIGN FIRM	Turner Duckworth	**DESIGN FIRM**	Selikoff+Company, LLC
LOCATION	London, England and San Francicso, CA	**LOCATION**	West Orange, NJ
CLIENT	Superdrug Stores PLC	**CLIENT**	Pomology

BE Simple, fresh, elegant, and clean: The kaleidoscope lends scientific cues, tying nicely into the concept of extracts; they almost look microscopic. This serves to beautify the ingredients and highlight the combinations of natural plants in a gentle and delicate way. The white background allows the ingredients to be fresh and vibrant, and the simple, authoritative type keeps this grounded and believable.

MK The symmetry of these beautiful herbs gently tumbling around the package gives tension and allure to what could be a fairly humdrum subject. An intelligent solution that visually implies "scientific" with structural forms and "herbal" with natural ingredients. I am intrigued by how the circular repetition creates inner graphical forms. The clean, open space and confident, modern, sans serif typeface add balance and give the brand a vivid, positive image. A nice linking of medicine, nature, and art.

RW What are you to do when the product inherently ain't so pretty? Use this beautiful example and assemble the product into an engaging kaleidoscopic presentation. This arresting visual product array turns nondescript herbs into intriguing patterns inside patterns. I love how the offset images bleed from front to top and/or side panels, encouraging the viewer to explore the entire package. This leaves the all-capital type to communicate the straight story. Playful, nostalgic, and yet sophisticated.

BE The genre tends toward hokey-pokey, overly chaotic design, or super-functional and slightly scary, whereas this is efficacious without being cold, and it has a touch of class. Black-on-black varnishes and vibrant color punches in the middle make this range cohesive and clear. The mass of information has also been ordered in a clean and efficient way that makes this easy to navigate, when there's so much to communicate, in a consistent and considered way.

MK There is definitely a positive energy emanating from these vibrant icons, pulsating from the black bottles. The subtle matte varnish dots add liveliness to the black background. The typography commands attention with the creative use of gray and white to highlight specific text. This line should be forceful on shelf.

SW A beautiful color-coded system for a category of products that is often confusing and aesthetically void. The logo nicely communicates the pomegranate-based products but it also exudes energy and vitality. That's appropriate; as the company adds more products, they won't be restricted. Highlighting key product attributes in bolder type works well in this design. It gives it an easy, conversational approach rather than bullet-pointing the information, which would feel cold. Even though this is a new product, it has a confidence I would trust.

PRODUCT	**Amie Skincare**	**PRODUCT**	**Sainsbury's Organic You Skincare**
DESIGN FIRM	Turner Duckworth	**DESIGN FIRM**	Paul Cartwright Branding
LOCATION	London, England and San Francicso, CA	**LOCATION**	Ramsgate, England
CLIENT	Beauty Buddy Ltd	**CLIENT**	Sainsbury's PLC

BE A charming naiveté, soft, flowery pastilles, and a fresh logo color create a fresh and fun design. The illustrative style, cute language, and lowercase logo all make for an ultra-girly range that I'm sure hits the spot (no pun intended) with the target market.

MK This sweet, young, fresh brand identity is immediately attractive, from the youthful characteristic of the "a "flipped over to become the "e" to the heart-shaped flower. I particularly like the message conveyed by the flower bud energetically asserting itself. A nice definition of harmony: "A pleasing effect produced by an arrangement of things, parts, or colors."

BE This is an archetypal own-brand design, with its simple design that easily extends itself. The choice of imagery here is key, and this soft, delicate floral shot exemplifies the product benefits fittingly. The soft pastilles, combined with this stylized imagery, lend this design an almost magical quality that befits the category entirely.

MK A dazzling demonstration of how the just-right photograph, utilized well, can capture the soul of a brand. With this use of duo-tone and the color gradient washing behind the image, the design feels fresh and gentle, which is the perfect message for this skin-care line. The type, scale, and positioning, however, do not do justice to the imagery.

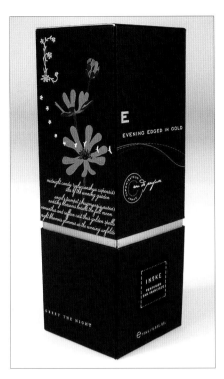

PRODUCT	**Perfume package for Evening Edged in Gold**
DESIGN FIRM	Helena Seo Design
LOCATION	Sunnyvale, CA
CLIENT	Ineke, LLC

 Lovely karma; this design has both body and soul. The signals this design sends out are intriguing, playful, and paradoxical—the stillness of the black and gold against the motion of the imagery and graphics. Lovely bottle graphics, and the gold band adds a refined structural element. A fantastically free-spirited solution except for the bottle cap that is a bit overwhelming.

 Much is expected of brand identity in the prestige fragrance category. Often these graphics and structures must tell a richly compelling story evoking a luxuriant experience that justifies the brand's ultra-premium price point. This identity does not disappoint. I do find the bottle's gold and black to be a bit matronly, the cap a bit heavy, and the overall impression perhaps just a little dusty for a young, contemporary, urbane woman. But the outer carton compensates with its light and dreamlike graphics.

 Wow! This package is a visual playground; in less adept hands, it could have been a mess. The elements flow, jump, twirl, and spin around all sides of the box and your eyes willingly dance along. It's girly and pretty, and yet it manages to be sophisticated. The burnished gold contrasted with the matte black and sparkles of white is both modern and art deco. It feels like an amazing night out with friends.

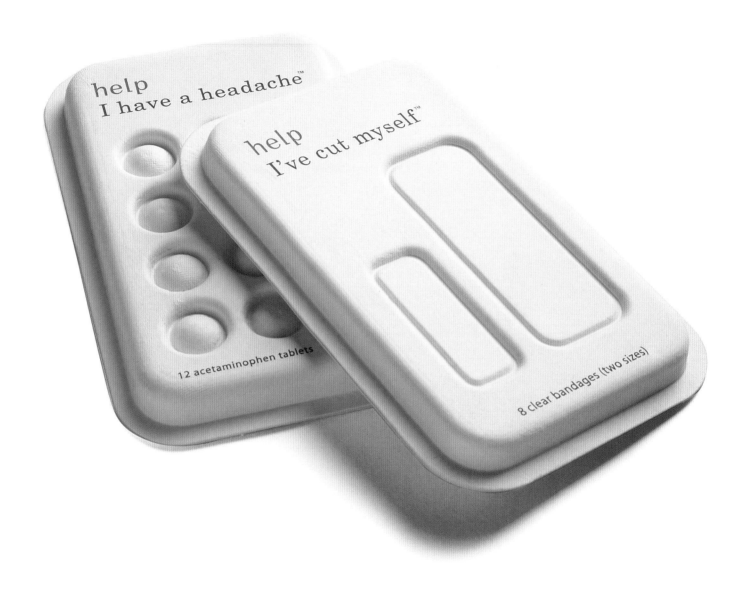

PRODUCT	**Help Remedies**
DESIGN FIRM	Little Fury and ChappsMalina
LOCATION	New York, NY
CLIENT	Richard Fine

 I'm so impressed with this totally unconventional take on a medical category, usually adorned with dubious-looking body parts, active arrows, and "breathable flashes"... [Shudder]. Its simple brand name, which is so direct and yet so personal, totally pared-down design, and beautifully simple use of embossing, which makes it tactile and almost sculptural, totally defies the expected. Bravo! It's almost a placebo in itself.

 Not only do I love the look of these molded–paper pulp cartons and the geometric extruded forms, but the tactile quality of them must be wonderful. The simple, respectful type that exclaims what help is needed is a very fresh divergence from an aisle of products that scream from the shelf. Kudos to the designer who created this refreshing approach in a typically boring and unhelpful category.

 This identity makes me smile. Sure, it breaks some of branding's cardinal rules, like having a brand name, for instance. (Is the brand name Help? "Go get me some Help!") Yes, it might lack effective shelf impact, making it hard to find. And yes, it might not communicate the efficacy and credibility demanded of other medications. But, damn, does it redefine the language of a monolingual category! I'd love to work for the courageous marketers who would embrace this strategy.

 Why, oh, why can't more packaging look like this? Please, enough of all the gradients and swooshes and swirls! This is brilliant, not because it's an over-the-top, beautiful design solution (although the rounded edges on the trays are lovely), but rather for all that it's not. It does its job concisely and manages to get in a little wink and a nudge. I wish I had designed this.

neral
etail

"This package design elevates a mundane
product into a branded experience."

— Rob Wallace, page 205

PRODUCT	**Casablanca Moderne Fans**
DESIGN FIRM	Terres Design
LOCATION	Pleasanton, CA
CLIENT	Casablanca Fan Company

PRODUCT	**Benjamin Moore: Ben Paints**
DESIGN FIRM	Sterling Brands
LOCATION	New York, NY
CLIENT	Benjamin Moore

 Of course, with a product that captures the best of machine-age industrial design, there is a clear strategy for the packaging design. That said, there are many directions this concept could have taken, but this one nails it with the rich artistic influence of artists such as A. M. Cassandre. The geometric, angular, layered graphics that feature the industrial feats of the moderne period serve as a well-suited means of positioning this product in the annals of outstanding design achievements. I appreciate the wrapping of the artwork around all sides of the packaging, making for an interactive experience and a gift-giving appearance. The car and man positioned in front of the billboard design give scale and presence to this impactful primary display panel.

 Great design often seeks to create a sense of place, intimating how the product would appear in a consumer's home or incorporated into her lifestyle. Here the design evokes a sense of both time and place with a 1930s aesthetic, reflected from the product design to the environment in which it is heroically featured. The retro illustration depicts a '30s cityscape, complete with idealized searchlights and all those Raymond Lowe icons, to support the hero-product, featured as a billboard and a sort of hood ornament and/or building cornice. The '30's aesthetic is reflected in the product design with its ornate windscreen and its architectural pedestal. I have nothing retro in my home or office, but I was curiously drawn to this because of the experience that the packaging promises.

 Can we really be on a first-name basis and call him Ben? What an incredible difference that makes—after all, manners dictate that one should not call anyone by his first name unless one really knows him quite well. If you know someone well, you tend to be loyal and trust him or her. So this brand now has a lot to live up to. The lowercase signature is personal and comfortable within an overall layout that is orderly and stylish. The transparencies of the well-constructed type communicate the evolution or transitional nature of the product. This good-natured disposition is a very smart strategy.

I can't help but compare this package to the Flawless paint package, designed by Turner Duckworth—which I think is brilliant, and that's a tough act to follow. I love Benjamin Moore paints and they have a loyal following among interior designers and architects, so to shorten the name to Ben is perfect for that group. In fact, I wouldn't be surprised if it is commonly referred to as Ben. The hierarchy of information is consistent and easy to navigate. I love the look of the overlapping transparent letterforms, but do they communicate that this paint takes three coats to cover?

PRODUCT	**Bookmarked**
DESIGN FIRM	Wink
LOCATION	Minneapolis, MN
CLIENT	Target

 A simple, smart, and straightforward strategy that is well crafted and effectively repeatable. The bookmark makes perfect sense, as do the background page graphics. The design does more than showcase what is basically a straightforward, reliable, and effective (perhaps even unexciting) line of products: It positions it as contemporary, even compelling. Of course, the color coding of black, white, and red (read) makes sense, too.

 There is little that is more effective than actually providing the consumer brand experience and being able to demonstrate its core product benefits on the package. I don't remember studying other magnifying glass packaging, but how intuitive is this? It literally encourages consumers to hold the product in their hands as they focus their attention on the brand benefit copy and its background story. I happen to wear my magnifiers at the end of my nose these days, but still this package made me want to buy this product—even knowing full well that I may never use it. That's a true test of all great packaging.

 I've always loved this Bookmarked logo of the B with a bookmark. So it makes me happy to see it expanded onto packaging for products that assist the reader. Although there isn't a lot that's earth-shatteringly new in the design, these packages let the product be the star—and they do it very handsomely and very appropriately for Target.

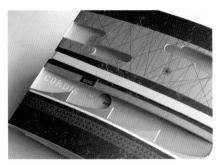

PRODUCT	**Cordis** *Here On Out* **CD**
DESIGN FIRM	Chen Design Associates
LOCATION	San Francisco, CA
CLIENT	Richard Grimes

 MK Even though it goes without saying that great packaging makes you want to explore the product further, this design exemplifies that expression. After examining this highly engaging design, I went on to search out the music of Cordis. The graphics perfectly capture the atmospheric, layered, rich, textural, and expressive quality of this band while the subtle use of both typography and die cutting is quietly inviting. I am glad to see this sustainable solution to the plastic jewel case.

 RW I normally have a negative visceral response to paper-wrapped CDs not in traditional jewel cases. It too often seems like a low-rent cop-out. Quite the converse here. The textured paper and precision die cuts add interest and value. I like the interplay between the wave and cloud graphics and the stark, haphazard lines. The steely grey and deep forest colors are also an attractive contrast. This package required a significant investment in detail and craftsmanship that has paid off well.

 SW I have a pretty high standard when it comes to CD design—there are so many amazing designs that for something to rise above and really stand out, it has to be stunning. I want to pick this package up and explore every nook and cranny of its 4 x 4 inches. The cloud and wave die cuts with type peeking through have the allure of a pop-up book.

PRODUCT	**Firelighters 251 degrees**
DESIGN FIRM	See7
LOCATION	Konstanz, Germany
CLIENT	Lindner AG / Switzerland

PRODUCT	**das comptoir Wine Bottle Tubes**
DESIGN FIRM	A. Egger, J.J. Lamut, B. Mayer
LOCATION	Vienna, Austria
CLIENT	das comptoir

 What an elegantly sophisticated way to approach a low-/ no involvement product category. The octagonal pack shape and its inset closures immediately signal something special. The smart type and descriptive icons contrast nicely against the natural textured background. The overall impression is one of a high-end gift! Not only does this identity add interest and value, it elevates a mundane product into a branded experience.

 I am mesmerized by this meneragie of paperboard wine canisters. Each one has a uniquely strong presence, yet as a collection they work harmoniously. They have a decorator style of modernistic interior wallpapers that makes them sophisticated, chic, and giftworthy.

 Traditionally, the wine category aesthetic has been so fussy and crafty, and—well—traditional. I love the irreverent vitality this identity brings to the wine-drinking and wine-gifting experience. Elegant without being boring or borish, these tubes and the wine labels within them represent a bold new statement. While this identity may disengage wine snobs, it certainly speaks to a new generation of visual and vinacious enthusiasts.

The product is beautiful, almost sculptural, and I applaud the designers for letting the texture of the product become a major part of the package design. The overprint of bold red reads well on top of the photographic pattern. The modular placement of *251* and illustrations demonstrating the suggested uses makes the product work from all eight sides. I would love to see these lined up to see the movement.

 These wine bottle tubes have amazing impact en masse. Individually, I definitely gravitate to some more than to others, as it should be. I love how the "das comptoir" logotype has been dissected, enlarged, repeated, and manipulated to make several of the stunning patterns. The color combinations are interesting and fresh. It would be fun to give (and even better to receive) this wine package as a housewarming gift.

PRODUCT	**Dr. Weil Cookware By Spring**
DESIGN FIRM	FAI Design Group
LOCATION	Irvington, NY
CLIENT	Dr. Weil Spring

PRODUCT	**Fullers Earth Cat Litter**
DESIGN FIRM	Turner Duckworth
LOCATION	London, England & San Francisco, CA
CLIENT	Waitrose Ltd.

 Lemongrass, with its long, fluid lines and vivid green hue, makes for an effective textural pattern. Its use in this line of kitchen products projects the fresh, healthy, green lifestyle that the guru of healthy lifestyle, Andrew Weil, promotes.

This design architecture resisted the temptation to "sell the sizzle" by emphasizing the end result of beautiful, healthy food. Rather, the product becomes the hero here, along with the heroic image of Dr. Weil. The clean, simple lines of the cookware designs are reflected in the clarity and simplicity of this identity. I am interested to see how well the natural green texture works both horizontally and vertically. Even though it is not always in the same staging area on all packages, it holds this line of very different package shapes together as a brand.

 A witty idea, simply executed with understated charm. The uncluttered nature of the design draws your eye to the idea, and the copy does its job in a simple and unobtrusive manner, leaving you with a smile and a pampered kitty!

 Simply purrrrrrfect!

A design so simply effective that one more element would be superfluous—and would detract from the premium and intuitive brand message. Imagine the client shrieking, "But we just have to make the odor-fighting message larger!" Nope. Doing so would just disrupt the balance and denigrate the brand. Nice work! But perhaps it could be even nicer with a resealable bag. Ever knocked over an opened bag of litter? It's a cat-astrophe.

 I'm becoming very irritated with Turner Duckworth. They can even make kitty litter look amazing; what will they package next? The idea of a cat-door plaque (like the generic men/women bathroom plaques) is hilarious. And this is perfectly executed, with just enough personality in the cat to make it cute. The typography is handled in a straightforward manner, letting the icon do all the work.

PRODUCT	Epson (redesign of logotype, ink, and paper packaging)
DESIGN FIRM	Nicole Splater
LOCATION	Thousand Oaks, CA
CLIENT	Epson

RW I'm actually a fan of the drop icon inside the logo, the oversized drop on the toners, and the angled paper geometry of the paper packaging. I like the use of color on the side, bottom, and front panels, immediately differentiating between ink products. I like the use of green on the paper, connoting sustainability. I also like how all ancillary type is controlled within one area so as to keep the rest of the identity open and simple.

SW I love Epson; I am very brand-loyal. Although I think this package design is really good, I don't think it quite lives up to my expectations of Epson. The new logo has strength and clearly communicates ink-jet printing. This is a product that lends itself to color-coding of all products, starting of course with the CMYK ink cartridges—the logo's ink droplet does this well.

PRODUCT	Guido's "Foodie" T-Shirts		**PRODUCT**	Herman Miller C2
DESIGN FIRM	Studio Two		**DESIGN FIRM**	felix sockwell, Inc
LOCATION	Lenox, MA		**LOCATION**	Maplewood, NJ
CLIENT	Guido's Fresh Marketplace		**CLIENT**	Herman Miller

 Maybe a bit novel, but that's its irresistible appeal. This is a clever way to create a tourist gift market for a non-food-related product, and it fits perfectly within a retail establishment that is all about fresh, quality food. The monochromatic color palette keeps it fashionable.

 Yes, we've all seen the vernacular of meat packaging used in many applications in the last few years, but I can't help it—I like this! The folding of the T-shirt to reveal "FOODIE" is funny and makes a great gift purchase. The packaging is elevated, albeit only slightly, by keeping a strict black-and-white color palette, which works well for the nutrition-panelesque branding.

 When a product originates from a company recognized for producing modern classic designs—Herman Miller, for example—the packaging must simply and skillfully address the same aesthetic. This package has a somewhat 1950s design aesthetic. Alexander Calder's wire-frame portraits and other modern classics may have inspired this whimsical and clever approach. The simple line art and flat use of color establish a classic, artistic, interpersonal connection between the viewer and the package. The fluidity of the line—the way in which it brings the eye around each panel and connects the story of the person and their product—is effectively executed.

 I am always intrigued and gratified by Felix Sockwell's illustrations, and this is one more good example of how a single well-executed line can convey an immediate personality. The line flowing from one colored panel to the next, and matching up from package to package, makes me want to pick this up and explore it. I can imagine it would be stunning when merchandised.

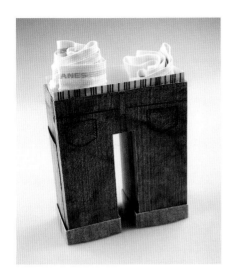

PRODUCT	**Hanes Designer Briefs**
DESIGN FIRM	Rubbish
LOCATION	Lombard, IL
CLIENT	Hanes

 Hey, you've gotta admire the balls of this design, with such an innovative structure built around a simple idea. I'm not sure how they're sealed, but what a great way to package your undies! I particularly like the details of the turn-ups, and the flexibility to carry the charity's identity and logo through the design of the pants. This is fun, frivolous, and so amusing. It's nice to see paper engineering for something so different, and I'm sure it will fly off the shelves.

 Packaging and product design need to lead—if not closely follow—trend, specifically in the ever-changing, hyper-kinetic fashion category. So now that it's a fashion statement to wear one's underpants well up over one's jeans, the waistband is suddenly self-defining. And underwear now makes a political and cause-marketing statement. You have to love the pack structure for these boxer-style briefs. But what's to be done for thongs? Hmmmm.

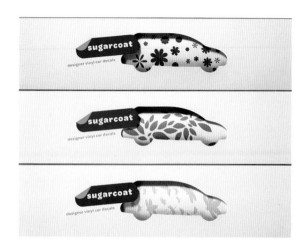

PRODUCT	Sugarcoat		PRODUCT	Tesco Eggs
DESIGN FIRM	Spunk Design Machine		DESIGN FIRM	P&W
LOCATION	Minneapolis, MN		LOCATION	London, England
CLIENT	Sugarcoat		CLIENT	Tesco

 I have always been amazed that Colorforms, one of my favorite childhood games, has never been adapted to customize cars. This packaging expresses the free expression of creativity conveyed through the wide array of vinyl shapes that defines this inventive product. There's a bit of '60s retro style to the type and graphics, and the saccharine-sweet green color with the peeled decals makes this design pop.

 Decals for your car! I could have really used these when I was in college with an old four-door Nova; it would have made it considerably more bearable to drive. Now, for the package: The turned-down corner on the logotype oval immediately describes the product. The alternating box sides of flat white/flat green mimic the flat color of the decals and give the package graphic punch.

 Great idea here, so simple—with just a few brush strokes, the product shot transforms into its particular attributes, neatly, with no fuss, in a simple and poignant way that is instantly understandable. This is particularly challenging on such a rough substrate with only two print colors to work with.

 I spent an exorbitant amount of time in the egg section of the supermarket on my last trip to London—the packaging design is far more well designed than any I have seen in my own country in the recent past. U.S. egg packaging of the 1930s had some lively designs, and this solution is no less compelling, from the tinted pulp cartons to the manner in which the print appears raw and unfinished. Of course, the humor of the egg telling its own story—free range or barn raised—is the defining personality. A great example of how the use of different print and illustration styles can turn a two-color job into a design that is rich and distinctive. What's not to love about these good eggs?

These are really cute—not a word normally used to describe egg cartons! I love the egg characters differentiating between "free range" and "barn" eggs. The tone-on-tone of the type and the egg carton works for the technical printing challenges on this material but also adds to the earthy, natural feel.

PRODUCT	**Jot-it**
DESIGN FIRM	Struck
LOCATION	Salt Lake City, UT
CLIENT	Cocoa

 MK Here's a case where the product design and the packaging structural design are equally impressive and innovative. The overall appearance of the packaging is striking and contemporary, and it functions perfectly to showcase this convenient desk accessory product.

 RW Here is packaging as architecture. The package frames the product beautifully, simply. It directs the consumer's attention to the organized layout of information. I adore the details—like the small die cuts in the top and bottom of the frame which allow the products to interlock when stacked. I'm not sure how stacking these packages adds value, but it does make for an impressive brand impression.

 SW Brilliant package engineering. It protects the product while letting the consumer actually see the product; what a great idea! And it seems as if this amazing feat is done without glue, staples, or those pesky twist ties. Every surface of this package is utilized to communicate the personality of the brand with chatty quips. The shape and structure are reminiscent of in/ out boxes of old, which seems appropriate for a product that is intended for jotting notes. The bright green color works well against the glossy white product and shades of gray—it feels like a tech product, but not too serious. When the Jot-It's are stacked, they become very sculptural.

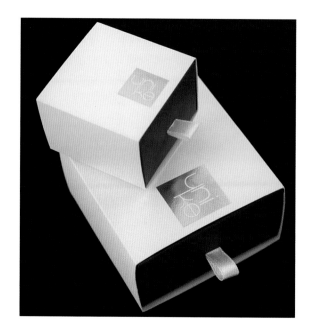

PRODUCT	**PARAD Shopping Bag**
DESIGN FIRM	Design bureau Proekt
LOCATION	Moscow, Russia
CLIENT	Parad

PRODUCT	**Unike Jewelery Packaging**
DESIGN FIRM	Ana Roncha	Jorge Jorge
LOCATION	Porto, Portugal
CLIENT	Unike

 A glamorously simple form that becomes an exceptionally intelligent icon. Love the sexy little beauty mark! The concept that the brand is on her lips speaks volumes.

 I agree, whole heartedly, with Marianne's insights. What further engages me is this design's urbane and distinctly feminine appeal, despite its rather heavy geometric shape. The bold type, metallic color, and minimalist simplicity are again a welcomed alternative to expected frilly, ornately feminine imagery. Lastly, I'm pleasantly surprised that the identity is a shoe brand. It would work perhaps even harder for cosmetics, making the lips and beauty mark that much more relevant. But then again it would be somewhat more intuitive. I applaud this design for its embrace of the unexpected.

 Compared to the Goliaths of the luxury jewelry market, this is young and fresh, keeping it simple with a white-and-silver brand that has an ultra-urban logo. I'm not sure I'd be able to read "unike," but the way it's knocked out of a silver square makes it highly versatile, and the foil is a luxurious touch.

 Beautiful! I love the logotype reversing out of the foiled silver off-center square. It looks very upscale, young, and classically hip. The ribbon pull is a nice touch. Every detail counts on such a minimal package.

PRODUCT	**The North Face Packaging Re-design**
DESIGN FIRM	Chen Design Associates
LOCATION	San Francisco, CA
CLIENT	The North Face

MK With a company that is always cutting-edge, it is no surprise that this redesign captures all of the tactile, environmental, and experiential traits that define this brand.

RW Here texture is taken to the extreme, and with a magnificent result. The deep embossings require significant investment and a committed partnership with the printer. The considered color palette is derived from the product and informs all brand communications. How smart to print information onto the sole inserts and wrapping tissue, an opportunity that other brands literally throw away.

SW I remember experiencing this box for the first time when a Zappos order arrived at the office. We were all running our hands across the heavily debossed box. From the printed tissue to the shoe-form inserts with detailed product copy, this was a completely enjoyable brand experience. I wish all packaging could perform at this level.

PRODUCT	**TIMEX Packaging for Target**
DESIGN FIRM	ATLASON
LOCATION	New York, NY
CLIENT	TIMEX

 Talk about reinventing American icons—where has Timex been in the new age of the everyday-watch-as-fashion-statement? Stuck in its John Cameron Swayze *"takes a licking and keeps on ticking"* 1950s perceptions? I have long grown weary of Swatch, and all those brands who knocked it off, with their ultra-simple, light-infused aesthetic, trying to justify a super-premium price for a rather cheap product. Into this void, Timex comes roaring back, reclaiming its rightful place as the value-based, but still valuable, everyday watch. I love the "view from the side" structure, with the strong Timex logo ghosted over the product, and the new "X." icon. (See how simply adding a dot next to a standard letterform transforms it into a brand mnemonic?) Strong insight, Target! Strong work, Timex! Keep it real.

 I've always loved the functional simplicity and economy of a Timex watch. This marriage between Timex and Target takes all that to a new level of cool. This package is ingenious. It hits all the designer hot buttons—bold, iconographically simple, tactile, and sculptural—all without being overly designed, just like a Timex timepiece. And they manage to do it in an environmentally conscious way.

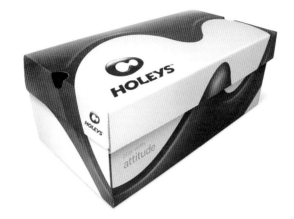

PRODUCT	**Jimmy Choo Bags**
DESIGN FIRM	Brandhouse
LOCATION	London, England
CLIENT	Jimmy Choo

PRODUCT	**Holeys Re-brand**
DESIGN FIRM	dossiercreative inc.
LOCATION	Vancouver, Canada
CLIENT	Holey Soles Holdings Ltd.

 Breathtaking, sexy, and elegant! A simple, classic shopping bag transformed into a powerful and evocative statement.

 This package is perhaps as precious as the products it contains. The reinterpretation of shoelaces as closure is quite brilliant. The subtle touch of color coming from the teal ribbon adds dimension. The logo, on its own, is worth note. I continue to stare at it. At first glance, I read it immediately and accurately, but in detailed examination, unless my eyes deceive me, it seems to be missing a descender, or even two! I'm wondering if adding all the proper vertical letterforms would actually have made this elegant logo less readable? Here is yet another great lesson for designers: Sometimes you may have to break the rules—even in how letters are formed—to be most effective. Great work.

When the brand icon is as ownable as this one is, the packaging design can be wrapped in it and work successfully. Seems like there's not much to it—in a good way—and yet the dimensional positioning feels especially interactive.

Here again, a brand icon becomes the central device of its entire communication architecture. Wrapping the package with the stylized shape is somewhat intuitive but still nicely executed, specifically in how it wraps around all six sides of the box. I admit that I did not originally see the "H" inside the icon, but it does not bother me. Sometimes it's nice to discover something unique inside an identity, kind of like the arrow in the FedEx logo. I'm wondering why the the actual hole in the top/side area could not have been punched with the same distinctive branded shape! That would have just completed the experience.

!!! These ballet-style shoes are sold from vending machines at nightclubs, offering female clubbers an on-the-spot solution to stiletto-sore feet. Entertaining copy is placed inside the shoes, creating a set of urban fairytales for modern girls.

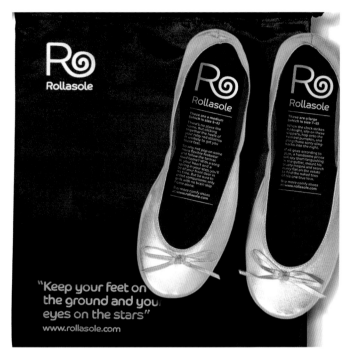

PRODUCT	**Rollasole Slippers**
DESIGN FIRM	Magpie Studio
LOCATION	London, England
CLIENT	Rollasole

 BE What works here is the idea in the logo—rather endearing, softly feminine without being too girly—that's neatly short-handed for application on the innersole. This is particularly pertinent as the brand is an impulse purchase from vending machines in nightclubs, meaning the logo communicates the product's uniqueness as well as the brand feel. The brand is then enhanced by the touching use of copy that's different each time. The idea of the modern fairytale fits perfectly with the target market—girls who need to change out of their stillettos at the end of the night.

 MK What a brilliant way to position these little slip-ons as high-end, irresistible fashion accessories! I imagine pocketing these little shoes in my handbag for those late nights when your feet hurt and you just want to walk home barefoot. The little black set-up box is classy and austere, yet the rounded, contemporary logo is friendly, approachable, and expresses the features of the enclosed product. Just visualizing the experience of opening the box to discover the gold or silver Rollasole makes me smile.

 SW First off, why didn't I think of this product? It's brilliant! And the package does it proud, from the logotype to the fairytale copy on the inside of the shoe. I've always loved the *h* logo with the roll that Paul Rand designed for the Helbros Watch Spring, so I am happy to see this done so smartly. I hate to have anything but good to say, but I wonder if such a lovely, sturdy box was really necessary? What do you do with this box in a club environment—stick it into your tiny clutch?

PRODUCT	**Kudos Collars**
DESIGN FIRM	Exhibit A: Design Group
LOCATION	Vancouver, Canada
CLIENT	Kudos Collars

PRODUCT	**T-Mobile Sidekick LX**
DESIGN FIRM	PhilippeBecker
LOCATION	San Francisco, CA
CLIENT	T-Mobile

MK This designer packaging for pet accessories fits within the glamorous-doggie world without being stereotypically cutesie. The packaging could have a second life as a treat container. The photography perspective—from the viewpoint of the dog—is smart, as is the dog-bone hang tag with the cord peeking out from under the lid. The command on the front of the label is quiet but effective. A fresh approach to canine culture.

SW Aww, the joy of walking your dog on a clear summer day, grass green, sky blue. I didn't realize a package could capture that experience. Kudos does it by what it's not—it's not cluttered with sell copy; it's not even showing you the dog—allowing you to imagine you and your dog in this place. The message is clear: "Walk Your Dog." The addition of the dog bone–shaped tag gives you all the information you need.

MK Ooohh, ahh...positioned there like an oh-so-skinny celebrity in the glow of the spotlight. This product is poised, onstage, and commanding attention, with its brand name clearly identifying itself and an image that reads "check me out." The matte black background and embossed, spot-varnished identity exude high style and luxury.

RW How smart and unexpected to showcase your product from its side view! It certainly communicates its super-slim product design. How nice are the black-on-black graphics and the considered logotype? How effective is the use of color to differentiate between product offerings—changing the product's halo clearly differentiates between identical-looking devices? Stealthy and simple. But what does it do? Perhaps this design has devoted itself to a simple aesthetic at the expense of communicating the product's function. I thought that form was to follow function.

SW Yet another saintly, glowing product! The difference is that this package gives the product the proper graphic space to be exalted and revered. Even the product name is toned back in reverence to the product. This is an elegant, sophisticated package. I like the silly upside-down "i" as a playful contrast to this very serious box.

PRODUCT	**Brockhaus Digital Encyclopedia**
DESIGN FIRM	Factor Design AG
LOCATION	Hamburg, Germany
CLIENT	Bibliographisches Institut & F. A. Brockhaus AG

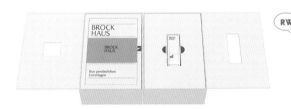

RW This is glorious product design. Slender, elegant, sophisticated, simple, and—with its sweeping cap serving as a pedestal—distinctively different! I like the translucent sleeve revealing the black box—a nice piece of theater. However, a couple important things concern me. First, I agree that the product depicted on the outside needs to look like what's inside. I missed the red product payoff. Second, the structure itself, with its white-on-white simplicity, its die-cut windows and zero-tolerance wells, looks way too similar to Apple's signature aesthetic. Imitation may be the highest form of flattery, but when it goes this far, it intrudes on another brand's equity. Expect a call from Cupertino, CA.

SW A beautiful merging of tradition, history, and modern technology. The designer's restraint with historical graphic embellishments on the package is admirable. This is an expensive product, so the packaging needed to feel monumental and duplicate the experience of purchasing the volumes of encyclopedia books and cracking open the covers for the first time. The overall size and structure of this cube does that well, without having to dedicate an entire bookcase to it. I especially like the package after the sleeve is removed—the type treatment on the matte black, then moving to the all-white inside is academically elegant and tasteful. The thin rule lines subtly suggest timelines.

PRODUCT	**Tolkowsky**
DESIGN FIRM	Brandhouse
LOCATION	London, England
CLIENT	Tolkowsky

PRODUCT	**EGel**
DESIGN FIRM	Antonio Castro Graphic Design Studio
LOCATION	El Paso, TX
CLIENT	Electrode Arrays

 There's the little blue box and now the "perfect" box. What a magnificently simple and perfectly appropriate product presentation. Talk about making the product the hero! I adore the innovative way this box folds back on itself, creating the perfect stage on which to reveal the heroic product. The magnets in the closure open and then reseal this package with confidence. With the surprisingly elegant experience this package creates, how could she possibly say no?

 This package does it's product justice and I might even venture to say it elevates it (literally and figuratively). The use of handstitched leather, the density of the wrapped board and the experience of the diamond rising to the surface, is beautiful theater. Don't you wish all packaging could provide a little more theater? The logo type is tasteful and feels appropriate but a bit expected, could this have been pushed a little bit more?

 There's definitely a scientific energy conveyed by the achromatic color palette along with the type and icons that convey credibility. The architectural design of the height of the white reads as pure, while the silver matte reads as modern, clinical, and effective. One caveat: I'm unsure why the color of the tamper evident label does not match the design.

 The designers have managed to find the spot where clinical and design-sensitive meet with great success. This product is primarily used in hospitals and clinics for EEG electro pads. This product has all the authority of a medical product and yet aesthetically, I wouldn't be surprised to find this in retail stores such as Sephora. The clean typography and the asymmetrical layout, along with the lovely matte silver and black, look very high end.

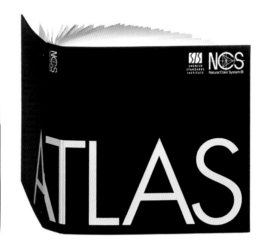

PRODUCT	**NCS**
DESIGN FIRM	BVD
LOCATION	Stockholm, Sweeden
CLIENT	Scandinavian Colour Institute

 These clear bold messages demonstrate the beauty and graphic impact of letterforms beyond their linguistic meaning. We judge letters based on their form which in this case is clean, modern, and powerful.

 I find it refreshingly bold that a company such as NCS that is dedicated to color would choose bold black and white to package and promote their vast color products. It is a nice foil for the color samples and chips inside. The typography wrapping around the sides makes these enticing as sculptural display objects, and as a frequent user of these products, I would assume the shape is more a clue to what's inside than the name of the specific product.

PRODUCT	**Askul , highlighter**
DESIGN FIRM	BVD
LOCATION	Stockholm, Sweden
CLIENT	Askul

 Color talks. This seems so obvious and yet so brave. I admire the client that sees the value in a design firm that not only conceives of but is able to execute this strategy.

 These boxes are so starkly simple and beautiful, there's really no need to say more. The vertical direction of the typography is not only a design element but it also mirrors the row of highlighters as they sit in the box. The intensity and vibrancy of the colored boxes captures the essence of the highlighters perfectly. On such a simple package, these elements elevate the package from functional to beautiful.

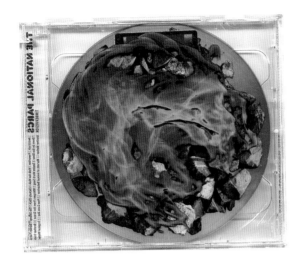

PRODUCT	**The National Parcs**
DESIGN FIRM	1F
LOCATION	Montréal, Canada
CLIENT	The National Parcs

 I was so fascinated by these graphics that I had to audio-sample the band, which turns out to be as inspired musically as the CDs are artistically. It is particularly intelligent, for the normal reference points for a CD are gone. The play of nature images in a plastic jewel case is pure entertainment.

 The merging of man-made and natural is intriguingly captured in the packaging as well as the music, which is a sampling of the sounds of nature, wood splitting, water dripping, etc. Peeling off the hyper-real photography overlays as you open the package is a wonderful experience. You can almost smell the moss-covered ground and freshly cut wood. It's so immediate to download music, but this CD package makes me realize I would be missing half the experience if I did that.

PRODUCT	OGO
DESIGN FIRM	Collins
LOCATION	New York, NY
CLIENT	AT&T Wireless

 BE Apart from Apple, this category is strongly gender-stereotyped, with techy, masculine, steel gadgets contrasted with pink, bubbly, frosted goodies for the ladies (so to speak). This packaging, however, effortlessly slots into a happy medium—young and punchy, with its rainbow of primary colors as the simple graphic backdrop. It might distract from the product visual slightly, but it would certainly attract your attention. I'm relieved the windows are transparent frosted, as I think an opaque box with that amount of vibrancy might be a little overbearing.

 MK In 1985, Paul Rand designed packaging for IBM that applied a similar, vertical color-bar format. That was more than twenty years ago, so it goes to show that really good design really is timeless. As a form of re-appropriation this design brings back stripes as a decorative and attention-grabbing graphic back into fashion.

 RW A nice exercise in visual contrasts. The cacophony of color on the front of the package is nicely balanced by the side panel's quiet elegance. I like how product features are called out in simple, tiny-but-readable black type, and how this again is contrasted by the huge, playful, geometric drop-out logo. The name and entire brand experience speaks directly to the millennium's kinetic, connected, "survival-of-the-fastest" culture.

 SW You can feel the energy pulsing through this brand. This is all about the constant flow of communication, using all sources—text, IM, and email. This is perfect for a young culture, but the design wisely manages to broaden that demographic. I love how OGO is reversed out of the stripes and becomes part of the energy. The translucent side panels add a sophistication and give the design room to breathe.

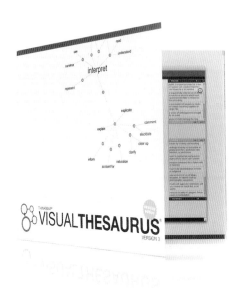

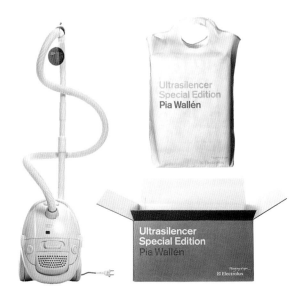

PRODUCT	**The Visual Thesaurus**
DESIGN FIRM	Thinkmap
LOCATION	New York, NY
CLIENT	Thinkmap

 I like to think that designers carry a visual thesaurus in their heads. We visually associate the connections between words and images, signs, symbols, colors, and shapes. But who would not want to use this product to get the juices going? The graphic map, positioned off-center as structures building in space, is a perfect means to visually identify this experiential process. The top horizontal color-coded band serves as an overhead boundary for the interconnected concepts and nicely balances the brand identity that grounds the overall architecture. The icon and brand identity lockup effectively communicates the character of this product.

 The Visual Thesaurus is an intriguing concept in and of itself, so to use one of the diagrams on the cover of the package was probably an obvious solution. However, the obvious is often overlooked. The orange band at the top feels too rigid for such a beautiful, exploding diagram. My eye bounces up there, when I really want to roam around the beautiful words. The booklike box structure with the wider sides feels sturdy and substantial, like an old-school thesaurus.

PRODUCT	**Ultrasilencer Special Edition**
DESIGN FIRM	BVD
LOCATION	Stockholm, Sweden
CLIENT	Electrolux Floor Care & Light Appliances

 A noise-free (noise as in clutter, uncontaminated by unnecessary elements) image for a vacuum packaging design is really quite cunning. The classic, clean typeface and color combination express a confidently modern design aesthetic. Creating silence with a pure white interior is beyond clever. Imagine the experience of opening a brown kraft–color corrugated box and experiencing the stark whiteness of the product and the inner environment. The white bag carries its branding proudly. The fact that the designers considered the interior structure as part of the experiential strategy is an added benefit that helps make this really good design.

 Cleaning might actually be fun if I had this vacuum. The product is beautiful, and the package it comes in is a perfect expression of the design aesthetic. The brown kraft on the outside of the box communicates the utilitarian aspect, while opening to the bright white vacuum surrounded by the white kraft would be almost surreal. The orange cord sold me.

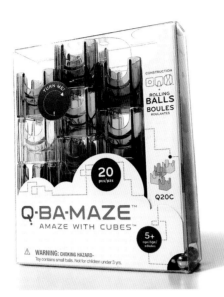

PRODUCT	**Q•BA•MAZE**
DESIGN FIRM	Spunk Design Machine
LOCATION	Minneapolis, MN
CLIENT	Q•BA•MAZE

 With product this graphic and colorful, incorporating it into the visual appeal of the design makes sense. The white label with die-cut arcs contrasts nicely with the structural forms of the products and with the dotted lines that bleed off the edges. The bold identity and graphics on a white background complement rather than compete with the vibrantly colored product. It's interesting how both the large and small black dots work effectively in symbolically expressing the purpose of the game.

 I'm not sure if it's the product or the package that I like more. Sure, your eye bounces around between the many elements, but that's part of the fun in the maze experience. The product name mirrors the clever tag line. I like the structural die cut and the graphic dotted line that continues through the lower right corner, revealing the final destination of the traveling balls. Bravo to the design firm who left the dual language and the warning statement on this submission! That's a requirement in the real world. So many others cheat by giving in to the temptation of removing the required disclaimers before entering a review process. I applaud not only the design but also the design firm's honesty.

 This straddles the line between adult product and kid product. Amazingly, the package manages to target both by giving the colorful, translucent maze pieces center stage. The pictographic quality of the logo and the primarily white package surface frame the product nicely. The dotted line running through the package tells a useful story of how the marble moves through the maze, but it also adds a sophisticated, playful element to the surface. Could this be the next Lego?

PRODUCT	**USB Cell**
DESIGN FIRM	Turner Duckworth
LOCATION	London, England and San Francisco, CA
CLIENT	Moixa Limited

 Great idea in the logo, nicely observed, that gives this tiny package relevance. Pastiching the generic language of batteries—black with green/orange; heavy, bold sans serif caps with some glowing energy cues—helps communicate the attributes of the product.

 The product is extremely clever, the effectiveness of this small design solution is equally bright, and the logo really nails it. At first glance, you assume it's a battery, then it's a flash drive, then it's a USB battery. Our immediate presumptions come from visual conditioning. Maybe you have to be pretty astute to see the flash drive symbol in the logo but once you get it, you really appreciate how one letter and one rectangle can be transformed into a clever brand identity. Nice little radiating energy graphics, too.

PRODUCT	**Yank DVD Burner**
DESIGN FIRM	Capsule
LOCATION	Minneapolis, MN
CLIENT	Yank

RW You gotta love a frog with bling, right? If one of brand identity's objectives is to surprise and delight, then this design is a contender. What a hip and trendy frog has to do with burning DVDs I don't know, but I do know that this will catch your eye and perhaps fire your imagination in the otherwise duller-than-dull electronics category. Check out the froggie icons that call out the brand's core benefits in equally delightful ways. Check out the vibrant color and the playful logo. Forgive the "yank 'n burn" brand motto on the top panel (again, I just don't get it.) However, sometimes it's worth going to this extreme to make a lasting impression. Even if that means kissing a few frogs in the process.

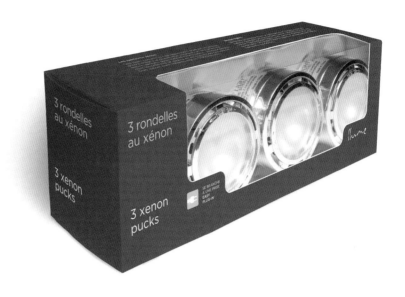

PRODUCT	Divcom
DESIGN FIRM	Nolin Branding & Design
LOCATION	Montreal, Canada
CLIENT	Divcom

 It often surprises me how poorly designed the packaging for interior design products is. This solution for under-cabinet lights demonstrates how a simple, clean, modern aesthetic can effectively distinguish a product from its competition. The die-cut window nicely frames the products, the combination of the silver-and-white product against the lime foil lining shines, and the matte gray structure with lime and white lowercase type all work together to give it a pleasing appearance.

 This is a beautiful package—clean, simple, elegant, and only two-color. The solid matte finish is a nice foil for the shiny chrome-and-glass finish of the product. The solid interior color gives the products a strong base. The simple diagrams/icons work especially well to keep the bilingual copy to a minimum.

PRODUCT	**Motorola Packaging**
DESIGN FIRM	Turner Duckworth
LOCATION	London, England and San Francisco, CA
CLIENT	Motorola

 As a range, these look great, colorful, slick—and yet each one has its own individual feel, held together by the consistent composition and Motorola logo. But the really great thing about this range is the fact that each one has its own idea. The middle one that slides out to become a speaker, using die cutting and BurgoPak sliding technology, instantly makes this stylish, interactive, and fun, and making a box into a giant gemstone certainly sparkles on shelf! The success here is to allow each product to have its own style and idea—yet together, they are strongly unified.

 These are totally rad. Each design is intriguing on many levels, from the printing mastery to the textural graphics. Just like the products they feature, each design—from tattoo art to gemstone facets to speaker graphics—has its own unique features and appeal. Individuality and choice are clearly expressed. The consistent positioning of the brand identity and the product holds this motivating line together.

 Product as hero and package as theater—a nice combination. The "kick-slide" package informs and transforms. It indicates how the product opens as it transforms the experience from that of a phone to that of a rock concert. I love the idea of tattoos, and how they continue from the package background to the phone itself. And who doesn't like jewel tones and textures?

 This is a brilliant range of packages. Motorola realizes that, with the type of product they sell and a particular demographic of consumer, their brand needs to have various faces. These packages manage to communicate product attributes as well as distinct personalities within the package design and still maintain a solid Motorola brand image. They do this with a strong, consistently placed logo and product name position. The die-cut speaker mesh treatment is stunning, as well as the reflective, jewel-like finish. The packages really become part of the product rather than a necessary evil you have to protect the product.

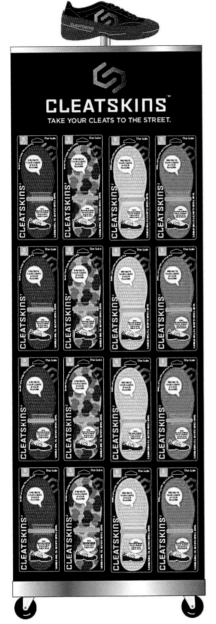

PRODUCT	**Cleatskins POP**
DESIGN FIRM	The UXB
LOCATION	Beverly Hills, CA
CLIENT	Cleatskins

MK A powerful effect created by the black background for the brightly colored products. The Cleatskin-wrapped cleat is a compelling graphic; followed by the strong brand identity, it's a real traffic-stopper. The bold graphic packaging conversing with the consumer through speech bubbles is engaging, persuasive, and speaks to the customization value of today's consumer.

RW As a system, both packaging and merchandising unit result in a smart identity. The interlocking CS graphic (which forms an "S") is a sporty and strong brand mnemonic. The packaging is well organized, highlighting unique selling features while allowing the product color to shine. And the merchandising unit, crowned by its sample shoe, immediately communicates the product in use. I also very much like how the "CS" graphic is debossed into the product tread itself, another visual and tactile reference point for the brand.

PRODUCT	**Shell Car Care**
DESIGN FIRM	Blue Marlin Brand Design
LOCATION	London, England
CLIENT	Shell

PRODUCT	**Copycats DVD**
DESIGN FIRM	Wink
LOCATION	Minneapolis, MN
CLIENT	Copycats

 Its not just the organized layout, the organic sweeping graphic which leads the eye to the key benefit, the master brand icon, nor the uniquely sensible structures that makes this identity work. Its *all* of that. The care taken in every element is evident from the matte silver substrate to the well-crafted textured illustrations inside the sweeping graphic. I specifically like the subtle variations of the sweeping graphic itself, breaking the traditional rules of consistent branding and forcing the buyer to reconsider this key element in every SKU.

 Wink does it again. The visual language of this design truly captures what was considered a classic design aesthetic style of the mid-twentieth century. The repeat pattern of the background, the abstraction of the video camera into bold graphic components, the choice of typefaces and mono-grams, and the monochromatic color tones feel completely authentic. This design tugs on the nostalgic heartstrings.

 This DVD package successfully marries old school and new school to create something fun and exciting. So often we see '50s-inspired design just regurgitated, but this does it in a way that creates something new and fresh with a wink of humor and keeps the best part of the era's imperfect design aesthetic—the human quality. I love the company name and how the logo is repeated, to reinforce the duplication CD/DVD process.

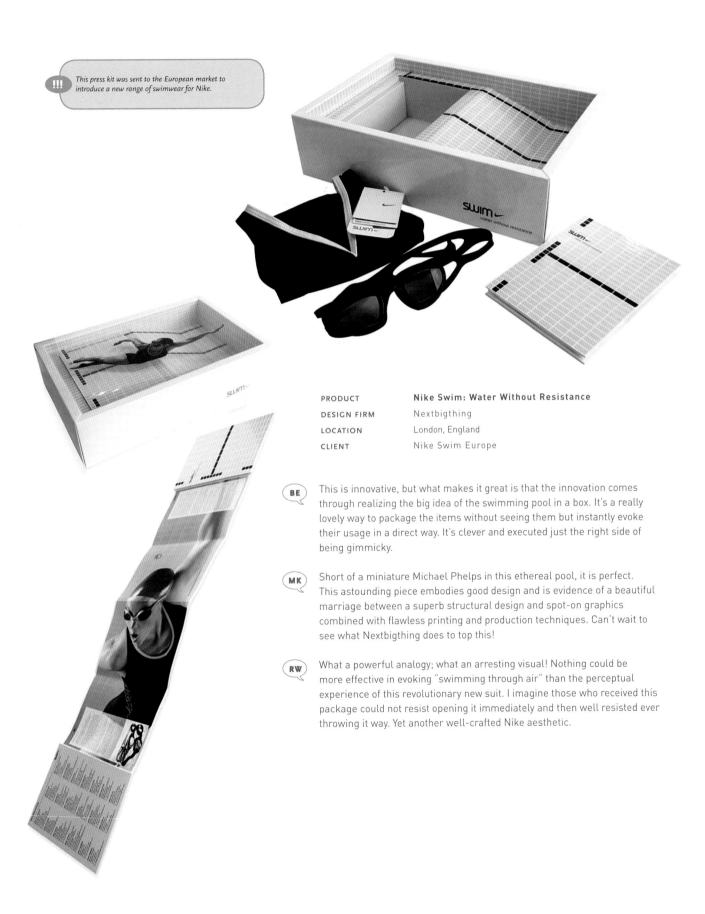

!!! This press kit was sent to the European market to introduce a new range of swimwear for Nike.

PRODUCT	Nike Swim: Water Without Resistance
DESIGN FIRM	Nextbigthing
LOCATION	London, England
CLIENT	Nike Swim Europe

BE This is innovative, but what makes it great is that the innovation comes through realizing the big idea of the swimming pool in a box. It's a really lovely way to package the items without seeing them but instantly evoke their usage in a direct way. It's clever and executed just the right side of being gimmicky.

MK Short of a miniature Michael Phelps in this ethereal pool, it is perfect. This astounding piece embodies good design and is evidence of a beautiful marriage between a superb structural design and spot-on graphics combined with flawless printing and production techniques. Can't wait to see what Nextbigthing does to top this!

RW What a powerful analogy; what an arresting visual! Nothing could be more effective in evoking "swimming through air" than the perceptual experience of this revolutionary new suit. I imagine those who received this package could not resist opening it immediately and then well resisted ever throwing it way. Yet another well-crafted Nike aesthetic.

PRODUCT	**Two Pianos**
DESIGN FIRM	Studio 360
LOCATION	Ljubljana, Slovenia
CLIENT	RTV Slovenia

 The origami-style folded appearance of this matte black design is intriguing. Traditionally, paper folded in halves, thirds, or quarters was often presented with objects that were high in value, and this design does convey excellence. The shapes created by the dividing lines convey two aspects to the content of this CD.

 I just want to touch this package. The matte-finished, highly textured substrate just draws me in. The rich, deep embossing almost looks like origami. I adore how this element reflects back and forth on the inside of the case, moving directly through the CD itself. I can imagine that this is no simple feat, ensuring that the CD is perfectly aligned with the inside graphics. It certainly sets the mood for the audio dance between classical and jazz.

PRODUCT	**Speck**
DESIGN FIRM	Liquid Agency
LOCATION	San Jose, CA
CLIENT	Speck

 Make the product the hero. It's a proven strategy. I like the sweeping lines, both top and bottom, acting almost like a stage for the floating superhero product. I appreciate how the side panels are cut away to allow the product to be viewed from every angle. I like the emoticon logo emblem and the complementing and quirky logo. I even like the die cut-violator, intrusive but not cluttering, violating without denigrating the design's simple integrity.

 I love that what seems to be a massive, heavy product appears to hover in the package. Overall, the package has an elegant simplicity. The Speck logotype adds a playful, fun quality that is unlike the product itself, which looks almost military in its Tuffskin seriousness.

PRODUCT	**Target Reusable Shopping Bag/ Zippered Tote**
DESIGN FIRM	Wink
LOCATION	Minneapolis, MN
CLIENT	Target

MK My initial take on this design was that it projected a seasonal appearance, not necessarily a sustainable one. Then I recognized that I was falling into patterned expectations and that the seasonal qualities—merry, joyful, community, nature—are qualities that speak year 'round. The design feels youthful, with a classic simplicity that is charming and appealing.

RW How smart an idea to brand your own reusable shopping bag made from 100 percent post-consumer water bottles (the number-one element in our solid waste stream.) How effective an execution in using the Target logo to represent the benefit of saving trees. How clever to use the vibrant Target red brand color rather than the expected green to get the green message across and still be somewhat of a fashion statement. I'd proudly carry mine—not just to Target, but to every other place I'm shopping. Smart work, folks!

SW A perfectly playful use of the Target logo. Based on personal experience, this bag takes away part of the chore of remembering to use the bag and actually makes me happy. What's not to like?

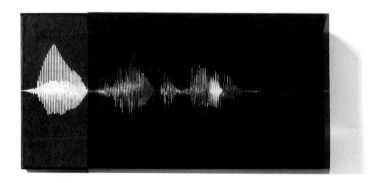

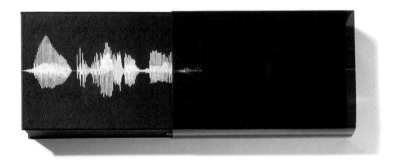

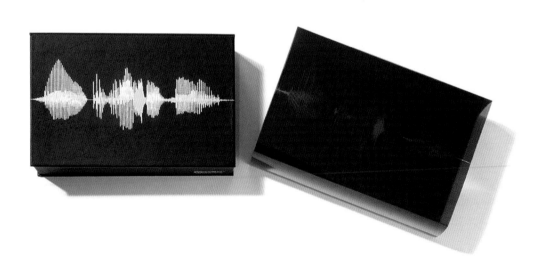

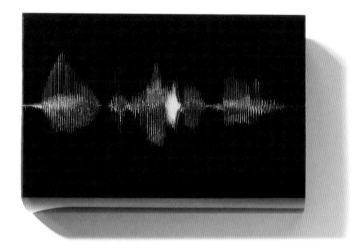

PRODUCT	**Widex Hearing Aid**
DESIGN FIRM	Goodmorning Technology
LOCATION	Copenhagen, Denmark
CLIENT	Widex

 This, to me, is one of the most innovative designs I have seen in ages. Yes, it's in a slightly unusual market because it's not sold in a competitive visual arena and has no branding or descriptive copy on it, but I would argue this would do equally well even if that were not so. The most rewarding thing about this design is the fact that the consumer interacts with it to animate it and therefore engages in a way far beyond where most packaging designs leave off. The simplicity of the idea—that it's a sound wave for a hearing aid—is brilliant, and when you see it move, it's strikingly effective for such a basic idea. The execution here is what makes this idea live, with its simple screenprinting on a matte jet black, solid, premium-looking case, sheathed in a glossy smoked plastic wrap. Yet again, having a great idea, then allowing it to breathe and be the focus of the pack works to make a stunning design. It boldly breaks every expectation in what can be a techy, patronizing and medical genre, making this product slick, young, and—for what might be a slightly self-conscious product—seriously cool!

 This package takes full advantage of the fact that it doesn't need to sell the product—since the hearing aid is already purchased by the time the consumer sees it, the brand name and supporting sell copy isn't necessary. This universal package is actually used for several different products and is modified by the doctors for each patient. The movement of the sound waves as you slide the sleeve across the surface is lovely and depicts the increased hearing performance as it opens. I can see playing with this package over and over; it's like watching ocean waves. Honestly, I think it could have been just as successful even if it had brand names and sell copy, but I'm glad it doesn't. It's a piece of art.

not as go
pack
explaine

aging

 All the elements of this identity look as if they came out of a standard design application toolbox. The stock container does nothing to reflect a unique product experience. The outlined typefaces are unimaginative. Nothing new about the layout. The background art looks like a stock texture. The resulting effect is less than brilliant.

 Lord knows there are enough great water brand identities around to float a boat, but this one misses the mark for me. Debossing this structure with the mountain relief is not an insignificant investment in design, and this specific execution looks cliché. It does not effectively echo the mountain icon behind the logo. The logo is weighty and stiff. In all, I find it less than refreshing, visually and perceptually.

 Hum drum. How often have we seen the stars and stripes reinterpreted? Can't we please be more imaginative? I like the product-as-hero, in-your-face photo perspective, but, like popcorn and chips, nuts just don't look beautiful when shown in a pile. Carefully craft your photo styling; focus the consumer on one or two beautiful peanuts and you'll drive their appetite appeal.

So, who is that masked man? There is no need for this cliché photo. The incongruous typestyles and garish colors are scary enough. At least this design uses the product to carry the brand mark. So often blister-packed products repeat the logo on both the product and the blister. That redundancy creates clutter. Just clean up these elements and create a hierarchy of messaging so the consumer's attention flows from the brand to the one unique benefit. Do so with smart type and perhaps a reassuring endorsement icon, and that is enough.

 Consistency at the expense of personality. A great design needs both. I assume from the name that this brand uses chocolate as a unique ingredient. This identity does nothing to explain that premise or its relevance in the hair-care category.

 I am so impressed with the breadth of the product offering. There are so many elements to this package that are really good, but they don't all add up to a great package. I think the reason is that every element of the package is asking for the same amount of attention, either by virtue of its physical size or color value. My eye doesn't know where to start and stop. The quotation marks are a great idea for this product, but because the photographed objects are large and all the type is large and the borders are bold and the colors are garishly bright, this big idea gets lost. I really want to go in and tweak everything just a bit.

 Arguably, there are too many elements on this package. The brand mark is oversized for the ordinary logotype within it. The logo leaf icon, the hand-drawn illustration, the overall layout of elements are all somewhat expected. The magenta logo outline is jarring and artificial. And yet, there is one element that draws me in: the flavor type. With its disintegrating elements, the type is literally falling apart, almost looking like a low-res printing flaw. However, it's specifically this low-tech, hand-stamped, hand-crafted impression that somehow makes the product more real. It all results in a nice visual impression, particularly when you consider that it's printed flexo on a film bag. Funny how sometimes all you need is just one emotion-driving element to make an entire brand architecture work.

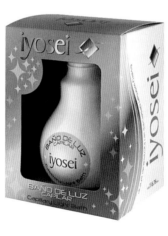

 Here is a design founded on one "cute" element that is not effectively leveraged across the rest of the identity. Every element of the design must complement the concept in some way. The carton design and its irrelevant die cut, the multiple typefaces, the dated sparkle texture, and the heavy metallic diamond icon all feel like they come from different places and do little to enhance the unique structure. And, while the light bulb idea may be cute, it does nothing to enhance the product experience.

 Once again, I'm not sure where to begin. I understand why this bottle was chosen in that it's a "capillary light bath" product, but that's not a good enough reason. From what I can understand, this is a hair treatment or shampoo product. I can't imagine trying to hold this bottle with wet hands in the shower, not to mention—how does this bottle sit? It's round on the bottom and I would guess that it's very tippy if balanced on its cap. There's something about the lavender color and sparkle graphics that feels vaguely like a feminine hygiene product.

MK I find it a bit frightening. (The logo would be great for a sports team! Mmm, meat!)

RW Duplicate icons. Too many typefaces. Changing baselines. A lack of central focus. Still, well-executed elements.

SW The eagle within the small crestlike logo isn't frightening, but the enlarged version with the beady yellow eye swooping in from the corner of the package, ready to attack the meat, is terrifying. The multiple baselines and directions of type are, in and of themselves, not bad, but if I turn the package to read the descriptive text, then that large, overbearing eagle is upside-down, as is the "Extra" on the side.

RW Some of the industry's most challenging assignments are those that reinvent an existing brand perception. It's often much easier to create a brand impression than to change one. While this design does not necessarily change the face of ready-to-drink beverage branding, it is a huge accomplishment for the Snapple brand. My only concern is that, now, Snapple is representing the same "great ingredient" story as many, many other RTD beverage brands. Where's that unique Snapple whimsy?

RW Here is a package innovation largely unsupported by its structural and graphic identity. This package heats or cools its contents, allowing for unprecedented consumer on-the-go convenience from a shelf-stable product. However, this benefit is not clearly communicated to the consumer, and the product doesn't appear especially appetizing. With this product, I can get a hot cup of soup anywhere, anytime, but the images make me wonder, what's it going to taste like? I suggest starting again: Change the functional brand name, invest in new typestyles, a cleaner layout, and much more indulgent photography. The innovation is too good not to be communicated clearly and effectively.

 BE The redeeming feature of these products—particularly the little one—is their interesting structure, which adds to the sense of being freshly prepared. However, the branding is rather insipid and recessive, and I have no idea what on earth the product is. If you were scooting around a kitchen in a hurry, you'd have trouble with these!

 RW Food service? Really? This identity will only work in a professional kitchen if there is either only one flavor per soup and sauce or there is a big honking descriptor on the lid. And even so, it would probably be way too precious for a high-functioning restaurant chef. If you've ever been in a fine professional kitchen, you know it's controlled chaos. There simply is no time to waste searching for an ingredient, and mistakenly using the wrong flavoring is verboten. Food service workers, some of whom don't readily understand the language of the country they are working in, rely on icons or dominant word cues to differentiate the dozens of canisters in their pantry. While this identity is stunning, it's unusable, and therefore it fails.

 SW Aesthetically, I really love the spare simplicity of these, but I also wondered what the actual product was. I assume these are starter items, like broths, and sauces, but I'm not sure of the specific flavors. These are definitely not speaking down to the audience, but maybe speaking a bit more clearly would be good. The large B of the logo and the simple photography are well balanced, but maybe just one teeny, little line of copy wouldn't have upset the balance, either.

 RW What is this and who is it for? Those need to be design's first objectives. The copy says "On or Off Scalp Lightening," but what does that mean? (Maybe I don't want to know?) If, as the website suggests, this is a hair-coloring product, then perhaps they should show the end result. If doing so makes it too polarizing (i.e., for both grannies and Goths), then have two very separate products, one for each consumer profile. Trying to walk the line between two worlds leaves you nowhere. Be a very specific something to a very specific someone, or create a new brand.

 SW From the name to the overall blue cast, this product brings to mind little blue-haired ladies. After visiting this company's website, I realized that many teens use this product at home to achieve white-blond hair. But certainly this package wouldn't appeal to that specific demographic— so who is it reaching?

Having worked a bunch in the razor category, I know that a consumer's first connotation of red is blood. It's a warning sign. A danger cue. And it's not just the color; the artificial, plastic product illustration doesn't project an image of quality. I imagine that Oster believes that the '50s sparkle inside the "O" is a core brand equity, but trying to bring it into the twenty-first century by adding the "O2" icon just does not work. Marketers and designers often misunderstand the relevance of brand equities. Sure, consumers might remember an element, but it's how they feel about what they remember that either makes it a true brand equity or an opportunity for optimization.

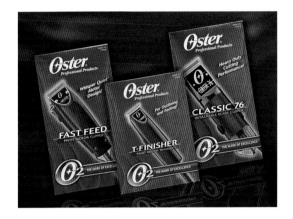

 Sure: This package does its job, highlights the product, and plays up an ownable Oster color. But it does nothing more than that to stimulate and entice the consumer. Granted, it maybe doesn't have to: When you venture out to buy a clipper or trimmer, you're not faced with a multitude of choices. The red product photo on the red background does nothing to improve the product's visibility or its image. Imagine if this product were floating on a sea of white or better yet, the red product on black: Suddenly it would have more attitude, be more enticing, more masculine. The Oster logotype is nice but has too much competition from the O2 logo—in fact, they appear to be nearly the same size.

 It took me a long while to "get" this design, but it does have merit. I am immediately drawn to the umbrella graphic, but if the side flap were not opened this idea would be lost. The negative space and cropping of this image is eye-catching; it is really a shame that it is positioned inside and with type running across it. Unless the consumer opens the side while looking at the front, the concept of the umbrella as a sunshade is lost. Additionally, the graphic styles of the sun and umbrella and the typography should be similar if they are to read as a story. Really a concept with potential that needs to be finessed.

 This identity can learn a lot from modeling design best practices, and all of us can learn from its optimization. The package structure appears to be a generic, stock bottle, but then again so are many of the exceptional concepts in this book. Not every brand can afford nor particularly benefit from a proprietary container. But with the proliferation of stock containers now available, there are lots of choices that could have enhanced this identity. What's harder to forgive is the generic look of the photographs, the expected "hand done" logotype, the lack of branded unity between adult and kid product, the shifting location of the "Bath Bubbles" type, and the disconnect between the top floral images and the main photo. What results is a less than imaginative identity that adds little to the brand experience.

 It is my belief that when a new product is added to the marketplace, it should bring something new to the category—ideally the actual performance of the product. It's then the designers job to communicate that point of difference through its package—but sometimes, its only difference is the package design. I would completely ignore this product on the shelf, its package does nothing to differentiate itself. If I were to critique this even further, one element that is so clear is the logo position on the "Happy Kidz" versus the other labels: Where is the top band of illustration on this label? These elements are all part of the brand architecture that should be considered when doing a brand line.

 I find the black logo-holding shape a bit strong, but I like how it is complemented on the Luxury Bathing Kit jar by the soothing illustrations behind it. Where is this balance across the rest of the line? I agree that the gift set must bring the brand to the next level of super-premium and unfortunately, this standard, windowed box with its overplayed graphics actually denigrates the brand experience for me.

 This design is almost there, but it would have been more successful had the designers (and client) used more restraint in the gift package and the product coloration. The intensity of the product color makes it look highly fragranced and inexpensive. If the colors had been toned down to about 1/4 of the color, this would have made a nice system with the black Kama Sutra logo.

SW There is nothing about this package that communicates a brand story—there is no personality here. It really just needed one element to be larger, or darker, make some statement, take some risk. It's the equivalent of white bread with butter—not offensive but not interesting, either.

BE I agree with the others that, alone, this is striking and has a premium beverage feel to it, yet I am unsure how consumers would navigate this range. If these came together, however, they'd work beautifully.

MK High-end, contemporary, classic style resonates from the box; you get the sense that the products must be equally aesthetically worthy. I assume that the letters wrap around three sides and the fourth side features text (perhaps on the black box there are outlines on three sides and no branding?). I keep trying to figure out how each letter translates to its respective utensil, but whatever the case, as a set this line has great shelf impact.

RW As beautiful as this identity is, I don't immediately get what the product is, and that's a huge problem. The ultra-simple identity does draw you in to want to learn more. But even on deeper exploration, I still can't tell if these utensils are metal or plastic, what the colors mean, and what's in the black box. As designers we must keep ourselves from falling so in love with design that we lose the product in the process.

SW I love this package design as a group or system, but I am confused as to how they work individually. I assume that each face of the box has a letter of "WUN" and the fourth side is descriptive copy. So is the full name "WUN" never visible? As a consumer, I would find the "U" above the word knives, and the "W" above forks, etc., confusing. And the full set of cutlery doesn't have the brand on the front face at all. I wish there were a way to keep the package this simple and beautiful and still accomplish the needs of retail. The color palette is really appealing to me, and the typography is minimal and perfect. Would this be as perfect-looking with more brand clarity?

 Creating a relevant brand identity within a well-established category is tough enough. But actually motivating a new consumer behavior and conjuring up a new brand experience is one of branding's greatest challenges. Yes, there is a lot going on here and your eye bounces between elements. The silhouettes and icon illustrations are both somewhat juvenile and generic. And I'm curious about the choice to break the pattern of using a complementing color palette by using green cartons against peppermint's strongly contrasting blue canisters. But I'm drawn to the sweeping, die-cut carton, the simple logo, and specifically the iconic way that the package teaches the consumers how and when to use the product.

 I don't read Cyrillic script, so I'm not quite sure if my comments are completely accurate. However, I can imagine that this identity's primary element, its typeface, might possibly detract from the desired brand experience. Even if it is immediately readable (which I question), the type is heavy, jagged, pointed, and sharp—not what I'd imagine the consumer is looking for in a cosmetic skin care brand. I'm more concerned about the brand colors. The black and white are a nice contrast, but the purple seems garish in comparison. Perhaps a silver or gray might have been more in keeping with the brand profile and still have been as distinctive.

 There is something quite lovely about the matte finish on the tubes and the reflective satin finish of the elegant leaf. The jagged brand name is difficult to read, which, in and of itself, isn't as bothersome as how it interacts with the leaf. Contrasts of sharp and smooth can work to create an interesting tension; however, the balance of each has to be just right. In this case, the jagged script and the smooth leaf are essentially the same mass, fighting for the same space. Hence, they don't feel cohesive.

The strategy behind this brand is interesting. I much prefer "anyware" as the brand name. It says it all. I certainly like the visual allusion that the laptop structure brings to the brand. It nicely houses all the well-designed literature. Here's my only concern: Look how much packaging it takes to brand a tiny little thumb drive! We as designers need to lead the cause for sustainability. Besides building materials, packaging is the single largest contributor to solid waste, and our planet is already overflowing with it. And it's our fault! While I like the allusion of the laptop, why not make the outer structure into something that can be repurposed and reused again and again? Make its afterlife relevant to the brand experience and you'll win big.

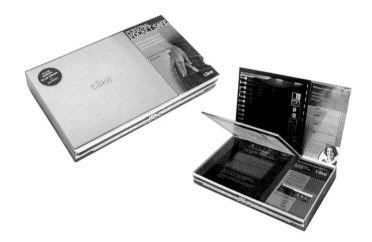

 Does every package need to be well-crafted and its every element well-considered? Isn't it enough for some products just to get the information across? Great designers prove over and over again that even the most mundane and functional of products can be elevated and made more valuable by effective design. This specific package actually makes the product feel cheaper. There is high romance and emotional indulgence in a proper bath. Own that experience and you can charge twice the price for this product.

 This is so difficult...if I saw this in a big box store, would I be attracted to the package? Would it make me think I needed a new tub spout? No. If I were looking for a new tub spout, would the package dissuade me from purchasing this? No, not if I liked the spout. But then I have to ask, would I pick this over something with more unique category packaging? Definitely no. Even in commodity products like this, the package design is important. I can't help but wonder: Do we really need to see the soft photo of the spout in action? I think we understand how the spout works, so this image only adds clutter.

 This big brand identity has almost every visual cliché going for it, yet somehow they all work in concert, specifically for the mass class of trade. Wishbone may never be a super premium brand and so dressing it up in a sophisticated design will never be authentic. Rather, the oval shape—reinforcing the logo icon—creates the age-old, hard-hitting "bull's eye" that targets your attention to the flavor and the food. The photography lacks luster and there is awkward spacing in some of the letter forms. There is a very 1990s reliance on Photoshop and Illustrator tools with all the blended backgrounds, faceted shapes, and dimensional swirls. There are too many type faces in play and none of them are distinct. And because of the heavy colors, there is little that communicates "light" or "better for you." And yet, I bet there's a lot of Wishbone Light being sold out there and this identity just might speak to this brand's loyal "grab and go" core target.

 Where to begin? There are so many beautiful elements of this package and others that merely get in the way. The package and structure are stunning, and the graphic patterns enhance the form perfectly. The designer should have stopped there. The typography is heavy-handed and cold, the hangtag gets in the way of the silhouette, and I would have preferred it without the fish icon—the wave pattern says enough.

A great design architecture is consistent yet differentiates all the products within it. Although the images created for this icon-driven architecture look like they come from different sources, at least they unify the brand. What concerns me most is the designer's choice to use a photograph of sea stones on only one package. Why? Designers must be disciplined and their work extendable so that there is no need to change the brand tool palette at random.

 There are many really nice elements to this package; unfortunately, the choice of color for the label background kills everything for me. I wonder if the intent was to "make it look like kraft paper," but the glossy finish and slightly fleshy pink tone aren't working. The aluminum bottles are nice, but they only make the fleshy color look more pallid. This label would have benefited greatly from white or real kraft paper. The type is generally nice, but sometimes it gets uncomfortably and inconsistently close to the trim edge, while other times it is quite spacious.

 OK. I've tried diet and exercise, all forms of powdered drinks, every manner of diet this and reduced calorie that, and even a few Extra Strength Excedrin with a Red Bull chaser (don't do that one), but I never considered that my shampoo was actually the secret to losing my beer belly. I hope that this is not some ploy, because brands need to be honest and authentic, first and foremost. However, if it does in fact work, I do like the tapered bottle design as a slenderizing cue, but I find the mono-color, black and blotchy, tape-measure graphic much too heavy and overt. Now, pass me that eight-hour energy shot and stop my legs from twitching.

 Big global brands like this one have a lot of cooks in the kitchen. Lots of folks need to sign off on the identity for this hundred million–dollar brand. The package must reference the tens of millions of dollars of global advertising that support it. And, all too often, that's where things get watered down. The Snuggle bear is the primary brand mnemonic. Having him float in space with no connection to the logo or the primary consumer benefit is a missed opportunity. The changing size ratio between the bear and the logo across product offerings is a mistake. Huge CPG corporations often look for what they call an "extractable branding unit"—the logo, core mnemonic, and ownable brand color all locked into a unifying device that can be extracted and applied to every consumer touchpoint. This identity has three separate elements—the bear, the logo, and the changing colors—that are inconsistently applied across the line.

 Okay, who doesn't love a cuddly little bear? But, this one looks a little like it's being flushed away. Why does re-branding of the large brands often include a swirl, and how does that say "clean"? I know my washer agitates the clothes; it always has. The detergent or fabric softener isn't going to change that. I do like the colors of these packages and the bear has a slightly different pose on each, which is a nice touch.

So the '60s logo is a bit hard to read and the color palette a bit too vibrant and juvenile. The red brand banner seems artificially imposed over a very different aesthetic (and a non-intuitive color choice for a brand named Ocean.) All this can be forgiven. What's less forgivable are the differences in the icon rendering style. The free-form, heavy-outlined apple graphic comes from one hand while the more textured flower comes from another one entirely. Look at the leaves on both icons, for example. Choose one icon style and use it consistently.

 I like the freshair logotype. It's very seventies, retro, cool— on a different package. But that logotype and the stilted fragrance illustrations forced into the corners are crowded and don't play well together. Everything is huge and there's no breathing space or "fresh air." My guess is the red bands are part of the brand dress, but they add a layer of disarray to this package.

 The only thing more difficult than creating a new brand ritual is recreating an established one. The wine-drinking experience is one of the most ritualized in all of consumer behavior. Storing the bottle, disrobing the foil top, the entire uncorking and tasting—all of this signals a super-premium experience that I contend actually makes the wine taste better. Now, put that same product in a flip-top juice container and try to evoke the same message. It's tough, and that's why wine-box graphics have to supersede their structure. They need to overbalance the absence of the wine ritual. For me, these do not. Tip this photo so that you view the package as the consumer will, and you'll notice it loses its energy from this perspective. The logo is too strong, the copy too overbearing, and the colors too acerbic and artificial to compensate for this structure.

auth
favo

HERSHEY'S

or
favorites

A collection of the authors' all-time favorite packaging.

Widex Hearing Aid
Brandhouse

This is a new one, but I think it's a perfect example of packaging challenging conventions to ultimate effect. It forces the user to interact with it in a way that is relevant to its most simplistic conclusion, creating animated sound waves, and it is so striking and unique that it doesn't even require any typography. Its power is in its simplicity and its loyalty to the big idea.

Harvey Nichols Food Range
Michael Nash Associates

Where to start? This range is iconic. Brilliant in its originality at the time, luxuriously indulgent, it's a vast, own-label range that could not be more engaging. This bucked the trend by using elegant and considered space while having not a single product shot in sight, not a single ingredient portrayed. Every item has been carefully thought about, with an idea relating to the product in the nostalgic black-and-white photography on the top half of the pack. Some are highly amusing, some are cheeky, and some are just adorable, but each one provokes a reaction and an emotional response—a real achievement for such a vast range.

Bassets & Beyond Frosties
Brandhouse

For a children's brand that has many variants, this creates an entire magical kingdom in which the sweets become the backdrop for our hero's adventures. The sheer crafting and imagination that has gone into this vast range is astounding, and it is perfect for an audience of children who love to get lost in their own imagined worlds.

Jif Lemon Juice
Bill Pugh

A classic that has inspired generations of designers, it's a blissfully simple structural idea that works brilliantly, is unmistakably unique, and conveys everything you need to know about the product. It even has a lemon texture, and the fact that you squeeze it to get the product out is inspired.

Wart Remover
Lippa Pearce

Take something traditionally quite embarrassing, wrap it in a humorous and witty idea, and you'd almost buy it anyway! It's all about what's unsaid and, as a result, it rewards the consumer with a smile.

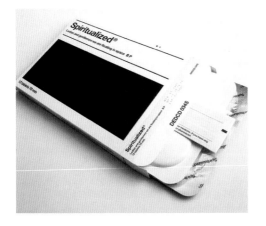

Spiritualized
Ladies and Gentlemen, We are Floating in Space
Mark Farrow

This broke the mold—literally and metaphorically—in terms of album art by creating a truly packaged design. Pastiching prescription drugs using the blister pack CDs is every student project's dream, but it had never been done before and has now become iconic. The idea came from the concept of music as a prescribed drug, narcotic and raw, and set the standard for medical-themed artwork thenceforth.

Nabisco Barnum's Animals Crackers
Nabisco (In-house)

A simple folding carton turned into an experience. I recall the sides having wheels that could be cut out from the bottom to put on the cage. The string handle makes for easy portability and was well ahead of its time. Educational, entertaining, experiential.

Hershey's Kiss
Milton Hershey

Incredibly, this silver foil packaging with the enclosed plume to identify the product was patented by Milton Hershey in 1923. It demonstrates the very essence of good design.

FUN FACT: "Hershey's Kisses Brand Chocolates, a little product with a big future, were first introduced in 1907. While it's not known exactly how Kisses got their name, it is a popular theory that the candy was named for the sound or motion of the chocolate being deposited during the manufacturing process."[1]

Screaming Yellow Zonkers
Milton Glaser/Seymour Chwast

Loved this packaging design as a child, well before I knew the profession existed. Milton Glaser's Baby Teeth typography, illustration by Seymour Chwast, and perhaps the first black packaging in the food category. A design that used space and color brilliantly. Although it broke convention in the '60s, it would be equally effective today.

L'eggs Pantyhose Egg
Roger Ferriter

This 1970 Roger Ferriter packaging design, created when he was working for Herb Lubalin, revolutionized how women perceived pantyhose. The word mark designed by both Ferriter and Tom Carnase epitomized outstanding type design. The possibilities for the packaging design's afterlife contribute to its significance in the annals of design.

FUN FACT: *On the morning of Ferriter's presentation to Hanes for a new low-cost pantyhose launch, he compressed a pair of pantyhose in his fist and noticed that the package could be an egg. Just as quickly, he realized that "egg" rhymes with "leg" and by adding the popular mid-century marketing boost of giving a product name some French-sounding twist, he incorporated the "l" (french for "the" when followed by a vowel such as the "e" of eggs) and arrived at L'eggs.*[2]

Egg Carton
Joseph Coyle (invented 1911)

The molded pulp cartons are not only recyclable and reusable, they hold the best packaging design of all.

Germanium

Another clean, simple design that hits the mark.

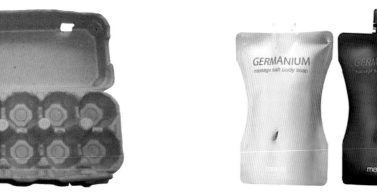

Evian
Tridimage

To my mind, this is the brand that made bottled water a multi–billion dollar business. Sure, other water brands are older or larger, but none have been more effective at elevating one of the most ubiquitous things on the planet to true prestige brand-badge status. People who buy Evian are not buying water. They are buying status. And only design can make this happen.

CK one
Calvin Klein (In-house)

Great brands communicate visually and not verbally. And those that speak most eloquently speak with simplicity. They strip away all the nonessential elements. They pare their choices down to a precious few, but as a result, every one of these choices has to work that much harder and in concert with each other to make simple into effective. That's what impressed me when I first saw CK One. It was, to my recollection, the first true dual-gender fragrance. Prior to this brand, it was thought impossible for a product as hyper-personalized as a fragrance to appeal to both men and women. This brand identity succeeds because it did not talk to the consumer, it talked to the experience and allowed the consumer to either accept or reject its authenticity. This brand stands for something. This package reflects that. And that's enough.

Harley-Davidson Motorcycles

Who has a Microsoft emblem permanently inked on their bodies? Where are the Oreo tattoos? Only this brand—and its iconic badge-and-bar emblem—codify its loyal brand enthusiasts into a tribe. You probably know that Tribe Harley is not all head-bangers. There are more than a few Fortune 500 CEOs and responsible clergy members who can think of nothing more liberating than donning their Harley-branded black leathers and proudly riding their hogs. Are there better, cheaper bikes? Most definitely. Are there other bike loyalists? Sure. But none with the feverish loyalty of Tribe Harley.

Like many brands, this one has strayed a bit in its history. I recently counted more than a dozen Harley logos. But I understand that current management is committed to reining this growing beast back to its core essence. In building a great brand, you have to be a very specific something to a very specific somebody. All too often, big CPG brands seek to be everything to everyone and as a result, they end up with the concept that the greatest number of people hate the least. This is the kiss of death to great branding. In being something to someone, you can't be afraid of pissing someone else off! Harley embraces that rule—and its loyalists reward the brand for it.

Orange
Mother Nature

C'mon, I challenge you. Try to think of a better package. It owns a color. It links that color to its proprietary and universal name. It owns a shape. It's simple. In fact, it requires no logo, no words, no imagery at all, and still it tells a compelling story. The package unmistakably signals the product inside. It could hold nothing else. It could be nothing else. The package engages all the senses with its tactile, visual, and fragrance cues. Even if you were shopping in the dark, you could easily find this product. It's easy to open. It's 100 percent organic and biodegrades faster than any other package substrate. It goes to prove that God is a really, really great designer. But He also leaves traces of his handiwork everywhere to inspire us. Own a color and a shape. Simplify your message. Engage all the senses. Be responsible to the earth. Be courageous.

Macintosh iBook
Jonathan Ive

 Having been an Apple loyalist since there were flying toasters—anybody remember them?—I could not wait to get my iBook home so I could open the box. I was already impressed with the outer carton, which had immediately engaged me at the point of sale and motivated me to buy the product, knowing full well that I was paying a premium to other brands with better features. Again, true to all other Apple products, I anticipated how the product and all its components would sit flush to the surface inside zero-tolerance, precision die-cut wells. I anticipated the completely intuitive way things were organized inside, encouraging me to immediately begin exploring. What I did not anticipate was what makes this my favorite package: I opened the carton and was greeted by the fragrance of fresh-picked fruit! The original iBook package had a small sachet of fragrance perceptually coded to the product color—in my case, tangerine. By fully engaging all the senses, the iBook has earned its place as my all-time favorite package and reconfirmed Apple as my all-time favorite brand.

Heinz Ketchup

 As mentioned, it's much easier to be creative with a tiny specialty brand than a global category leader. Just look at how many specialty brands are highlighted in this book! Although huge, monolithic, category-leading, billion-dollar brands may move more slowly, their identities are often most creative. In fact, I'd argue that it takes much more creativity to effect a change in brand perception when you are working with deeply engrained brand recognition and tightly defined parameters. Heinz has done just that.

Like Coke, Heinz has a heritage that stretches for well more than 100 years. The white keystone label shape with the all-capitalized Heinz logo in its arched top area has been a consistent carrying device all these many years. Amplifying its heritage, Heinz has never been dusty or retro or kitsch. It has always remained tried and true to both itself and its consumers. And once trust is built, it then gives the latitude to explore. Several years ago, Heinz began adding whimsical phrases like "Caution, Slow-Moving Condiment," literally making a negative brand experience into a celebration! Great brand identities are at the same time reassuringly familiar (visual shorthand for our grab-and-go culture) and refreshingly engaging. Balancing these two extremes is where the creativity comes in.

Coca-Cola Classic Bottle
Earl R. Dean

I woke up alone from a voodoo nightmare in an old and assuredly haunted New Orleans hotel room at 3 AM—probably because of the rich and deliciously fried food I had consumed (it could not have been those SoCo Hurricanes!).

I was sick to my stomach and desperately thirsty. Seeking a cool drink, I ran the tap. The water went from tepid to downright warm and smelled of sulfur. There was only one thing that would settle my sour stomach and my jangled nerves, and I had to have it. Out into the humid after-hours I went looking for a vending machine. I was immediately swept into the sweaty sensuality of Bourbon Street, where every manner of beverage awaited. I wanted only one thing.

I was pushed into a tiny bar and asked the bouncer. He pointed me to a red coffin cooler (remember those?) at the very back of the room. I opened it and was immediately embraced by a refreshing fog. And there, in a bed of cracked ice, was the last green-tinted, red-capped, contoured bottle. Ahhhhh.

Coke's identity is almost undeniably the most powerful in all global branding. Surely there is no magic in the color red or the Spencerian script or the voluptuously curved bottle shape. Admittedly, there are other colas that taste better. What makes Coke a great brand is simply the fact that this product and its iconic identity have for so long stood the test of time while remaining ever relevant.

Great design like this is memorable, transferable, and—with proper care—virtually immortal. Believe me, if I had opened that cooler and found a Pepsi, I probably would have drunk it, but I would never have remembered the story.

Wonder Bread
Sidney Peers

The Wonder Bread branding and packaging worked amazingly well, whether you liked the product inside or not. It was identifiable from the end of the grocery aisle no matter what shelf position it was given. It was fun and kid-friendly but also clearly communicated its added nutrient value to parents. It managed to bridge the generation gap. It has become an icon of bread packaging—in fact, it has a cult-like following. Over the years, the package has evolved to its present incarnation, which isn't nearly so kid-friendly.

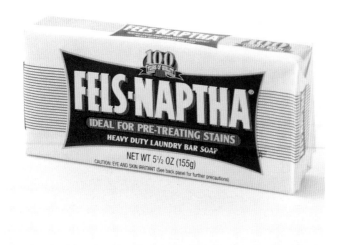

Fels-Naptha

It's hard to say exactly why I selected this package, but I've always gravitated to it. It could be fond memories of my grandmother using this soap for everything and that the packaging has not changed since then. The packaging wasn't "reinvented to be more relevant to today's homekeepers." The product is as honest and hard-working as the package indicates.

FUN FACT: Fels-Naptha is a brand of bar laundry soap used for pre-treating stains on clothing and as a home remedy for exposure to poison ivy and other skin irritants. Fels-Naptha is manufactured by and is a trademark of the Dial Corporation.[3]

First Aid kit
David L. Romanoff

Of course, I've always loved the Red Cross logo, and this first aid kit from the '60's is so obviously simple, which is what makes it brilliant. It's immediately recognizable from across the room, which is very important. A few years ago, the cross-shaped medicine cabinet was reissued—lucky me!

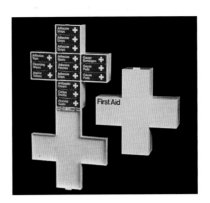

Salmiakki

I love this package and always have. The bold colors and simple typography are timeless, yet they manage to feel fresh and new. This just says licorice to me. I realize that although this is candy, the packaging doesn't necessarily appeal to kids—but who says all candy has to be for kids?

Wine Glass Packaging
Alfred Lutz

I love the simple linear drawing of the wine goblets contrasting the undulating, bold, fluid colored shapes. It feels solid, yet liquid. The typography is kept very simple, letting the graphics tell the story.

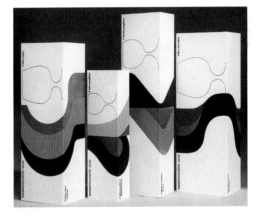

Asian take-out container

Brilliant structural design. Immediately and universally identifiable. The container with the wire handle and staples was amazing but it continues to get better with innovation: The new generation no longer contains any metal parts, which not only makes it microwavable but, I assume, easier to automate the manufacturing process.

Bazooka Bubble Gum

MK This tiny packaging design has great impact and lasting power. Patriotic colors, a flag-style layout, a brand identity that is fun and memorable—and of course the comic enclosed—make this a classic.

SW Like most young kids, I didn't really care about packaging, with one exception: The Bazooka Bubble Gum package. The bold red-and-blue graphics on the waxy paper, so meticulously folded at the ends like a gift-wrapped box. And then you carefully opened it and popped that pink powdery piece of bubble gum into your mouth—ahh, heaven. But that wasn't all...oh no, that was just the beginning. There was the cherished Bazooka Joe and His Gang comic concealed inside the wrapper. This tiny piece of paper, no more than an inch and a half square, made all the difference in the world. And all that could be mine for less than five cents. I think this is when I first understood that packaging could create a memorable brand experience and it didn't have to stop on the outside—it could continue as you open the package and discover the surprise inside.

Banana Juice
Naoto Fukasawa

BE I love this because—again—it's the most simple, intrinsic idea executed to best impact: Clean, clear design that simply emulates the natural qualities of the product in a clever and unexpected way. Little touches, like the way the design even follows the folding, make this elegantly executed, elevating the idea from good to great.

MK Anything that Naota Fukasawa designs becomes a classic. With the banana being as good a packaging design as nature could invent, this aseptic packaging is the next best thing. Love the technical mastery, from the color, the tactile banana quality, the iconic sticker graphic to the end of the banana incorporated into the fold. Perfection.

Method
Karim Rashid

MK Karim Rashid's packaging design for household products revolutionized the industry. Method has raised consumer design consciousness and—through a continuous stream of innovative designs—has practically created a cult following. The "form follows fluid" approach was the hallmark of Rashid's aesthetic, and this design exemplifies that idea.

RW This brand has taken its lumps in recent times, but it still remains a favorite for its courage to challenge convention. P&G, Clorox, Colgate could never have embraced design as a core competitive advantage. Convention would have you leverage your ownable bottle shape across all product forms. Not here. Every product form is different and still somehow united under a common aesthetic. Props go to Target for recognizing the power of this design-driven brand. Together both Method and Target have enhanced their individual brands because of their association and their passion to make the ordinary extraordinary.

Chanel No.5
Gabrielle "Coco" Chanel

MK The simplicity of the beveled bottle structure with an equally brilliant, emerald-cut glass closure epitomizes luxury. The white label and sans serif type uses proportion, balance, and hierarchy with perfection. The secondary packaging equally demonstrates the understated, classic elegance of this fashion brand.

SW This is lovely packaging, simple, yet elegant and sophisticated. Every detail is perfect, from the faceted stopper to the airy letter spacing of Chanel. This has become the icon for upscale perfume and cosmetic packaging.

Absolut Vodka
Gunnar Broman

What other package warrants its own coffee-table book? Talk about owning a recognizable mnemonic! This iconic bottle has evolved from a vessel that holds vodka, to a revered brand equity, to an internationally acclaimed art object. Again, there is no magic in the bottle shape itself. Turn it upside down and it's the same shape as those old glass intravenous bottles. But use it consistently as a core brand mnemonic in increasingly interesting ways, and not only does the shape come to define the brand, it transcends every other package in the hyper-trendy vodka category, preventing imitation and becoming an absolute (pun intended) brand beacon.

FUN FACT: In 1879, Lars Olosson Smith, the King of Vodka, created his masterpiece Absolut pure vodka which is created by a continuous distillation process. He had very high standards which helped to set Absolut Vodka apart. You will still find him, keeping a watchful eye, on each and every bottle.[4]

Angostura bitters
J. G. B. Siegert

Some things are charming in their lack of design, and I hope Angostura bitters never sees the hand of a client who feels the brand needs "updating to keep in line with consumer trends." Its cluttered, clumsy typography and lack of any taste values or brand values whatsoever has somehow stood the test of time. The endearing un-designed feel and the fact that the label is too big for the bottle (something nobody would dream of nowadays) add to its immense charm and appeal. A timeless classic.

FUN FACT: According to the website, many stories surround why the label ended up being too large for the bottle but probably the most well known is that it was simply a result of the laid back Caribbean attitude. When someone ordered the wrong size of label and the mistake was spotted, everyone thought someone else would correct it. When no one did, they decided to stick with the oversized label rather than change it and so it became the trade mark of the brand.[5]

Ty Nant water
Ross Lovegrove

Again, a structure whose idea is deeply rooted in the product attributes, creating a beautiful water effect that is elegant, unusual, and aesthetically appealing via its simple execution. The strength of this, again, requires very little typographic support: The idea speaks for itself.

FUN FACT: Boasting a form that was described as "impossible to produce," Ty Nant's fierce determination and passion for innovation brought the ground-breaking bottle to life. The asymmetrical bottle was designed to evoke the fluidity of water.[6]

Hovis Bread
Williams Murray Hamm

 This took a category which was full of bread wrapped in images of wheat and upended it completely. What consumers really know of bread is the end product, smothered in beans, or cucumbers. This design brought bread into much more relevant territory in a beautifully simple way that's colorful and has immense standout and differentiation.

Classico Pasta Sauce
Duffy Design

 Perhaps this is the design that made me decide to pursue packaging design as a profession. I distinctly remember its impact on me. The total package epitomizes the qualities of really good packaging design—timeless, transporting, aspirational. If I recall correctly, the printing technology used thermography, which added texture and an innovative quality to the nostalgic design.

The Thymes – Azure
Duffy Design

 This is a lovely package, from the soothing colors to the beautiful type which is similar to that of Chanel No. 5. Every aspect of these highly designed packages is perfect. This package feels timeless and will feel fresh 10+ years from now.

Index of Design Firms

Notes

1 History of Kisses, http://www.hersheys.com/kisses/about/history.asp

2 History of the L'Eggs plastic egg, http://en.wikipedia.org/wiki/L'eggs

3 History of Fels-Naptha soap, http://en.wikipedia.org/wiki/Fels-Naptha

4 History of Absolut, http://www.vsgroup.com/en/Key-brands/Vodka/Absolut-vodka/History-of-Absolut/

5 History of Angostura bitters, http://www.angosturabitters.com/history.htm

6 Ty Nant bottle, Design and Production, http://www.tynant.com/main.aspx?pID=40-0